WOUNDED CITY

WOUNDED CITY

Wounded City

Violent Turf Wars in a Chicago Barrio

ROBERT VARGAS

OXFORD
UNIVERSITY PRESS

OXFORD
UNIVERSITY PRESS

Oxford University Press is a department of the University of Oxford.
It furthers the University's objective of excellence in research, scholarship,
and education by publishing worldwide. Oxford is a registered trade mark of
Oxford University Press in the UK and in certain other countries.

Published in the United States of America by Oxford University Press
198 Madison Avenue, New York, NY 10016, United States of America

Library of Congress Cataloging-in-Publication Data
Names: Vargas, Robert, 1985– author.
Title: Wounded city : violent turf wars in a Chicago barrio / Robert Vargas.
Description: Oxford; New York, NY: Oxford University Press, [2016] |
Includes bibliographical references and index.
Identifiers: LCCN 2015032693| ISBN 9780190245900 (hardcover : alk. paper) |
ISBN 9780190245917 (pbk. : alk. paper)
Subjects: LCSH: Urban violence—Illinois—Chicago. | Inner
cities—Illinois—Chicago. | Gangs—Illinois—Chicago. | Ethnic
neighborhoods—Illinois—Chicago. | Police-community
relations—Illinois—Chicago.
Classification: LCC HN80.C5 V37 2016 | DDC 307.1/40977311—dc23 LC record
available at http://lccn.loc.gov/2015032693

MIX
Paper from
responsible sources
FSC® C004071

1 3 5 7 9 8 6 4 2
Printed in Canada by WEBCOM, Inc.

This book is dedicated to Professor William A. Sampson for sparking my intellectual curiosity with the workings of power, politics, and race in Chicago.

CONTENTS

ACKNOWLEDGMENTS

The process of constructing a book necessarily involves insight, support, and inspiration from a broad network of people. I hope to do them justice by acknowledging their role in the production of this manuscript.

At Northwestern I have been blessed by the support of the sociology faculty. Northwestern Sociology is truly a special place for graduate training. Working with Mary Pattillo and Gary Fine made me the ethnographer I am today. Mary's intense attention to detail made me a better writer and more observant ethnographer. When I hit a wall at my field site, Gary challenged me to step outside my comfort zone, which always led to deeper findings. Carolyn Chen provided great support during my search for a topic and offered valuable advice on how to organize my loosely connected ideas and how to ask good research questions.

My participation in the Multi-Disciplinary Program in Educational Sciences immersed me in rigorous methods training that made me a better scholar. I am indebted to Tom Cook, David Figlio, and Lincoln Quillian, whose statistics training helped me think of new ways to approach my research questions. Other

Northwestern faculty provided support to this book project in smaller yet highly significant doses: Hector Carrillo, Tony Chen, Jeannette Colyvas, John Hagan, Barnor Hesse, Chieko Maene, Christine Percheski, Jim Spillane, and Celeste Watkins-Hayes.

Jeremy Freese, my dissertation advisor, is an excellent mentor. Though his research topics overlap little with my own, Jeremy never lost interest in this project or my development as a scholar. In fact he was the only professor I met who did not raise an eyebrow when I proposed designing and fielding a survey on my own. Jeremy's critical eye pushed me to explain my work in terms that scholars outside my field would understand. From help restructuring data sets to feedback on grant proposals, he provided the full package of support anyone could hope for in a mentor. He is an exceptional role model I can only hope to emulate in my own career as a scholar and mentor.

Many colleagues also provided fresh eyes and one-on-one meetings that helped improve the book immensely. Colin Jerolmack, Andrew Papachristos, and Nicole Marwell were especially helpful as they read the entire manuscript and provided invaluable feedback. Colin pushed me to refrain from using a pseudonym for the neighborhood to make findings more transparent. Andrew provided Chicago expertise and let me know when my take on Chicago politics or violent crime trends needed further consideration. I am especially indebted to Nicole, who encouraged me to theorize neighborhood governance. My many exchanges with her fundamentally shaped my thinking on neighborhood politics, nonprofit organizations, governance, social organization, and collective efficacy. The manuscript also benefited from shorter exchanges and conversations with Jason Beckfield, Scott Decker, Matt Desmond, Sylvia Dominguez, Kathy Edin, Mike Geruso, Dan Gillion, David Harding, Tiffany Joseph, Armando Lara-Millan, Rob Sampson, Clarence Stone, Todd Swanstrom, and Kathy Swartz. James Cook at Oxford University Press was an extremely patient and helpful editor. I am thankful for his faith in me and the manuscript as it went through two rounds of review. I am also grateful to the lengthy, engaged, and extensive reviews from my anonymous reviewers. Their feedback helped me strengthen the book and flesh out its theoretical contribution. Jessica Cobb provided much needed critique and editing toward the end of revising that pushed the book to another level of clarity and theoretical sophistication.

My colleagues at the University of Wisconsin–Madison have been wonderful. I feel lucky to have their personal and intellectual support. John Delameter, Mustafa Emirbayer, Myra Marx Ferree, Robert Freeland, Alice Goffman, Chaeyoon Lim, Michael Massoglia, and Pam Oliver all provided feedback to help polish the manuscript. Erik Olin Wright read multiple drafts of chapters and provided an unrelenting high level of intellectual engagement and feedback each time. I also benefited greatly from audiences at the annual meeting of the American Sociological Association, Northwestern University, Brown University, Harvard University, the University of Wisconsin–Madison, the University of Michigan, and the University of Chicago. I am grateful to my great friends Melissa Abad, Vanessa Cruz, Eva DuGoff, Anthony Johnson, Josh Kaiser, Armando Lara-Millan, Freeden Oeur, Liz Onasch, Aliza Richman, John Robinson, Ricardo Sanchez, Brian Sargent, Saher Selod, Nicole Gonzalez-Van Cleve, and Juhi Verma, who helped keep me sane as I worked on the manuscript in Chicago, Boston, and Madison. This book was made possible by funding from the National Science Foundation and the Robert Wood Johnson Foundation.

This book would never have been written without the help of my second family at DePaul University, where, during an office hours meeting, a brilliant and charismatic professor, William A. Sampson, dragged me to the office of the McNair Scholars Program to encourage me to pursue a PhD. Professor Sampson's course on power, politics, and race in Chicago ignited my intellectual curiosity in urban politics. His lectures left a deep impression on my intellectual thinking that is visible throughout the manuscript. I am also grateful for the opportunities, knowledge, advice, and support I received from other DePaul faculty and staff: Monique Payne, Traci Schlesinger, Kelly Tzoumis, Fassil Demissie, and Rafael Hernandez-Arias. At the McNair Scholars Program, Michael Aldaronado-Jeffries, Doreen Hopkins, Luciano Berardi, and all of the McNair scholars pushed me toward a career in academia.

I appreciate as well the mentoring and encouragement of Irene Bloemraad at UC Berkeley. My experience as a research assistant on her Mexican American Political Socialization Project introduced me to the joys of conducting sociological research. Her encouragement and vocal support made me believe that I could thrive in a premier sociology graduate program. I am thankful to Heather Zenone and Gloria Chun, whose work at the UC Berkeley Summer Research Opportunity Program made my experience with Irene possible.

I thank the Little Village residents and community organizations who participated in this study for their willingness to share intimate details of their lives. In addition I am grateful for the excellent research assistance of Manuel Beltran, Ogarita Deloera, Erika Gutierrez, Andrea Guzman, Christina Hernandez, Ruben Ornelas, and Yvonne Valencia. Their hard work and good spirits made canvassing blocks fun even on the hottest, coldest, and rainiest days.

My family has been an incredible source of support and inspiration over the course of writing this book. The example set by my parents, Tomas and Maria, on an everyday basis reminded me that if they could come to the United States with just a suitcase, learn a new culture and language, and work long hours to take care of me and my siblings, then I could make it through to the PhD. I am grateful for their unwavering support as I pursued dreams beyond their own realm of experience. My brother, Tom, his wife, Maggie, and my beautiful niece and nephew have been a source of joy and renewal during much-needed breaks from research and writing. My sister's love and playful reminders that I will always be her little brother keep me grounded. Finally, my wife, Kimberly Hoang, has been tremendous. She always brought calm during storms and fun on sunny days. Her support and sacrifice provided me with the energy needed to finish this book.

WOUNDED CITY

1

Introduction

IN JANUARY 2013, ONLY ONE week after she performed at an event for President Barack Obama's second inauguration, Chicago high school student Hadiya Pendleton was shot in the back and killed. In response to her tragic death, the president remarked, "When a child opens fire on another child, there is a hole in that child's heart that government can't fill.... Only community, and parents, and teachers, and clergy can fill that hole." One year later, after a warm Easter weekend punctuated by nine homicides and thirty-six shootings, Chicago's mayor Rahm Emanuel told rows of reporters at city hall, "The neighborhoods that make up this city cannot live by a code of silence.... When some people go: 'Well, it's the weather.' No, it's whether you have values." Michael Chandler, alderman of Chicago's 24th ward, agreed with the mayor's diagnosis. "People have to get engaged," he said. "You can't just come home from work, see ten young kids on the street corner, fix dinner, sit down, watch TV and cross your legs and don't say nothing to those kids on the street corner."

When episodes of violence break out in Chicago, the leaders responsible for protecting life in the city often respond by questioning the motives of residents in Chicago's most disadvantaged neighborhoods. They assume that poor communities lack the capacity to prevent violence—at worst because of deficient

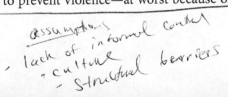

cultural values and at best because of structural conditions like poverty. For this book I set out to reassess dominant under-standings of violence and a community's struggles to prevent it by studying the Little Village neighborhood of Chicago, a Mexican enclave with one of the highest violent crime rates in the city.

I began my research canvassing the west side of Little Village. As I walked the streets, I observed countless instances of residents working to end the violence on their block; they called police, lobbied their alderman for resources, signed petitions to close liquor stores, and even worked with landlords to evict gang members living on their block. Despite living under condi-tions of residential instability and concentrated poverty (neigh-borhood factors known to suppress collective action), residents were often successful in their efforts.[1] Equipped with interper-sonal ties to neighborhood nonprofits and politicians, they were able to access much-needed resources to combat the violence. On warm days when residents of other poor communities re-mained inside out of fear, the west side of Little Village was full of life, with neighbors hanging out on their front steps and chil-dren playing on their front lawn.

If I walked only five minutes east, however, I found myself on an entirely different cluster of blocks. On the east side of Little Village, streets and sidewalks were desolate except for the occasional group of gang members hanging out or riding their bikes. Graffiti marred garage doors and garbage bins. It was harder to canvass here because more homes were blocked by tall wrought-iron fences that prevented me from even ringing the doorbell. Pit bulls added an extra layer of security to many front yards. Residents who answered their door quickly ushered me inside, away from public view. Our conversations revealed their paralyzing fear of both the police and the gangs and their frustration at the lack of support from politicians and nonprofit organizations.

To make sense of this contrast I analyzed violent crime statistics in Little Village by block and census tract. I found that most of the violence was concentrated in clusters of blocks located primarily in the east side. On average neighborhood violence was twice as common in these eastside blocks as it was on the west side. How could different blocks in the same neighborhood have such different experiences with violence?

To understand inner-city violence, scholars must scale down the level of analysis from neighborhoods to blocks and, most important, explain how violence becomes concentrated in particular areas within a neighborhood. Artists and journalists use terms like *Chiraq* to describe the threat of violence as omnipresent throughout Chicago, but evidence shows this is a myth. Violence does not occur everywhere, and it does not occur randomly. Outside Chicago criminologists studying cities like Seattle, Boston, and Vancouver show that violence tends to concentrate in very small geographic units or hot spots and that 3 to 4 percent of blocks within a city account for nearly half of all its crimes.[2] It makes little sense to blame urban violence on an entire neighborhood's values or capacity for collective action. Rather scholars and politicians should focus on understanding the causes and effects of violence in particular hot spots. This task is especially important given that levels of violent crime remain high in particular blocks within cities despite the massive drop in crime in U.S. cities overall.[3] In Chicago, violent crime persists in pockets of neighborhoods like Little Village, Englewood, West Garfield Park, and Fuller Park. Unpacking the forces concentrating violence on clusters of blocks in these neighborhoods is key to understanding the persistence of urban violence.[4]

Scholars of urban violence tend to study gang members, police, and nonprofit intervention programs separately; however, recent advances in the social science of violent crime suggest the need to study relationships among these actors.[5] The logic is simple: individuals do not engage in violence simply as a result of living in or next to a high-risk area; rather violence is an *interaction* sparked by relational conflict.[6] For example, gang violence is often sparked by competitive relations over turf. A gang's turf has economic and symbolic value: the gang regulates who sells what on its street corners, and gang members take pride in controlling the blocks where they grew up.[7] Encroaching on another gang's turf can trigger violence and a series of retaliations as gang members avenge fallen comrades.

Just as relationships are important to violence, so too do they matter for violence prevention. Organizations like Cure Violence employ reformed former gang members to mediate disputes among gangs and prevent violent retaliations.[8] These workers, known as "interrupters," arrive at the scene of a violent crime and work to convince victims, their loved ones, and friends from retaliating. Like a public health worker trying to stop the spread of disease, violence interrupters try to stop the transmission of violence from one relationship to another.

Using the case of the Little Village neighborhood in Chicago, I argue that, to understand the persistence of violence, we must examine the consequences of competitive relationships among not only gangs but also politicians, nonprofits, and police.[9] Chicago's blocks may reside in gang territories, but they also reside in police beats and political wards where groups compete for city resources and control of streets. Police officers compete over blocks against gang members as they seek to establish social control. The strategic actions taken by police officers, politicians, nonprofit organizations, and gangs to collaborate or compete for power and resources can vary block by block, triggering violence on some blocks while successfully preventing it on others.

In addition to gangs' violent competition, this study identifies two other types of turf wars that contributed to the concentration of violence on blocks located mostly on Little Village's

[handwritten margin notes: "turf wars → violence / disagreement practice"]

east side: political turf wars and street turf wars. First, political turf wars were competition over blocks' ward designation, a process commonly known as ward redistricting. The decennial battles to reassign blocks' ward designation among Chicago's Democratic Party and politically independent groups produced two very different organizational infrastructures for violence prevention in Little Village. Since 1986 Mexican activists have succeeded in defeating the Chicago Democratic Party in aldermanic elections in the 22nd ward, which covers the west side of Little Village. The leaders of the 22nd ward funneled city resources to nonprofits and blocks for violence prevention, securing state contracts to implement social programs, installing surveillance cameras, and opening green spaces and schools.

The rise of independent political leadership supported by a Latino majority in the 1970s threatened the Chicago Democratic Party. In 1980, Mayor Jane Byrne and the city council passed a redistricting ordinance that carved up the east side of Little Village into three different wards. By gerrymandering ward boundaries so that Little Village blocks constituted less than 5 percent of the electorate in each ward, the Democratic Party successfully prevented the east side from becoming another independent Latino majority ward. These practices enabled the Democratic Party to maintain its majority vote in the Chicago city council. In the 1990s and 2000s ward redistricting continued to split eastside blocks into multiple wards. As a result of these political turf wars, Little Village's east side still has little organizational or political infrastructure to respond to residents' efforts to prevent violence.

Political gerrymandering was the first type of turf war to concentrate violence in blocks primarily on Little Village's east side; the second type was a street turf war between gangs and police over the social control of blocks. Besides fighting off rival gangs, gangs also fought with police over blocks to maintain their drug operations and control over residents. To combat police, gangs enforced a code of silence to prevent residents from reporting crimes or cooperating with police investigations. When residents violated the code, gangs responded by setting informants' homes on fire to intimidate others into complying. The police's failure to protect informant identities routinely triggered acts of aggravated arson in Little Village's east side.

In their efforts to retake the streets from gangs, the police appropriated violence by arresting gang leaders. The arrests had the intended effect of dismantling the gang's drug-selling operations, but they also sparked violent competition among gangs in adjacent territories who fought over the new turf made vacant by the police raid. In February 2010, one month after the arrest of a major gang leader, there were three shootings and several unreported violent altercations among gangs that made residents afraid of venturing outside. The street turf wars between gangs and police further concentrated violence in Little Village's east side.

The goal of this book is to convince citizens, organizers, and policymakers to think differently about the forces sustaining violence in poor neighborhoods.[10] While many blame residents for the violence that plagues their blocks, this book shows that we cannot assume that all areas within the city have equal access to the organizations, politicians, and city officials necessary to address the problem of violence. Preventing violence requires collaboration among numerous actors at the residential, organizational, and political levels. Residents cannot be held fully responsible for organizing this collaboration. Cities must take a hard look at the political structures that inhibit or support collective action to address violence. Building organizational infrastructures within gerrymandered areas of the city, like Little Village's east side, may provide a mechanism to address neighborhood violence. I hope to focus public discussion on the sources of violence away from scapegoating the supposed deficiencies of poor people and toward a real accounting of the wounds inflicted upon violence-plagued neighborhoods by turf wars among the city's dominant and subordinate political groups.

This book advances the work of scholars Todd Clear, Victor Rios, and others who show that the U.S. criminal justice system is doing more harm than good to low-income communities.[11] In the turf war between gangs and police in Little Village, it was impossible to discern a winner. Police arrests of gang leaders resulted in a period of violence before a new gang leader stepped into place and street activity continued. Gang retaliations against citizen informants prompted only temporary adherence to the code of silence. When new residents moved in—a common occurrence in a neighborhood with high residential instability—the gang was forced to continue retaliations or run from the police. Neither the police tactic of gang suppression nor the gang tactic of informant suppression proved effective in this turf war.

Violence prevention experts across the country agree that suppression and punishment alone are not sufficient to address criminal groups.[12] Suppression tactics must be integrated with social interventions to help people find jobs, social services, medical care, and support networks. It is time to take up these alternative approaches. In places like Baltimore, Maryland, and Ferguson, Missouri, the growth of the criminal justice system has burdened local governments and sparked civil unrest rather than address violence. This book demonstrates that in Chicago, where collaborations between the police department and violence prevention organizations have largely ended in failure, groups need to heal from their political wounds and collaborate to stop the violence.[13]

I use pseudonyms to disguise the identity of research subjects and nonprofit organizations, but I use the real name of the neighborhood, of politicians, and of several major streets. Doing so gives the findings greater utility for violence prevention policy and allows for fact checking, falsifiability, and replication.

However, this also made it more difficult to anonymize research participants who shared sensitive information on violence and gangs. To maintain individuals' anonymity, I used pseudonyms and changed details about their block, occupation, age, gender, and home. These minor alterations helped me stay true to the major threads of their stories.

LITTLE VILLAGE

Little Village is one of seventy-seven community areas in Chicago (figure 1.1). Latinos compose 85 percent of its population, African Americans 12 percent, and whites 3 percent. Bordered by railroads to the north, the city limits to the west, the Chicago River to the south, and Western Avenue to the east, the neighborhood is regarded as the Mexican capital of the Midwest. Little Village's 26th Street is home to a healthy ethnic business district catering to the local Mexican population. Spanish is regularly spoken on the street, and many storefront signs are printed in Spanish. Scores of clothing stores, restaurants, immigration law offices, and small grocery stores run along the street, providing a strong source of sales tax revenue for the city. Aside from two busy streets and six major avenues, the neighborhood is predominantly residential, with 1940s red-brick single-family homes concentrated on the west side and more affordable rental units on the poorer east side. Figure 1.2 presents demographic data from the 2010 census, showing that 27 percent of Little Village families live in poverty, and 62 percent have less than a high school education. The neighborhood is very young, with a median age of 25.3 years. Nearly half of residents are foreign-born.

Several street gangs occupy the residential blocks outside 26th Street, most notably the Latin Kings, Two Sixers, 22 Boys, and Satan Disciples. These gangs gave Little Village its reputation

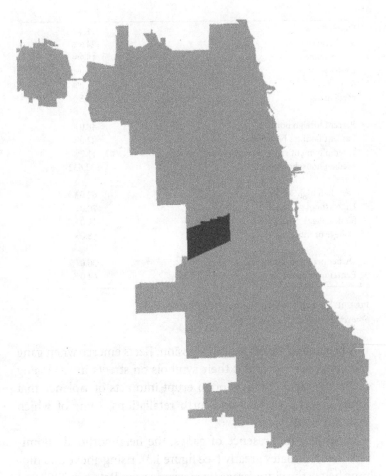

FIGURE 1.1 Location of Little Village in Chicago.
Source: Map produced by author.

as a violent and uncontrolled place; however, most of the gang violence stems from disputes over honor and respect rather than drug trade disputes. The gangs are more involved in wholesale drug deals, not in direct sale to consumers on street corners. Most drug activity is conducted behind closed doors, yet

Under 5 years	11.4%
5–17 years	24.6%
18–24 years	15.9%
25–64 years	44.9%
65 years	3.2%
Median age	25.3
Percent foreign born	48.0%
Percent families below poverty	27.0%
Unemployment rate (16 years old and over)	11.7%
Median household income	$32,632
Less than high school	62.0%
High school graduate	20.0%
Some college no degree	11.0%
College or more	8.0%
Owner occupied units	36.0%
Renter occupied units	64.0%

FIGURE 1.2 Little Village demographics.
Source: U.S. Decennial Census 2010.

this has not curtailed gang aggression. Beefs emerge when gang members enter or paint their symbols on streets in rival gang territory. Small conflicts often erupt into acts of violence that ignite a series of back-and-forth retaliations, some of which result in homicides.

Despite the presence of gangs, the neighborhood's homicide rate fluctuates greatly (see figure 1.3), rising above and dipping below the city average from year to year. Between 2002 and 2012 fifty-four homicides occurred in the neighborhood.[14] Most neighborhood violence comes in the form of aggravated battery or physical attacks using a weapon where the victim suffers severe injury such as broken bones, loss of teeth, or loss of consciousness.[15] Figure 1.4 shows that the Little Village aggravated battery rate was consistently about 1.3 times the city average.

Though the homicide rate fluctuates from year to year, the amount of nonlethal violence in Little Village places it among the

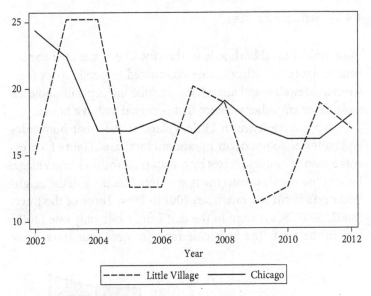

FIGURE 1.3 Chicago and Little Village homicide rates (per 100,000),
2002–2012.
Source: City of Chicago 2015.

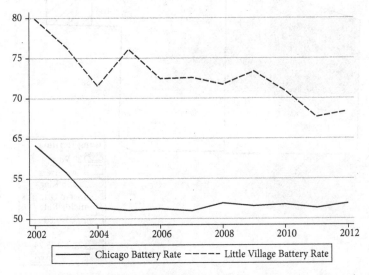

FIGURE 1.4 Chicago and Little Village aggravated battery rates (per 100,000),
2002–2012.
Source: City of Chicago 2015.

most violent neighborhoods in the city. The aggravated battery data in figure 1.4 reflect crimes committed in public space (e.g., streets, sidewalks, and alleys) and exclude incidents of domestic violence or any other violence that occurred within a home.

Mapping violence in Little Village reveals that homicides and batteries do not occur in random locations. Figure 1.5 presents a map of homicide rates by census tract within Little Village. Four of the twenty census tracts accounted for most of the neighborhood's homicide rate from 2001 to 2014. Three of the tracts (3002, 3003, 3010) were in the east side, while only one (3018) was in the west. The homicide rates in these four tracts were

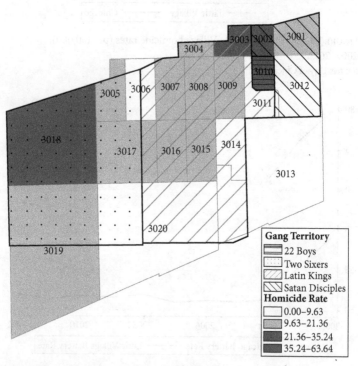

FIGURE 1.5 Map of homicide rates by Little Village census tract.
Source: City of Chicago 2015; map produced by author.

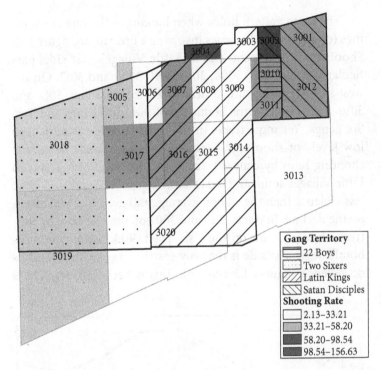

FIGURE 1.6 Map of shooting rates by Little Village census tract.
Source: City of Chicago 2015; map produced by author.

between 21.36 and 63.64 per 100,000 citizens, much higher than the city average of 18.5. All other tracts, especially those located in the south and central areas, had homicide rates that would rank them among the safest neighborhoods in the city. Interestingly, figure 1.5 also shows that homicide is concentrated in particular areas even within gang territories. For example, in Two Sixer gang territory on the west side, homicide is concentrated in tract 3018, far from the gang's border with their rival, the Latin Kings. On the east side homicide is concentrated in pockets of various gang territories, while adjacent areas have extremely low levels of homicide.

The same pattern holds when looking at the rate of shootings (or aggravated batteries involving a firearm; see figure 1.6). Shootings are concentrated in Little Village's east side, particularly tracts 3002, 3004, 3010, 3011, 3001, and 3012. On the west side shootings are concentrated in just tracts 3017 and 3016, which overlap the boundary of the Latin Kings and Two Six gangs. Yet most tracts in the neighborhood experienced low levels of shootings. Figure 1.7 shows change in annual shooting rates by census tract from 2006 to 2014.[16] Tracts in Little Village's south and west sides, such as 3020 and 3016, have less violence than the city on average, and even that violence is on the decline. In tracts 3010 and 3002 on the east side, by contrast, shootings are on the rise. Tract 3013 in the neighborhood's southeast side is the only eastside tract with low levels of violence (figures 1.5 and 1.6). This is because tract 3013 is

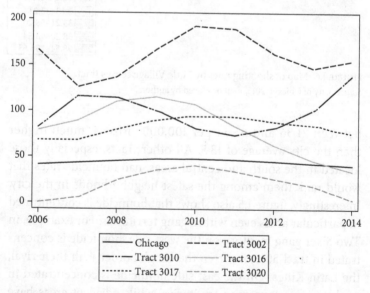

FIGURE 1.7 Chicago and Little Village census tract shooting rates, 2006–2014.
Source: City of Chicago 2015.

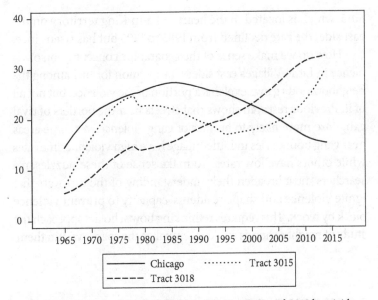

FIGURE 1.8 Chicago and Little Village census tract 3015 and 3018 homicide rates, 1965–2014.
Source: City of Chicago 2015; Chicago Homicide Database.

Cook County Jail, a ninety-six-acre facility that houses 12,700 inmates.[17]

Homicides are on the rise in just two tracts within Little Village. Figure 1.8 presents annual homicide rates for these two tracts and the city of Chicago from 1965 to 2015. Like cities across the nation, most Little Village census tracts experienced declines in homicide during this period. For purposes of presentation, I did not include all tracts in the graph, but most Little Village census tracts had homicide rates following the declining trajectory of the city average. In these tracts homicide rose in the 1960s and 1970s, peaked in the 1980s, then declined in the 1990s before leveling off. Yet in tract 3015 on the east side the rate has increased steadily since the mid-1970s. And in tract

3015, which is located in the heart of Latin King territory on the east side, the rate declined from 1985 to 1995 but has risen since.

How do we make sense of the geographic concentration of violence in Little Village's east side? Competition for turf among the neighborhood's gangs explains a portion of the violence, but not all of it. Previous research shows that streets near the borders of rival gangs are more likely to be sites of gang violence, yet some areas near gang boundaries in Little Village have high violent crime rates while others have low rates. To make sense of these puzzles, researchers must broaden their understanding of the turf wars that ignite violence and shape residents' capacity to prevent violence block by block. This requires rethinking how scholars approach the study of neighborhoods and conceptualize the spaces within them.

THINKING OF NEIGHBORHOODS AS FIELDS

When criminologists or policymakers try to understand violence in neighborhoods like Little Village, their standard approach is to measure the neighborhoods as geographically bounded places (see figure 1.9). The first step is to calculate a violent crime rate based on incidents within neighborhood boundaries and then to search for explanations by looking at other neighborhood characteristics or the neighborhood ecology. For example, a researcher might examine the effect of a neighborhood's poverty rate, level of trust in police, or collaborations on neighborhood violence.[18] While intuitive, this line of thinking has one major shortcoming: it cannot identify the mechanisms triggering or preventing acts of violence. Using statistical averages of neighborhood characteristics identifies risk factors that make individuals more or less likely to engage in violence, but this does not account for the relationships, events, or situations that trigger violence.[19] For example, in Little Village fifty-four homicides occurred between 2002 and

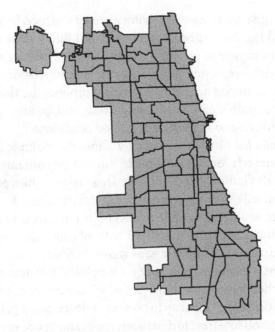

FIGURE 1.9 Chicago neighborhoods as bounded places.
Source: Map Collection, University of Chicago Library.

2012. Assuming that all perpetrators were from Little Village, this means that, out of the entire neighborhood population (79,238), fewer than 1 percent of the population committed a murder. An exclusive focus on individuals obscures the importance of political relationships needed to secure resources for implementing violence prevention programs or relationships among actors in the criminal underworld that might spark violent conflict.

This study advances an alternative approach to thinking about violence in neighborhoods, a framework that focuses on relationships among actors in a field in addition to aggregate statistics. Studying a neighborhood like Little Village as a field means identifying relationships among people and organizations whose collaboration or competition triggers or prevents violence.[20] For example, gangs are key actors in Little Village's field whose competitive relations over territory trigger violence. In addition to thinking that exposure to poverty in Little Village induces youth to engage in violence, a field approach enables scholars to see violence as stemming from competitive relationships, or turf wars, among actors. Just as neighborhoods are thought to influence individuals' relationships, relationships among actors in a field can also shape neighborhood conditions.[21]

Wounded City takes a deep look into the multiple political and social relationships that contributed to the concentration of violence in Little Village's eastside. These relationships provided the west side with an organizational infrastructure to prevent violence while concentrating violence in small areas of the east side. I focus in particular on two types of competitive relationships, or what I call turf wars, as shown in figure 1.10.

First, I examine competition for political turf among political parties or groups within a city, which can enable or constrain residential blocks' capacity to prevent violence. Second, I look at competition for street turf between gangs and police who inflict violence upon the community in their efforts to socially control residential blocks. In this framework it's not simply exposure to an environment that triggers or prevents violence but rather conflict or collaboration among actors engaged in relationships.

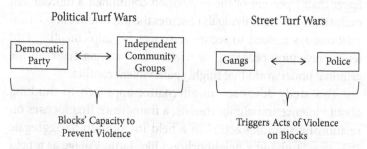

FIGURE 1.10 Turf wars triggering violence and shaping blocks' capacity for violence prevention.
Source: Figure produced by author.

THE CONSEQUENCES OF POLITICAL TURF FOR VIOLENCE PREVENTION

Gangs battle for streets year round, but battles for political turf unfold at two particular times: during election years and the decennial redrawing of the city's ward boundaries. When election season comes, campaign advertisements are visible throughout Chicago on private lawns and in apartment windows, on billboards over highways, and posted on trees and telephone poles. The gang graffiti that marks so many walls in poor neighborhoods is joined by campaign posters as political candidates compete block by block for votes, like gangs competing for turf. Some might argue that these political battles have higher stakes; instead of fighting for economic control over a particular corner, elections can determine the balance of power between the dominant Democratic Party and independent political groups in the city council, the governing body that allocates city funds and contracts and creates city ordinances.

Elections are not the only time when political battles emerge in Chicago. Though less public, a battle is also waged over the city's fifty ward boundaries each decade when they are redrawn to ensure each ward represents a similar proportion of the total city population. The new boundaries can save or kill an alderman's political career overnight. Radical shifts in a ward's demographics (such as a shift from a majority-white to majority-Latino ward) can leave an alderman vulnerable to electoral defeat. To combat such threats, dominant political parties have been known to gerrymander the redistricting process, drawing boundaries that favor their party. Political scientists show that gerrymandering can have severe consequences for the disenfranchisement of minority populations and for the types of policies and budgets passed by legislative bodies.[22]

These political turf wars over ward boundaries affect blocks' ability to address violence because acquiring violence prevention resources depends heavily on relationships with ward leaders. Criminologists like Robert Bursik refer to the relationships between residents, nonprofits, and public officials as systemic social organization.[23] Residents or block groups with strong relationships to ward officials and nonprofits can request resources like violence prevention programs, job programs, surveillance cameras, and street cleaning. In Little Village westside residents have a strong relationship with the alderman of the 22nd ward, who provides resources to address violence. By contrast the majority-Latino east side has been gerrymandered into three wards such that Little Village residents constitute less than 5 percent of each ward's constituents. These residential blocks do not have relationships to nonprofits or public officials who can broker violence prevention resources. In addition to enduring gang turf wars, these blocks suffer the consequences of political turf wars that turn sections of neighborhoods into gerrymandered areas where residents lack access to the systemic social organization necessary for preventing violence.

By recognizing that blocks within neighborhoods constitute political turf for city political groups, it becomes possible to understand why residents living in the same neighborhood access different levels of resources and institutional support for violence prevention. Instead of questioning residents' capacity to engage in collective action to prevent violence, which public officials are quick to do in the media after violent tragedies, a focus on political turf wars asks whether public officials and institutions adequately respond to residents' resource requests and violence prevention efforts.[24] The existence of gerrymandered areas, like the one in Little Village's east side shown in figure 1.11, may be a piece of the puzzle for understanding the persistence of violence within a handful of urban communities despite the dramatic decline in violence in cities over the past couple decades.

This framework advances sociological understandings of how the state contributes to the persistence of violence in low-income

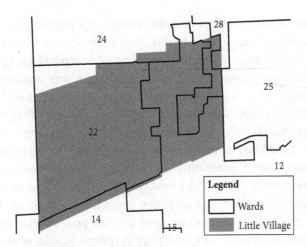

FIGURE 1.11 Little Village ward boundaries, 2015.
Source: Map Collection, University of Chicago Library.

communities. For decades scholars have criticized the ecological approach for its lack of attention to the political economic forces shaping neighborhoods.[25] While some social scientists have theorized how government policies like welfare retrenchment and mass incarceration affect neighborhood conditions, these studies cannot explain how state action can affect different neighborhoods in different ways.[26] The cases of Little Village's west and east sides demonstrate the usefulness of studying how neighborhoods are embedded in competitive relations for political turf among state actors whose actions have consequences for the geographic concentration of problems like violence.

HOW TURF WARS BETWEEN GANGS AND POLICE TRIGGER VIOLENCE

Gangs and police are locked in a seemingly eternal battle for control of both streets and residents' cooperation, yet few scholars or public officials consider how this antagonism triggers violence.[27] As noted earlier, violence results from a conflict in a relationship and functions as a mechanism for asserting dominance. Gangs and police engage in violence to assert dominance over one another, although in the United States studies of gangs show that they rarely engage in violence against police officers.[28] Hurting or killing police officers results in repressive retaliation from local law enforcement who, in addition to maintaining law and order, are interested in avenging their fallen comrade by making an example of the gang through mass arrests and brutality.[29] Given the consequences of engaging in violence against police, gangs instead target residents in their efforts to assert dominance over the police. Police rely on residents to report crimes, identify perpetrators, cooperate with investigations, and testify in court. By undermining resident cooperation with police, gangs gain an advantage over their adversary.

Gangs achieve this by enforcing a code of silence, an informal street code asserting that residents should refrain from reporting gang crimes or cooperating with police investigations. Ethnographies show that, in exchange for residents' cooperation with the code of silence, gangs and criminal groups provide resources like protection from robbers or even direct bribes.[30] Mutually beneficial relationships between gangs and the community allow gangs to survive and operate their illicit enterprises. Yet not all residents abide by the code of silence. Police departments fight back against the gang's code by operating anonymous tip hotlines and public relations campaigns. As a result many residents violate the code and report gang activities despite the risk of violent retaliation.

In this competition for resident cooperation, police do not always adequately protect informant identities. When police disclose an informant to the gang by, for example, knocking on an informant's door and questioning him or her in public, this sometimes triggers violent retaliation from the gang. Publicly punishing informants reinforces the code of silence that protects gang activities. In Little Village the Latin Kings street gang often violently retaliated against informants who broke the code of silence by setting their house on fire or throwing bricks through the windows. These acts were triggered by the police's inadvertent disclosure of informant identities.

In addition to triggering acts of violent retaliation against residents, police suppression of gangs triggered episodes of violence between gangs by igniting competition for street turf. Research on gang violence suggests that it erupts as a result of acts that trigger conflict between gangs. This can involve an economic dispute over control of drug selling territory, occupying a rival's street corner, disrespecting or insulting a rival gang, or disputes over romantic relationships.[31] *Wounded City* shows how law enforcement efforts to suppress gangs have the unintended consequences of triggering such conflicts. If we think of neighborhoods as a field of actors, it becomes possible to observe how a law enforcement strategy targeting one gang affects the gang's competitors as well. In Little Village's east side, the arrest of the 22 Boys gang leader and the gang's subsequent disorganization created a pocket of vacant territory for rival gangs in adjacent territories to fight over. In the month after the gang leader's arrest, the blocks once occupied by the 22 Boys experienced the highest number of shootings in a decade.

By demonstrating how competitive relationships between gangs and police trigger violence, this book highlights the importance of studying the effects of police interventions not just on blocks or neighborhoods but also on relationships among community members. By studying neighborhood fields, we can identify the harmful effects of police interventions and the processes through which they occur. In the case of Little Village there was good reason for the police to do something about high levels of violence in tract 3010, but when they acted, they did not take into consideration how the intervention would affect relationships among rival gangs in the neighborhood's field of actors. The criminal justice system needs to understand that suppression strategies affect far more than just the targeted individuals or criminal organizations. By incorporating the relational perspective on violence described in this book, law enforcement could engage in more responsible interventions that do not inflict more harm than good upon the community.

GENERALIZABILITY BEYOND CHICAGO

Achieving generalizability through a single neighborhood case study is, quite simply, an impossible task. The structure and level of organization among gangs vary from city to city, as do city politics. And some regard Chicago as an exceptional case with a unique political culture.[32] Thus, it is important to clarify that this book is not an effort to put forward a general, all-encompassing theory of urban violence.

These limits on generalizability, however, do not mean that scholars have nothing to learn from case studies. For example, as Mario Small argues, when Clifford Geertz wrote about "cockfights in a small Balinese village, many expected his *theoretical model* (of how games can embody societal power relations) to be applicable to other sites, but few expected the empirical findings to be so applicable—that is, for cockfights to look similar outside Indonesia."[33] In a similar sense this book does not argue that the empirical findings related to violence in Little Village will look similar in other cities. Rather, I present a theoretical model for scholars to better understand how competitive relationships, or turf wars, are critical for understanding the forces triggering or preventing violence on blocks within a city. Building a theoretical base through small in-depth empirical case studies is a common approach for advancing knowledge of processes that are often difficult to access, measure, and sample in large quantities.[34]

This book provides a conceptual roadmap for future studies to understand how relationships among actors in a field have consequences for the geographic concentration of problems like violence. Previously, urban sociologists argued that changes in urban political economies produced neighborhoods with high levels of concentrated poverty and a dearth of collective efficacy, both of which are highly correlated with neighborhood violence.[35] *Wounded City* illuminates how relationships among actors—residents, nonprofits, aldermen, and city-level officials— mediate this process. For example, in the same time period (1970–2000) that poverty was increasing in Little Village, most of the neighborhood's south and west sides experienced declines in violence as a result of relationships among residents, nonprofits, and public officials. The neighborhood's east side did not have these relationships and had a consistently high rate of violent crime. Relationships among actors in a neighborhood's field can amplify or diminish the effects of structural factors on block-level conditions. The case of Little Village demonstrates that, even within the same neighborhood, blocks vary in access to resources and institutional support for violence prevention.

Sampson and Wilson

While the political turf wars in Little Village were rooted in competition for power within the city council, turf wars can look different outside Chicago. For example, in Boston relationships among churches, academics, and public officials helped reduce violence in the 1990s, but these relationships fell apart as churches disputed who deserved recognition for this accomplishment.[36] As a result, Boston struggled to combat the resurgence of youth violence in the 2000s. In *Don't Shoot*, David Kennedy describes how political turf wars among government bureaucrats in Boston and law enforcement agencies in Baltimore made it extremely difficult to implement violence prevention initiatives in these cities.[37] Although the actors and political dynamics vary across cities, the case study of Little Village demonstrates the importance of studying relations among gangs, residents, police, nonprofits, neighborhood politicians, and city officials to understand the forces triggering and preventing violence, as well as the forces enabling or constraining violence prevention interventions.

THE APPROACH

The data collected for this project emerged in several phases between 2007 and 2012. The first phase took place from summer 2007 to summer 2009 and involved a pilot study of twenty-four high school students at a local community organization youth group. In this phase, I immersed myself in the lives of three friendship groups and shadowed them as they attended youth group and hung out in various spots in the neighborhood. Spending time with youth showed me firsthand the geographic concentration of violence that structured their everyday decision making. Young people told stories of avoiding particular streets in the neighborhood because of the threat of violence from gang members.

To better understand young people's experiences with violence in Little Village, I designed a survey and hired five research assistants to accompany me as I canvassed blocks in the neighborhood. I randomly sampled 20 percent of Little Village's 290 blocks to arrive at a list of sixty blocks to canvass. For all of 2010, five research assistants and I repeatedly canvassed these sixty blocks to recruit and administer a survey of youth between fourteen and nineteen years old using a handheld iPod Touch device to record survey responses. While piloting the survey, it was difficult to prevent parents from checking up on (and biasing) their child's answers. To distract parents from interfering with their child's completion of the survey, I asked them three open-ended questions: What do you think of the violence on your block? What do you think of police? And what do you think of the local alderman's effort to prevent violence? Though these questions were initially designed to distract the parents, their responses turned out to be an incredibly rich source of qualitative data. Parents shared stories of encounters with aggressive police, negotiating their children's safety with street gangs, their efforts to prevent violence, and recent trends in violent crime on their blocks.

After one week of canvassing, the research team and I decided to record daily field notes. The canvassing phase of research ultimately produced over one hundred field notes, survey data from 355 youth, and interviews with 355 parents. This research phase provided the bulk of block-level observations for this study.

Because residents' stories raised numerous questions about relationships among gangs, police, elected officials, and nonprofit organizations, I embarked on a third data collection phase, of ethnographic fieldwork and interviews with these actors. I began by volunteering for a small neighborhood collaborative of organizations working to reduce gang violence in Little Village's west side. I conducted interviews with five supervisors and staff members at the neighborhood's two largest violence prevention organizations, as well as fifteen other neighborhood organizations involved in violence prevention work. I also shadowed the daily routines of three violence prevention workers.

Through my relationships with violence prevention workers, I gained access to members of the Latin Kings street gang. In collaboration with a local school, Youth Inc. put together a basketball league of various block sets of the local gangs. As a player on the violence prevention workers' team, and with the workers vouching for my integrity, I was able to ask questions of various gang members, although without the use of an audio-recording device. (Gang members refused to be audio-recorded.) Unlike traditional gang ethnographies, my access to the gangs' organizational structure and leadership was limited. Our interactions

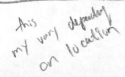
this my very depending on location

largely took place on streets as I canvassed the neighborhood or through informal interviews at the basketball league.[38] This book is therefore not an in-depth account of gang life or activity.

These data collection practices produced a large amount of qualitative data, which I analyzed. I then mapped violent crime statistics in Little Village to discern patterns and returned to the field to reinterview research subjects to improve the accuracy of my findings. I then revisited my quantitative data analysis to further refine my theoretical frame. I offer a more detailed discussion of the methods and analysis used in this study in appendix B.

OUTLINE OF THE BOOK

Chapter 2 provides important context for the rest of the book by describing the battles for political turf that significantly shaped Little Village's west and east sides. While blocks may be grouped into a neighborhood, city and state political boundaries overlap with neighborhoods, dividing them into spaces with varying levels of resources and institutional support. By describing Little Village's political battles, the chapter demonstrates that political turf wars can shape blocks' capacity to prevent violence.

Chapters 3 and 4 use the case of several blocks in Little Village's west side to show how political turf wars shaped their capacity to prevent drive-by shootings and street violence. Chapter 3 tells the story of residents who benefited from city resources and nonprofit organizational work to transform their blocks into fortresses that gangs had difficulty entering and exiting. In addition it describes the hardships of some residents who, despite living in the west side, still struggled to obtain support to reduce violence on their blocks. Chapter 4 details violence prevention organizations' successful and extraordinary effort to reduce violence on the blocks around Farragut High School, one of the most violent high schools in the city.

Chapters 5 and 6 focus on the east side of Little Village, where political turf wars gerrymandered the area, starving it of violence prevention resources and making it the site of violent competition between police and gangs for control of streets. Chapter 5 shows how competition between gangs and police triggered aggravated arson as the Latin Kings took advantage of instances when police inadvertently disclosed informant identities to retaliate and enforce a code of silence on certain blocks. Chapter 6 demonstrates the consequences of the police's turf war with gangs by describing the negative consequences of arresting a gang leader. Specifically the arrest of the 22 Boys gang leader triggered violent competition among rival gangs in adjacent territories who fought over territory made vacant by the police operation.

Chapter 7 concludes the book by describing the important contributions that relational criminology makes to the study of urban violence in particular and urban inequality more generally. I bring together the book's arguments to make the case that scholars and policymakers should seriously consider the role of political conflict in creating the neighborhood social conditions that sustain social problems like gang violence. I suggest that solutions to gang violence must involve not only additional resources but also efforts to identify and target areas that are underserved as a result of political competition. To thwart community violence we must rehabilitate relationships, in addition to places, in poor neighborhoods.

PART ONE

POLITICAL TURF

2

Battles for Political Turf in
Little Village

TWO VIOLENT BORDER STREETS DIVIDED gang territories in
Little Village (figure 2.1). On the neighborhood's west side
Ridgeway Avenue divided the Two Sixers from the Latin Kings,
gangs that have been at war since the early 1980s. To the east
Marshall Boulevard, Cermak, and California Avenue divided
the Latin Kings, 22 Boys, and Satan Disciples. On most days
Little Village residents steered clear of these streets, which had
been the site of dozens of shootings over the years, but on a
blazing summer day in July 2008 approximately two thousand
people occupied Ridgeway Avenue in an effort to rally the community against violence. The event was called Stop the Violence,
and it was intentionally held on the border between the Latin
Kings and Two Sixers to transform these violent blocks into a
space for building community solidarity. On that summer day
Ridgeway Avenue was alive with blaring music, street vendors
selling Mexican food, tables and booths staffed by community
organizations, and the sounds of youth playing basketball. Signs
posted on fences along the street read, "Stop the killing between
our people."

"Stop the violence is part of a comprehensive effort to bring
people together," said Steve Beltran, director of the PCG. "It's
not where we start, and it's not where we end." The event was an
annual summer event in Little Village's west side.

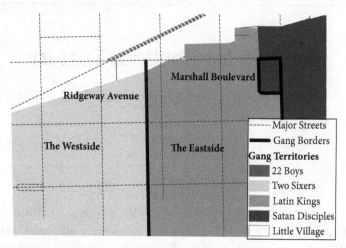

FIGURE 2.1 Map of Little Village's west and east gang borders.
Source: Map Collection, University of Chicago Library.

While the festivities continued well into the late afternoon on Ridgeway Avenue, it was like any other day on Marshall Boulevard, a major border street in the neighborhood's east side. No residents chatted on the streets, there were no shouts of children playing, no music filled the air. Only the sound of cars driving by broke the silence. On Marshall Boulevard, brick apartment buildings and sidewalks were marred by competing graffiti from warring gangs. In some places the back-and-forth graffiti between the gangs created layers of spray-paint that turned the wall into a dense cloud of black and gray paint.

Marshall Boulevard did not have any events like Stop the Violence; residents had to find their own ways to cope with the warring gangs. Eduardo and Cynthia were a married couple who had lived in 22 Boy gang territory for fifteen years. "You can't call the police," Eduardo told me from his front porch, "they're too afraid, and when they do come here, they come in packs." Eduardo got down on one knee and started petting his pit bull, who served as a security system for his apartment. "The best way to protect yourself and your property is to get yourself one of these."

Cynthia came downstairs to join the conversation. "We look out for each other here," she said. "There was a flood a couple weeks ago, and neighbors came out to help each other clean and suck out the water from our basements."

"Where do you go to complain about the violence?" I asked.

"We don't know," Cynthia answered. "When I call the police to complain about damage to my property, they just tell me to call my insurance company. We have no other way to voice our complaints. There's just nothing going on around here, no community meetings. Even if there were community meetings, we wouldn't know where to find out about them."

Just as I was about to ask another question, a group of Latin Kings started walking down the street toward us. "If we're going to keep talking," Cynthia said, her eyes fixed on the gang members, "we're going to have to move this conversation inside."

The contrasting scenes on Ridgeway Avenue and Marshall Boulevard that day were puzzling. How could blocks in the same neighborhood and located just one mile apart have such different levels of organization for preventing violence?

Little Village's east-west bifurcation was produced by two political battles with very different outcomes. In the 1980s Little Village's west side was the site of the battle between Mexican activists and the city's Democratic Party machine for the 22nd ward. Since 1986 activists have consistently won this electoral battle. In the process of advocating for resources and surviving political challengers, these activists built a nonprofit infrastructure equipped to funnel city and foundation resources to blocks in need. By contrast, the battle over Little Village's east side was won by the Chicago Democratic Party, which gerrymandered blocks in and around Marshall Boulevard to maintain a majority in the city council. Over the past three decades the Marshall Boulevard area has, for varying lengths of time, been part of the

12th, 24th, 28th, and 25th wards. Each time, the area's Latino population was carved up and absorbed into white- and black-majority wards. Decades of ward redistricting inflicted political wounds on residents in the Marshall Boulevard area.

These two political turf wars resulted in very different access to violence prevention resources for different areas of Little Village. The west side was home to several nonprofit organizations, community centers, and block groups. By contrast, the only formal organization dealing with the violence problem in the east side was the police, who implemented a unilateral strategy of gang suppression (a strategy that triggered violence, as I show in subsequent chapters). These political turf wars help explain the concentration of violence in pockets of Little Village.

POLITICAL TURF WARS IN CHICAGO'S CITY COUNCIL

Chicago's city council represents fifty wards spread throughout the city (figure 2.2). Historically the council's political turf wars have been fought between "independents," or far-left-leaning liberal democrats, and "machine democrats," or city council representatives loyal to the national Democratic Party.[1] Beginning in the 1950s, Chicago was a powerful player in national presidential elections as Illinois was a swing state for presidential elections. Though most of Illinois's rural and suburban population voted Republican, Mayor Richard J. Daley organized the Democratic Party in Chicago and Cook County into a powerful political machine to boost Democratic presidential candidates. For example, with Daley's support, John F. Kennedy won Illinois by just nine thousand votes in his 1960 presidential election victory over Republican Richard Nixon.[2]

Mayor Daley's political machine commanded a corps of supporters to campaign for candidates and turn out voters in

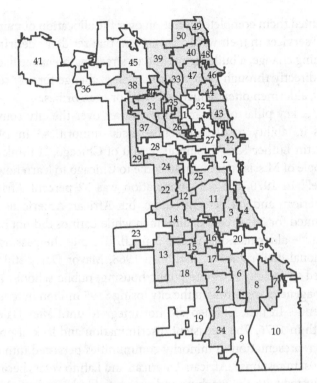

FIGURE 2.2 Map of Chicago's fifty wards.
Source: Map Collection, University of Chicago Library.

exchange for favors. The city's aldermen (city council members) were key players in this system. They voted to pass most of the mayor's ordinances and helped court votes in their wards for state and national Democratic Party candidates. The rise of the Chicago political machine created what Dick Simpson calls a "rubber stamp city council."[3] To maintain control the mayor fiercely disciplined aldermen who voted against him by shouting threats or insults at them in city council meetings, turning off their microphones, or even funding candidates to oust them from office. To reward aldermen for their compliance, the mayor granted them complete discretion over the allocation of municipal services in their ward.[4] This meant that residents desiring a zoning change, a building permit, or street maintenance had to go directly through their alderman. In exchange for city services, aldermen often demanded votes or even bribes.[5]

A key pillar of the machine's power over the city council was its ability to disenfranchise racial minorities.[6] In 1966, Martin Luther King Jr. famously said of Chicago, "I think the people of Mississippi ought to come to Chicago to learn how to hate."[7] In 1970, the city's population was 32 percent African American and 7.4 percent Latino, but African Americans accounted for 28 percent of aldermen while Latinos did not have a single alderman on the city council.[8] Despite the passing of national civil rights legislation in 1968, Mayor Daley still refused to racially integrate public housing, public schools, and city agencies, resulting in the city losing $195 million in federal revenue. In fact, Chicago did not integrate until after Daley's death in 1976. The persistent discrimination and lack of political representation in minority communities persisted into the 1980s. In response, African American and Latino voters became disgusted with the machine and supported independent aldermen in elections to defeat segregationists.

To deal with the threat of increasing numbers of minority voters, the mayor and his machine redrew ward boundaries after every decade to protect white incumbent aldermen who represented majority-black and -Latino neighborhoods. For example, between 1970 and 1980 African Americans in the 37th ward grew from 12 percent to 76 percent of the population. The mayor and machine Democrats redrew the ward's boundaries to include seventeen thousand more whites, creating a ward that was 50 percent white and 37 percent African American. This gerrymandering helped Alderman Thomas Casey win reelection.[9] These political battles heavily shaped Little Village's west and east sides.

THE BATTLE FOR THE 22ND WARD ON LITTLE VILLAGE'S WEST SIDE

"We know it's not their ward!" exclaimed Jesus "Chuy" Garcia, the former alderman of Little Village and a founder of the PCG, at a political rally at PCG headquarters. "Thanks for changing politics! Thanks for bringing change!" A large and worn PCG banner hung across the stage, providing a physical symbol of the neighborhood's scars accumulated from decades of battles with Chicago's political machine. Yet, the neighborhood's progressive and independent leadership endured through this struggle, bringing resources to the 22nd ward in Little Village's west side (shown in figure 2.3).

By 2015, Little Village's independent political leaders represented a significant challenge to the city's dominant Democratic Party. That year, Garcia fell just 12 points shy of defeating the incumbent mayor Rahm Emanuel in the first mayoral runoff election in city history.[10]

If we were to go back in time thirty-five years, we would find an entirely different political climate in Little Village. In

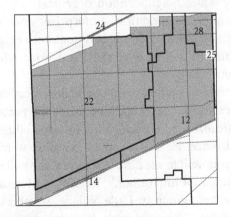

FIGURE 2.3 The 22nd ward in Little Village's west side.
Source: Map Collection, University of Chicago Library.

1980, one in seven Chicagoans was Latino, yet there were no Latino majority wards in the city. Mayor Jane Byrne and the machine-dominated city council passed a ward redistricting plan that severely undermined Latino and black efforts to unseat machine aldermen. While dominant political groups in Chicago readily incorporated immigrant groups like the Irish, Polish, and Italians into positions of power, the machine's approach to Spanish-speaking immigrants was different. When Mexican or Puerto Rican newcomers challenged the ward bosses who ran their neighborhoods, they were told they did not know their place.[11]

In Little Village the white population dropped from 33,963 to 12,032 between 1970 and 1980, and the Latino population grew from 19,497 to 55,650.[12] Frank Stemberk, the white machine alderman of the 22nd ward, did not adapt his governance to this shifting population. Instead he spoke derisively about his Mexican constituents, once telling a reporter, "These people better learn something about America or go back to Mexico where they belong."[13] Stemberk was a close ally of Mayor Daley and worked exclusively with predominantly white neighborhood organizations such as the Home Owners Preservation Enterprise and the South Lawndale Chamber of Commerce to maintain neighborhood infrastructure in the areas of the 22nd ward where whites resided (figure 2.4).

"[Stemberk] was very insensitive and disrespectful," said Jesus Garcia. "Despite the neighborhood being 70 percent Latino, mostly Mexican, he didn't even bother to have a bilingual person in his ward office. He was a typical machine ward alderman that, when you went to see him, he'd look at the poll sheet to see if you had voted for him or not."[14] Even after Mexicans became the largest ethnic group in Little Village, Stemberk remained alderman of the 22nd ward with the support of white homeowners who constituted just 17 percent of the neighborhood population in 1980.[15]

FIGURE 2.4 Mayor Richard J. Daley (far right) and Alderman Frank Stemberk (next to Daley).
Source: Frank S. Magallon Collection.

As unemployment and poverty rose in Little Village during Stemberk's tenure, gang violence spiraled out of control. Gangs had existed in Little Village since the 1960s, but the influx of Mexican immigrants into the predominantly white 22nd ward sparked new conflict. White gangs such as the Ambrose, the Saints, the Clowns, and the Ridgeway Lords fought with Mexicans to protect the neighborhood from the "Spic invasion."[16] Some Mexican gangs developed to fight back.

"There was tons of racial animosity with the white gangs," said Carlos, a fifty-seven-year-old former Latin King. "You had to at least be friends with a Mexican gang like the Latin Kings to protect yourself."

Initially most Mexican gangs in Little Village were informal social groups, but as the neighborhood experienced economic decline in the 1970s, two gangs evolved into large players in Chicago's informal drug economy: the Latin Kings and the Two Sixers. Johnny, a former leader of the Sin City Boys street gang explained, "You had gangs, but back then they were either party crews or movements. Like we [the Sin City Boys] were a party crew, we got people on our block together to hang out, drink, and, if necessary, throw down [fight]. We were all about having a good time. But the Latin Kings, they were a movement. You had to swear your loyalty to their nation. It meant something to be a Latin King. It brought you honor and respect."

With poverty increasing and the *Chicago Tribune* describing Little Village in 1979 as "forgotten by the city's urban planners," the neighborhood became a hot spot for the city's drug trade.[17]

"It got to a point in the late seventies for us to decide whether we were going to go the route of the drug trade like some of the other gangs," said Johnny. "But by then we were all in our thirties and had families to support. So we split up."

Led by ambitious entrepreneurs, the Latin Kings and Two Sixers evolved from street corner groups to large economic enterprises.[18] David, an ex–Latin King, explained, "Raul Gonzalez was the first leader of the Latin Kings in Chicago, and he made business ties with the Mafia, who supplied drugs to sell." While in prison for murder in 1977, Gonzalez wrote a constitution for the Latin Kings that included the creation of a hierarchical organizational structure with an executive board and smaller block-level committees.[19] Like the leaders of other corporatized street gangs in U.S. cities, Gonzalez controlled the drug operations of the Latin Kings from within prison.

Simultaneously Alfonso Ayala, a drug dealer residing in the suburban town of Westchester, also sought to capitalize on the neighborhood's growing drug market. Fernando, a thirty-two-year-old former Two Sixer (whose father was one of the gang's founding members) recalled the gang's transformation: "[Ayala] opened a clothing store in Little Village's west side that catered to party crew gangs by making custom logos and clothes. The Two Six were recruited by Ayala to operate his drug operations in the 'hood." The Two Sixers were originally a group of friends on a local softball team, Fernando explained. "With Alfonso Ayala's money, [the Two Sixers] grew into a large organized gang, and the street operations were run by his son David." Using the clothing store to store drugs and weapons, the Two Sixers grew into the Latin Kings' primary competitor for Little Village's drug market.

Competition in the neighborhood's underworld transformed into a full-fledged war after Ayala was shot and killed at a tavern located on 27th Street and Karlov on January 25, 1981.[20] The exact details motivating the murder remain unknown, but Two Six gang members suspected that the Latin Kings hired a hit man.

"The Two Six street gang promised a $500 reward to its members for every Latin King street gang member they killed," said Manny, a former Two Sixer. In 1981, Little Village experienced a record high eight gang-related homicides. Two months after Ayala's murder, his son David was arrested for the deaths of two innocent teenagers who were struck by stray bullets during a drive-by against the Latin Kings.[21]

The gang violence in 1981 transformed the 22nd ward's gang territories from an archipelago of small gangs to a terrain dominated by two large gangs whose territory was divided by a lone border street, Ridgeway Avenue. "The Latin Kings and Two Six would look at our blocks and see opportunities [for selling drugs]," said Johnny. "Sometimes the Two Six and Latin Kings would go up to the leader of the party crew and demand that they either join up or move out of the neighborhood. Some party crews just opted out and left the neighborhood or joined the Kings or Two Six without even being asked." Smaller gangs like the Sin City Boys and Ridgeway Boys disbanded or moved out of the neighborhood to avoid being caught in the middle of the violent war between the Two Sixers and Latin Kings.

Activists like Chuy Garcia and Rudy Lozano organized residents to bring neighborhood problems like violence and overcrowded schools to the city policy agenda, but their requests for help were ignored. With the neighborhood on a steep decline, Garcia and Lozano traded their picket signs and bull horns for suits and cameras and organized a campaign to oust Alderman Stemberk and give the ward its first Latino alderman.

"We were very active in the community, but we saw ourselves as militant and very pure, and we struggled," said Garcia. "We felt that electoral politics was kind of establishment, selling out, compromising on principles and so on, but we recognized that if we wanted to empower our people we had to find some practical ways of doing it."[22] For neighborhood activists this meant mounting a political campaign and running Lozano (a labor organizer) for 22nd ward alderman in the 1983 election.

The timing of the Little Village activists was perfect because in 1983 the Chicago political machine was divided into camps supporting either Mayor Byrne or Richard M. Daley, the son of the former mayor. With political experts anticipating a close race, the mayoral candidates descended upon Little Village to court Mexican votes. That election year, 26th Street was full of posters and billboards reading "Amigos for Daley," a slogan devised by Daley's campaign to attract Mexican voters.

"Daley came with all these signs and had a mariachi band playing on the street corner," said Garcia, "but he never actually came to the neighborhood to meet people."[23]

While white politicians courted Mexican voters from a distance, Harold Washington, a progressive black lawyer running for mayor, came to Little Village to build an alliance with activists. "Harold's approach was different," said Garcia. "[He didn't make] the grand entrance with a mariachi band. He came and reminded us that he was a state legislator, that he was defending bilingual education. He was defending immigrants' rights and fighting and stopping discrimination against immigrants. Harold was saying 'You need to have your own representatives. You need to have your own agenda. I want to take that agenda and implement it when I'm elected mayor.'"[24]

Washington won the support of Lozano, Garcia, and other Latino activists, such as Jose "Cha Cha" Jimenez, a Puerto Rican. They helped him court the Latino vote. "His whole theme of neighborhoods first was in line with what we believed in," said Jimenez. "It fit right in with our philosophy. So I just started organizing."

With the help of Latino voters, Washington defeated Byrne and the younger Daley to become mayor of Chicago in 1983. Winning the Democratic primary in Chicago usually guarantees a victory in the general election because Republicans hold little power in the city. However, the city's white Democratic leadership strongly supported a white Republican candidate against Washington in a highly racialized general election. Yet despite facing a formidable opponent in Bernard Epton, Washington won the general election with 51 percent of the vote over the 49 percent of his Republican challenger. The 1983 general election saw the highest turnout (79 percent) of any Chicago election in history, and Latino turnout was at a record high 62 percent. The Latino vote was essential to Washington's victory; he captured 82 percent of Latinos. If that number had been 4 percent less, he would have lost.[25]

Lozano lost to Stemberk in the 1983 race for 22nd ward alderman, but Washington's victory and subsequent battles with the majority-white and -Democratic city council presented Little Village activists with a new opportunity to gain power. Mayor Washington needed more independent allies in the city council. Machine aldermen comprised the majority in the council and refused to put Washington's proposed ordinances up for a vote. As a result, activists in several black neighborhoods filed a lawsuit against the city, charging that Mayor Byrne's 1980 ward redistricting discriminated against black and Latino voters. That redistricting cut the number of black-majority wards from nineteen to seventeen, even though the city's black population had increased by more than a hundred thousand in the previous decade.[26] The numbers were even worse for Latinos, who accounted for 14 percent of the city population but had no Latino-majority wards. To the delight of Little Village activists, the courts ruled the redistricting unconstitutional and ordered Chicago to host special elections in seven of the city's fifty wards, one of which was to be in the newly drawn Latino-majority 22nd ward. The court's redistricting in 1986 presented Mayor Washington with an opportunity to flip the city council majority in his favor. Washington needed allies to win at least four of the seven special elections to have the first independent-majority city council in the city's history.

Lozano, who fell seventeen votes shy of a runoff in 1983, planned to run again but was tragically murdered in June 1983.[27] He was gunned down in his home by a gang member, but many Little Village organizers suspect his assassination was politically motivated. At the suggestion of campaign supporters, Lozano's campaign manager, Jesus Garcia, ran in his place. With Mayor Washington as an ally and a new Latino-majority electorate in the 22nd ward, Garcia was set to achieve his goal of improving the neighborhood by being elected into city council. All signs pointed in his favor leading up to the 1986 election. Editorials by both the *Chicago Tribune* and the *Chicago Sun-Times* criticized Stemberk for ignoring the needs of his Mexican constituents.[28] Then the *Sun-Times* investigative reporting unit revealed that Alderman Stemberk had not even lived in the 22nd ward since at least 1983.[29] "The situation got so bad," Garcia recalled, "that [Alderman Stemberk] moved out of the community, was living in suburbia, contrary to law."[30]

Garcia won the 1986 special election over Stemberk's hand-chosen successor, Guadalupe Martinez, with 55 percent of the vote.[31] The victory transformed the 22nd ward, opening access to city resources for the neighborhood's Mexican residents. With Mayor Washington as an ally, Garcia moved quickly to direct money toward neighborhood improvement projects, block groups, curb and gutter repairs, street resurfacing, and the construction of new health centers.[32] For the first time in Chicago history, the mayor's office had a commission on Latino affairs, composed of fifteen leaders from Chicago's Latino neighborhoods who had direct access to Mayor Washington to express their needs or concerns. The number of Latinos in the city administration rose from three under Mayor Byrne to twenty-seven under Mayor Washington.[33] After years of being ignored and excluded by the mainstream Democratic machine in Chicago, the Mexican community in Little Village's 22nd ward finally had a voice in city politics.

Alderman Garcia brought public attention to the problems facing Chicago's growing Latino communities, such as the need for bilingual education and the protection of immigrant rights. With the help of the Latino Institute, a nonprofit advocacy organization, he and others engaged in research-based advocacy and founded community organizations to serve the Latino population. Alderman Garcia and Mayor Washington worked together to ease racial tension between African Americans and Latinos over policy issues such as immigration. Negotiations were not always easy, but Washington eventually signed an executive order that removed citizenship questions from all city applications and prohibited the city from collaborating with federal immigration investigators.[34] Garcia also helped push through some of the mayor's initiatives, such as an ethics ordinance, a tenant's bill of rights, and a gang violence prevention program spearheaded by Irving Spergel at the University of Chicago.[35] The year 1986 was a historic time for Little Village (figure 2.5).

It all came to an end on the morning of November 25, 1987. Two days after Thanksgiving Mayor Washington was talking with his press secretary at his city hall office when he collapsed on his desk and died of a massive heart attack. His death fractured the fragile coalition between politically independent African American and Latino leaders. It fell to the Chicago city

FIGURE 2.5 Alderman Garcia (left), Mayor Washington (center), and Cesar Chavez (right).

Source: Chicago Public Library (photographer unknown).

council to elect an interim mayor to finish the remainder of Washington's term. Just hours after the ambulance left city hall, white Democratic machine party leaders Ed Burke, Richard Mell, and Ed Vrdolyak worked to splinter the African American–Latino coalition, and they were ultimately successful.[36] After days of intense negotiation and political maneuvering, an African American machine-backed candidate, Eugene Sawyer, was elected interim mayor by the city council, ending the powerful alliance between Little Village and the mayor's office.

Despite the collapse of the interracial coalition that followed Mayor Washington's death, Little Village activists continued to expand their power base. After serving another term as alderman, Garcia ran for state senate in 1992 and won, allowing an ally, Ricardo Muñoz, to take over as alderman of the 22nd ward. Washington's death was a huge blow to independent political groups in Chicago, but the machine could no longer ignore and exclude the Mexican community in Little Village's 22nd ward as it had under previous administrations.

The election of Mayor Richard M. Daley in 1989 reinvigorated the Chicago machine and ushered in a new stage of political turf wars in the 22nd ward. Shortly after his election victory, Daley's "closest confidantes—Tim Degnan, Bill Daley, and Jeremiah Joyce—reached out to political mercenaries in Chicago and developed alliances that evolved into potent political patronage armies loyal [to his administration]."[37] Two machine-backed Latino organizations emerged from these efforts: the Hispanic Democratic Organization (HDO) and the United Neighborhoods Organization (UNO). Al Sanchez, a founder of HDO, and Juan Rangel, director of UNO, organized hundreds of Latino volunteers to raise votes for Daley and his allies in the city council in exchange for city jobs.[38]

With a reloaded political machine, Mayor Daley used his army of Latino supporters to try to oust Little Village's politically independent politicians from office.[39] The first challenge unfolded in 1995, when Rangel challenged Muñoz for 22nd ward alderman. The election was heated and contentious. Rangel confronted Alderman Muñoz, a former member of the Latin Kings, on gang control, saying, "We didn't invite Muñoz [to a violence prevention event] because we don't support the active recruitment of street gangs into politics."[40] But independent Latino politicians retained support of a growing political base in Little Village, and Alderman Muñoz won reelection by 19 percent.[41]

Muñoz's victory was crucial to bringing alternative gang violence interventions to the 22nd ward, where the Chicago police long operated under the exclusive approach of gang suppression. In 1995 Irving Spergel, a professor at the University of Chicago, hired and trained former gang members to respond to

incidents of gang violence in Little Village and prevent retaliatory violence between gangs. Spergel described Muñoz as "concerned with social reform and improvement of living conditions
in Little Village." Spergel's project resulted in significant de-
creases in violence and arrests among Little Village youth.
Muñoz became an active participant and supporter of Spergel's
project, but the two aldermen on Little Village's east side were
"strictly beholden to the Mayor and the Chicago Democratic
Party Machine and had no interest."[42] Mayor Daley made it
clear, Spergel lamented, that "the destruction of gangs would be
accomplished almost exclusively through police suppression."
Even though Spergel's program was successful, Mayor Daley
and the police department refused to fund its operations, and
the project was ultimately terminated.

The 22nd ward faced another setback in 1998, when a
Daley-backed candidate, Antonio Muñoz, defeated Jesus
Garcia in his bid for reelection to the state senate. "I spent too
many resources in the 25th Ward and on [a colleague's] campaign and not enough time campaigning in areas where we had
done very well in '96, two years prior," said Garcia. "We had not
factored in the number of bodies the Hispanic Democratic
Organization could pull in on election days. Daley had built an
old-style patronage army that was called out on election day. It
was downtown versus the neighborhood, it was Mayor Daley
versus Jesus Garcia."[43]

Garcia's loss raised fear in Little Village that a Daley-backed
candidate might oust Alderman Muñoz. After Garcia's loss, an
HDO worker was quoted in the *Chicago Reader* saying, "Rick
Muñoz [is next], the writing is on the wall for him. They're
gonna take him out next....One by one. We're gonna get 'em,
each election. We're gonna bring 'em down one at a time."[44]
Upon losing the 1998 November election, Garcia immediately
went to work to assist Alderman Muñoz in his reelection bid in
February 1999. Muñoz won reelection with 66 percent of the

vote, but Garcia's loss forced Little Village political leaders to reassess their strategies for improving the 22nd ward.

The Development of a Nonprofit Infrastructure

Rather than reenter the political field, Garcia became executive director of the Puebla Community Group, a nonprofit organization established in 1990 that had been involved in small efforts to form block groups in the neighborhood. Though the wounds of his campaign loss were still fresh, he carried on the 22nd ward's political turf war against the Chicago machine by holding Mayor Daley and the Chicago Public Schools (CPS) accountable for a promise they made to build a new high school in Little Village. Originally, Alderman Muñoz had successfully lobbied the city to purchase a property in Little Village for the construction of a new high school to ease overcrowding at Farragut High School. Plans were set for construction in 2000, but the city never started the work and instead opened two new high schools in more affluent Chicago neighborhoods.[45] In response the PCG, led by Garcia, organized a public campaign to lobby the city for construction of the school. Gabriel Cortez's ethnographic study of this campaign describes the mobilization of Little Village residents: "Many individuals, from educators to factory workers and local politicians to community activists, were involved in spreading the awareness and importance of the campaign [for the new high school]. It was a conversation that took place at local grammar school councils, town hall meetings, and block parties."[46]

To mobilize Little Village against the city, Garcia hired Tomas Gaete, a Chilean political activist who had been exiled by the Pinochet regime. Gaete revitalized Little Village's block club organization by working long hours and knocking on doors to inform residents about the city's broken promise for a new high school. One block group participant describes Gaete's efforts: "A lot of people preferred to talk to Mr. Gaete and Mr. Gaete would get the permits [for block parties] from [Alderman] Muñoz. And that's how we organized. Blocks, blocks, and blocks, and that's how we connected."[47] This mobilization resulted in the creation of the "parents committee for a New Little Village High School." In April 2001, the PCG arranged a meeting between the parents committee and CPS administrators.[48] Parents were told there were no longer funds for the school and that they should lobby Illinois state legislators for funding. After meeting with representatives of Governor George Ryan, parents were told CPS had been given the money allocated for the school, and that they should ask CPS how those funds were spent.

Frustrated with the inadequate answers from government officials, Gaete and four members of the parents committee began a hunger strike on May 13, 2001, Mother's Day.

"Tomas [Gaete] forbade any community organization from putting their banners on the hunger strike," said Maria Senna, one of the original hunger strikers. "He said that he wanted it to be truly representative of the community, and not to advance the cause of any particular organization." Alderman Muñoz and fifteen more mothers would go on to join the group of hunger strikers in their effort to bring national attention to Mayor Daley's broken promise.

After two brutal weeks, CPS President Paul Vallas finally met with the hunger strikers and verbally agreed to construct the school, but he refused to commit in writing. Gery Chico, president of the Chicago Board of Education, met with several protestors and explained that the funds originally allocated for the new school had been spent on the construction of Walter Payton High School and Northside College Prep in white middle-upper-class neighborhoods. After this startling truth emerged in the national media attention brought by the hunger strike, both Chico and Vallas resigned. On May 30, the state legislature approved a $148 million funding allocation to CPS for the construction of the new Little Village high school.

After this major political win against the city, the PCG grew into a large nonprofit overnight. CPS and foundations funded the nonprofit to oversee the school planning process. As described by ethnographer Gabriel Cortez, "Little Village's victory elevated the PCG to new heights as a community organization.... Through the effort of community activism, [the PCG] were recognized as a prominent community organization and were rewarded hundreds of thousands of dollars to [oversee the school planning process]."[49]

The PCG's rapid ascent angered some hunger strikers and led to some small political turf wars among neighborhood activists. "We [the hunger strikers] had no say," said Senna. "The PCG was running the show, hosting community meetings but with the intent of saying, 'Here are your choices: A, B, and C,' while not letting anyone else set the agenda." She also complained that language barriers excluded residents from the deliberation process with the city: "You can't be talking in English at community meetings. You're shutting out the community when you do that."

Sitting across the table from me at the PCG headquarters in Little Village, Steve, the PCG director, recalled, "I think [the hunger strike] helped launch us, but the biggest challenge was managing, compromising the ideas and participation of everybody. You had educators at the table, parents, youth, bureaucrats, different agendas. CPS didn't know how to deal with community folks, and community folks didn't know they needed to compromise sometimes. Hunger strikers wanted there to be even more involvement from the community. A lot of relationships were damaged, severed."

"What couldn't people agree on?" I asked.

"The biggest tension was that there was a particular group of people who weren't satisfied with the level of community participation. They felt that every meeting there needed to be five hundred people involved in every single decision, and that's just impossible." Steve paused, leaned back, and continued, "We were involved in every decision, and they were happening quickly. At one point people wanted to delay the opening of the frickin school!"

"Was there ever a concern you might lose the school if you took too long to make decisions?"

"No," said Steve, "the tension was that if we didn't agree on stuff on time, [CPS] was going to move forward without us and make decisions for us."

The bittersweet success of the hunger strike taught PCG organizers a valuable lesson that would help in their approach to violence prevention work, namely, that open dialogue with city officials was crucial even if it came at the cost of some resident participation.

"There's a limit to community input," said Steve. "What ends up happening is that there's always an initial interest in the beginning, a lot of people come, but work turns people away. Like, we have to meet weekly, set up committees, create a vision, raise money, create an agenda—it's work. And what ends up happening is that the people who are willing to come put the work in are the people who become the decision makers." While collective action among residents was important for advocating for city resources, it also had drawbacks in the form of delays or failures to make use of the resources that arrive. The aftermath of the hunger strike forced the PCG to make tough decisions regarding whether to prioritize the interests of residents or city officials. They chose city officials, which helped the school open on time but alienated some hunger strikers.

"Good relations with local political leaders is critical," said Steve. "If you don't have many political relationships, you ain't gonna do much, period. That's the name of the game, that's the city we live in."

"Do you worry that this might alienate some residents?" I asked.

"You can't please everybody," Steve answered. "We don't have no magic formula. We've got two elected officials that got

our back: Jesus Garcia and Ricardo Muñoz. And those are political relationships with two progressive independents, not the
political machine."

The PCG's approach to working with the city after winning
some key political turf wars had advantages and disadvantages
for violence prevention. On the positive side, the PCG's relations with 22nd ward independent politicians helped bring
more resources to Little Village's west side, especially for violence prevention. Agencies like the Chicago Violence Prevention
Authority and Ceasefire preferred funding nonprofits recommended by local aldermen.[50] With Alderman Muñoz's support,
the PCG was funded to implement Ceasefire, the largest violence prevention program in the city. The PCG's work with
Ceasefire opened doors to funding to organize the Stop the
Violence event on Ridgeway Avenue. This series of successes
helped the PCG win a large grant to implement the Culture of
Calm programs, which hired dozens of community members to
watch over street corners and reduced violence around Farragut
High School. The decades of victories by activists, organizers, and
politicians in their political turf wars with the machine over the
22nd ward created what Robert Bursik would describe as systemic social organization, or an organizational infrastructure
that could funnel city resources to reduce violence.[51] Without these
political victories, events like Stop the Violence and programs
like Ceasefire may not have come to the 22nd ward.

On the downside, the neighborhood remained heavily underresourced, forcing the PCG and the alderman to select some
neighborhood areas to assist over others. Even in the 22nd ward
some blocks remained underserved. Residents who wondered
why their block did not receive the resources they requested,
such as a surveillance camera, art mural, or recreational activity,
accused the alderman and the PCG of favoritism. For example,
Violeta, a resident who was frustrated by her inability to schedule
a meeting with Alderman Muñoz, said, "The alderman is not

accessible and does not care [about your problem] unless you show what's in it for him." Violeta's harsh criticism indicates the 22nd ward's continuing struggle to advocate for sufficient resources to assist its large, economically disadvantaged population. The ward is dependent on the mayor and city council for resources, a situation that forced the PCG to dampen its social activism and resistance toward city government.

I asked Steve Beltran, "Would your organization [the PCG] ever put together another hunger strike against the city?"

"I think a lot of other channels would have to be exhausted," he replied, "because we have so many relationships with government officials and there are a lot of resources that we've got from the state and the city. I think a lot of people would have second thoughts about what the backlash of that could be. Could we be losing a lot of the resources that we worked so hard to get over these years? It's hard."

The 22nd ward still faces challenges meeting residents' needs, but through their decades of political turf wars against the machine, local independent politicians and community leaders carved out a position of power within the city's political structure. The 22nd ward, which once excluded its Mexican population, is now controlled by Mexican progressive politicians and nonprofits. These political victories opened the doors for the neighborhood to receive violence prevention resources like Professor Spergel's violence reduction project in the 1990s, Ceasefire and Stop the Violence in the 2000s, and the Culture of Calm in the 2010s. These resources made gang violence in Little Village's 22nd ward more manageable than the violence in the east side.

GERRYMANDERED AREAS IN THE EAST

For decades, the 22nd ward was the epicenter for Mexican political activism in Chicago, but Little Village's east side was gerrymandered and incorporated into numerous wards over the same period. In 1975 (see figure 2.5, left map) almost the entire east side resided in the white-majority 25th ward led by Alderman Vito Marzullo, a machine stalwart who had been in office since 1953. During the 1970s the Mexican population quickly grew in Little Village and the 25th ward. After decades of running unopposed, Alderman Marzullo finally faced a challenge in 1979 from a Mexican community activist, Juan Velazquez. Though Velazquez lost that race, the election made clear to the Democratic machine that it was only a matter of time before the growing Mexican population in the 25th ward would oust Marzullo. Consequently, Mayor Jane Byrne and the machine-majority city council passed a ward redistricting plan that gerrymandered Little Village's east side in 1981. Figure 2.6 (right map) shows the splintering of Little Village's east side in 1985. The Mexican population on the east side was split in half, absorbed by the white-majority 12th ward to the south and the white-majority 25th ward to the east.

The courts struck down this redistricting plan in 1986 and mandated the creation of Latino-majority 22nd and 25th wards. Yet, the gerrymandered ward boundaries in the east side remained unchanged. The 22nd ward needed to incorporate only one precinct each from the 12th and 25th wards to become majority

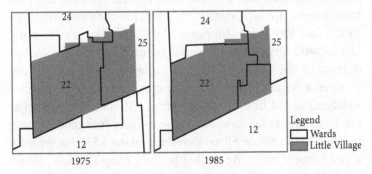

FIGURE 2.6 Ward boundaries in Little Village's east side, 1975 and 1985.
Source: Map Collection, University of Chicago Library.

Latino. Similarly, the 25th ward became majority Latino by absorbing Latinos exclusively from the 1st ward to the east. Little Village's east side remained splintered in the 12th and 25th wards.

While the court's ruling created four Latino-majority wards, the political damage to Little Village's east side went unaddressed. The 12th ward remained majority white and later made history when Alderman Aloysius Majerczyk became the first alderman in decades to endorse a Republican for mayor in the general election after Harold Washington's victory in the Democratic primary.[52] The 25th ward was represented by Juan Soliz, a Mexican attorney who originally fought alongside independents Rudy Lozano, Chuy Garcia, and Harold Washington. But after being passed up for jobs in Mayor Washington's administration, Alderman Soliz switched sides and became a vocal critic of Washington and a Democratic machine loyalist.[53] Even as progressive independents won the battle for the 22nd ward, Little Village's east side was still governed by machine loyalists in the 12th and 25th wards.

The 1995 ward redistricting changed Little Village's east side again, pushing the 25th ward farther east and out of Little Village and expanding the 12th ward to cover the majority of Little Village's east side (see figure 2.7, left map). This redistricting plan transformed the 12th ward from white majority to Latino majority, and Ray Frias (supported by Mayor Daley's Hispanic Democratic Organization) would become the first Latino alderman of the 12th ward in 1995. Alderman Frias quickly developed a reputation as "an alderman activists love to hate." Residents asked him to attend community policing meetings, but he always failed to show. Just two years into office he was indicted in Operation Silver Shovel for taking a $500 bribe from a government mole. According to the *Chicago Reader*, Frias's ward office seemed designed to keep the public at bay, with partitions that allowed no more than three people to enter at a time.[54]

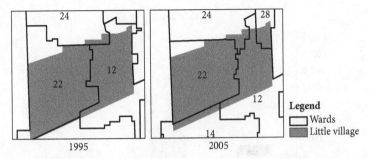

FIGURE 2.7 Ward boundaries in Little Village's east side, 1995 and 2005.
Source: Map Collection, University of Chicago Library.

In 1999, Mayor Daley and HDO supported George Cardenas, an unknown newcomer, in the race for 12th ward alderman. This loss of support surprised Frias and left him scrambling for resources to survive this challenge. It is unclear why the HDO withdrew its support; Frias may have upset HDO officials when he supported the candidacy of several Republicans in the Illinois state legislature. With three hundred volunteers and $50,000 in campaign contributions from the HDO, Cardenas forced Frias into a runoff election.[55] Seeing the writing on the wall, Frias withdrew his bid for reelection, and Cardenas became the new alderman of the 12th ward.

Little Village's east side was ready to embrace Cardenas, but the ward redistricting in 2005 carved up the area once again (see figure 2.6, right map). In addition to the 12th ward, chunks of the east side were absorbed into the 24th and 28th wards. The 24th ward was home to Alderman Michael Chandler, whose main constituents resided in the predominantly African American West Garfield Park neighborhood north of Little Village. Alderman Ed Smith governed the 28th ward, where the majority of blocks in the panhandle-shaped ward resided in Austin, another low-income African American neighborhood. It is worth noting that, amid all the ward boundary changes in Little

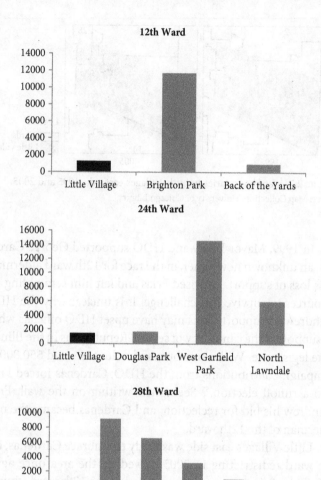

FIGURE 2.8 Number of neighborhood votes cast in aldermanic elections for ward 12, 24, and 28, 2003–2011.

Source: Chicago Democracy Project.

Village's east side, all maps in figures 2.5 and 2.6 show little change to the boundaries of the 22nd ward. While ward boundaries routinely splintered the east side, the 22nd ward in the west side remained remarkably stable.

Three graphs in figure 2.8 show the total number of neighborhood votes cast in each ward. In the 12th ward, Little Village precincts accounted for just 9.2 percent of the total votes cast in three aldermanic elections from 2003 to 2011, 6.1 percent in the 24th ward, and 2.1 percent in the 28th ward. Little Village accounted for four of the twenty-four precincts in the 12th ward, two of fifty-nine precincts in the 24th ward, and two of seventy-three precincts in the 28th ward.

In contrast to the 22nd ward in the west side, whose boundaries changed little and where over 90 percent of the votes cast were from Little Village residents, the decennial redrawing of the city's ward boundaries prevented blocks on the east side from being fully incorporated into any ward. The voter base of eastside Little Village residents is too small to significantly shape the outcome of any aldermanic race in the 12th, 24th, or 28th wards. While the 22nd ward's victorious political turf wars built systemic social organization that funneled resources for violence prevention through the PCG and alderman, the east side had no meaningful political victories. In fact, Little Village activists never had a real opportunity to obtain political power over the east side because it was split into several wards.

* * *

The disparate outcomes of political turf wars for the neighborhood's east and west sides are highly visible as one walks the streets of Little Village. The east side has more cracks in the pavement, more potholes, less green space, and fewer community centers.

The gerrymandered area in the east side of Little Village is not unique. Comparing the 2015 Chicago ward boundaries with the city's seventy-seven community areas, one can easily identify small pockets of neighborhood blocks that are splintered among several wards. For example, some of Chicago's most violent neighborhoods, like Englewood and Back of the Yards, are carved into four wards, while more affluent neighborhoods, like Bridgeport, Jefferson Park, and Rogers Park, are home to just one ward. Unraveling the persistence of violence in pockets of Chicago might entail unpacking the black box of the city council's decennial ward redistricting process.

The drastically different political histories of Little Village's west and east sides help explain how, on the same day, Ridgeway Avenue was the site of a major violence reduction event (Stop the Violence) while Marshall Boulevard was as eerily quiet and desolate as a militarized border. The two diverging tales of development in Little Village illustrate the importance of understanding how political turf wars for neighborhood space can shape residents' capacity for addressing problems like violence. These political turf wars had important consequences for the geographic concentration of violence in Little Village.

3

Burbs and Violent Blocks

MARCH 17, 2012, WAS a warm spring day in Little Village. On their front porch six-year-old Aaliyah Shell sat between her mother's legs, getting her hair untangled with a comb. A pickup truck pulled up to the house, and a man leaned out of the passenger-side window, shooting a revolver. Aaliyah's mother pushed her two-year-old brother to the ground and grabbed Aaliyah, hugging her tightly. But it was too late.[1] Aaliyah had been shot several times and died in the hospital later that afternoon. The perpetrators were two members of the Latin Kings looking to shoot their rival Two Sixers. Witnesses stated that the gang members shouted gang slogans before firing multiple times at a man standing near Aaliyah and her mother.[2]

This tragic scenario is all too common in Little Village. A gang member spray-paints gang symbols on rival turf, desecrates the memorial of a deceased rival, or gets into a verbal altercation on the street, and soon members of the rival gang are in a car, on the prowl to shoot dead not just the offending individual but any member of his gang. When pursuing rivals, gang members often look for an easy hit-and-run target, taking no precaution to protect bystanders. One of the easiest targets is an individual or group of gang members standing on a street corner or sitting on the front steps of a house, especially on streets that allow for an easy getaway by car. Many of the gang shootings on Little Village streets occur in this drive-by fashion, and tragic deaths like six-year-old Aaliyah's remind residents about the dangers of being in the wrong place at the wrong time.

For these reasons, one of the most common strategies residents took to prevent violence on their block was to stop gang members from loitering on sidewalks, street corners, or front steps. Clearing gang members from the block meant eliminating easy targets for rival gangs looking for someone to shoot. Yet, some blocks were better than others at getting gang members out of public spaces. While canvassing, I learned that blocks had different resources and institutional support to control their sidewalks and street corners.

To illustrate this difference, this chapter shares the stories of seven blocks in three different sections of Little Village: an area residents called "the burbs" (tract 3020), "the westside borderlands" (tracts 3017 and 3016), and "the eastside borderlands" (tracts 3002 and 3010).[3] The burbs, located south of 31st Street, had one of the lowest violent crime rates in Little Village. Residents referred to this area as the burbs because its mostly redbrick single-family homes resembled a suburb. The westside borderlands were a stretch of ten streets, five to the west and five to the east of the borderline dividing Two Sixer and Latin Kings territories. The eastside borderland was a smaller stretch of ten blocks that separated the Latin Kings and 22 Boys. Figure 3.1 is a map of the three regions. To maintain respondents' anonymity, I use pseudonyms for block names, but the regions shown in figure 3.1 approximate the location of these blocks within the neighborhood.

Figure 3.2 shows the number of reported shootings (aggravated battery with a firearm) between 2007 and 2012 on the seven blocks.[4] The blocks in the burbs (3100 Beaver, 3200 May, and 3100 Menard) had few incidents of gun violence, averaging just 0.66 shootings per block for the entire period. The borderland areas had more violence, with an average of 1.2 shootings per block on the west and 1.6 on the east. Shootings were unequally distributed

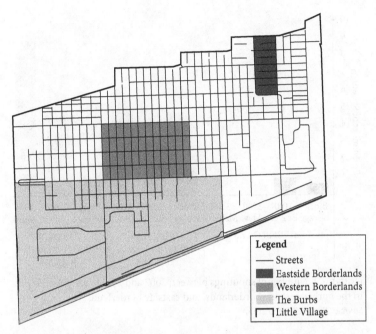

FIGURE 3.1 The burbs, westside borderlands, and eastside borderlands.
Source: Map produced by author.

across blocks in these regions. Three shootings occurred on 2800 Shedd and five on 2700 Bell, accounting for 34 percent of all shootings in the entire west side of Little Village. On the east side seven shootings took place on 2800 Pitt and nine on 2500 sword, accounting for 47 percent of the shootings on the entire east side. These blocks, which contained different levels of gun violence, present useful cases to help determine the forces behind the concentration of violence in Little Village's east side.

The political turf wars in Little Village's west and east sides heavily shaped these blocks' capacity to control gang members' use of space. On the west, side blocks in the burbs and western borderlands had more nonprofit organizations and city resources to socially control gang behavior and alter the local

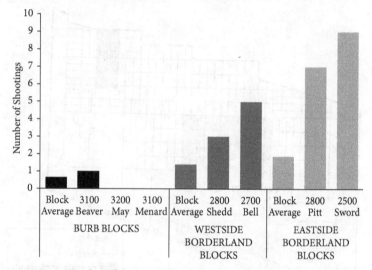

FIGURE 3.2 Number of shootings between 2007 and 2012 in canvassed blocks in the burbs, westside borderlands, and eastside borderlands.
Source: City of Chicago 2015.

ecology to prevent drive-by shootings. Residents benefited from resources like graffiti removal, surveillance cameras, and violence prevention workers who were effective at getting gang members off the streets when fights were brewing. Yet, these resources were still insufficient to meet the needs of every block, and pockets of blocks in the western borderlands stills struggled to control gang shootings. This situation was far worse on the east side. With fewer organizational resources and ties to political representatives, eastside residents were alone in their effort to curtail gang behavior and, as a result, were largely unsuccessful.

Social scientists tend to think of neighborhoods as places that either do or do not have the capacity to work collectively to address problems like violence, yet the divergent cases of Little Village's burbs, westside borderlands, and eastside borderlands demonstrate that the dynamics of collective action against violence vary block by block within neighborhoods.[5] Researchers need to recognize that systemic social organization, or the relationships among residents, organizations, and public officials needed to create social control, can vary even at the block level. In this study the political turf wars over Little Village blocks produced a west and east side with vastly different levels of systemic social organization for controlling gangs. As the following stories demonstrate, the political turf wars over blocks in violence-plagued neighborhoods can enable or constrain blocks' capacity to address violence.

THE BURBS

"What do you think of the violence on your block?" I asked seventeen-year-old Eddie as we sat in his living room after he completed a survey.

"What violence?" He replied. "Nothing ever happens around here."

"Oh yeah?" I responded.

"Yeah, everybody calls these blocks south of 31st Street the 'burbs' of Little Village, because they're like suburbs."

"In what ways?"

"Well, it's the only part of the neighborhood where some white people still live, but for the most part, it's because nothing really happens out here. It's quiet, and the people around here are really good."

Many of the forty-eight residents I interviewed in this region of the neighborhood described the burbs as a place where "nothing really happens." The burbs are located in the southernmost region of Little Village and are cut off from traffic by the Chicago River to the south and Lawndale High School to the west. Frederico, a longtime resident of the burbs, told me, "The only gang members I see are the ones that walk on the abandoned railroad tracks next to the river to avoid being seen by the cops or other gangbangers."

Despite the burbs' low violent crime rate, the area was not completely immune to incidents of violence. Aaliyah Shell's tragic murder occurred here, as did the murder of a Two Sixer who was lured into an alley and shot dead by Latin Kings. With the threat of violence always lurking, residents stayed vigilant to make sure their block never got out of control.

On the 3100 block of South Menard residents were careful to remove any gang graffiti from their walls or signs, and they benefited from the alderman's swift responses to their requests. "The graffiti is a big part of the problem," said Lorenzo, a resident of the burbs. "When [gangs] go back and forth spraying, they get mad, and start shooting each other. So we worked with the alderman to get the city to blast the graffiti. It was a pain in the ass, 'cause every time we painted over it, the gangbangers would just spray again. But eventually, [the gang members] got tired because we kept on painting over it. So the graffiti just stopped." Several residents of this block spoke positively about 22nd ward's alderman Ricardo Muñoz, who, in addition to graffiti removal, went out himself to fill potholes and remove tree branches from the street after a big thunderstorm.

Two blocks away, on 3200 South May, residents relied on relationships with the neighborhood's political leadership to alter physical features of the block to make it safer. My first encounter with the block happened on a 95-degree summer day. As I stopped for some water at a corner grocery store, I passed a resident watering his grass and saying hello to each of his neighbors as they walked by. "How's the fumigation going?" he asked a neighbor who stopped to chat for a few minutes.

After finishing my drink, I walked over and introduced myself. His name was Ed, and he was a firefighter who had lived on the block for fifteen years. Ed told me, "This block is the greatest and safest block in Little Village because of Ronny Santos who [pointing] lives in that big house with the garden. He got us that [traffic barrier], as well as surveillance cameras along 31st Street. He is the ward's precinct captain and the superintendent of streets and sanitation for the ward."

"What's a precinct captain?" I asked.

"Ever wonder who steals opposition political signs from your front lawn?" Ed asked. "That's a precinct captain."

In Chicago the position of superintendent for streets and sanitation for the ward is a government job appointed by each alderman. Appointees often serve as precinct captains who collect signatures to place aldermen on the ballot and who organize volunteers to get out the vote on election day. Though Ronny Santos politely refused to be interviewed for the project, his son, John Santos, said they had lived in the neighborhood for twenty-five years and advocated for physical barriers and speed bumps to block cars from entering and exiting the block quickly, to make drive-by shootings more difficult. "Our block is one of the most organized in the neighborhood. Do some of the resources come from guys my dad knows? Probably, but wouldn't you do the same thing for your kids?"

Julio, another resident on 3200 South May, described how over the years the block received a number of resources to reduce traffic. The direction of the streets surrounding South May were changed to make it difficult for any drive-by shooter to escape because getting to the nearest busy street would require driving in the wrong direction on a one-way street. "We also got these speed bumps and traffic circles at the end of the blocks to slow traffic down," said Julio. "It's not easy to get in and out of here."

These physical barriers made drive-by shootings difficult, a benefit that Two Six gang members on the block enjoyed as much as residents. A family of Two Six gang members lived two houses down from Julio, who hung out in front of their home at night. While one of the teenagers in the home completed a survey, his brother Anthony (a Two Sixer) said, "The [Latin] Kings are too afraid to come around here. They might get in, but they definitely ain't getting out."

Instead of directly confronting gang members and forcing them off the streets and sidewalks, residents on 3200 South May built several physical barriers to prevent rival gang members from quickly entering and exiting the block. "They [the gang-bangers] keep to themselves and don't start any trouble," said Julio. "I think they live here too because it's safer." The block's relationship with the ward's leadership helped facilitate access to the city resources and agencies needed to make these physical changes to the blocks.

In addition to the strong relationships between residents and the alderman and precinct captain, the burbs were located near several community centers and organizations that gave young people an alternative to spending time on streets and sidewalks. This was especially true of the 3100 block of South Beaver Street. Located a few blocks from Ridgeway Avenue, the dividing line between the Two Six and Latin Kings territories, Beaver Street was just a block away from one of the most active hot spots for gang violence. But when I asked a group of three teenagers sitting on the front steps of a house, "Are the gangs a problem in this block?," they replied in the negative.

"Not really," Jose said, "a lot of bad things happen on Ridgeway, a few streets away, but all the kids on this block just walk to the basketball courts by Gary Elementary School. There's other stuff to do besides gangbang around here."

"I go to the open gyms at this church around the corner," Ethan interjected, "because they have it there three days a week."

"We don't have to worry as much," said Stephen, "because we don't have to go far to get to these places. Like, I can walk straight down this street and get to Piotrowski Park or the gym at Little Village High School."

As the boys indicated, several organizations in the burbs provided spaces for young people, especially boys, to spend time playing sports. These included Boys and Girls Club locations, several basketball courts and soccer fields on elementary school grounds, and community organizations with weekly youth groups. Each of these places provided young people in the area with activities to keep them away from the street.

The police surveillance cameras on 31st Street, the northern border of the burbs, also made residents feel safe. "There used to be a lot of gang activity," said Lalo, a fifty-four-year-old resident on Beaver Street. "You used to see gang members running on the streets with bats and knives, but you just don't see that anymore where they put up the cameras."

Ignacio, a twenty-year-old Two Six gang member, lived a few houses down from Lalo. "Do the cameras make a difference?" I asked him.

"They're only good for one thing, stopping drive-by shootings because they can catch the license plate of the car. For anything else, all you need is a hoodie or mask to protect yourself."

Even gang members admitted that surveillance cameras made a difference in their use of space. Though Ignacio dismissed surveillance cameras as "only good for one thing," deterring drive-by shootings was an important goal in itself.

Figure 3.3 shows the location of police surveillance cameras, youth resource centers, and parks in Little Village. The Chicago River to the south served as an ecological barrier to traffic, and surveillance cameras and additional community resources were just blocks away to the north. Beyond the burbs, as the map shows, the west side had far more resources and green space than the east side. The geographic concentration of resources in the west was correlated with higher rates of participation in organizations and extracurricular activities among surveyed youth. In the burbs, 83 percent of surveyed youth (twenty out of twenty-four) participated in at least one organization or extracurricular activity, but the participation rate was

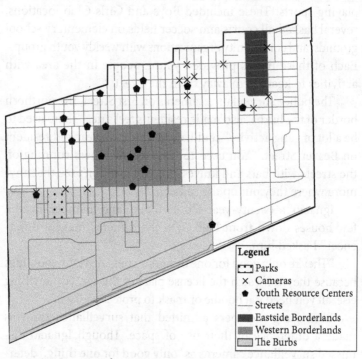

FIGURE 3.3 Location of cameras, community resources, and parks.
Source: Produced by the author.

only 73 percent in the west side borderlands (thirty-four out of forty-seven) and 36 percent in the east side borderlands (five out of fourteen).

While the burbs had the lowest violent crime rate in the neighborhood, not all blocks in the 22nd ward could easily prevent violence. The ward lacked the resources to give every block the same physical barriers as in the burbs, so small pockets on the west side were unable to alter gang behavior. Despite insufficient resources, the neighborhood's nonprofit and political leadership still found ways to prevent gang violence, though not to all residents' satisfaction.

THE WESTSIDE BORDERLANDS

A black cross and bright yellow flowers, colors of the Latin Kings street gang, lay next to lit votive candles on the corner of 28th Street and Shedd after a Latin King was shot and killed there. The Two Sixer who shot him was able to easily escape to his home turf only four blocks away. The three streets on either side of Ridgeway Avenue, the gang dividing line, were hot spots for shootings and homicides, according to both police and residents. When gang members stood on corners and sidewalks on these blocks, they were easy targets for a car driving through from rival territory. The adjacency of the two territories and the openness of the blocks that lined Ridgeway Avenue constituted what Peter St. Jean calls an "ecological disadvantage" by presenting opportunities for violent crimes to occur.[6] Due to a lack of resources, residents in the westside borderlands could not alter their physical environment in the same way as residents in the burbs. As a result, westside borderland residents needed to engage in face-to-face interventions with gang members to alter their behavior.

One day, as I canvassed the westside borderlands, I encountered twelve gang members standing on the sidewalk in front of two adjacent brick homes on 2800 Shedd in Latin Kings territory. The block was simmering with gang tension, and very few residents answered their door when we knocked.

"There was a shooting here yesterday," said Santiago, a resident, from the crevice of his chain-locked door, "but nobody got hit. The Kings and Two Six have been going back and forth shooting at one another for the past week."

As we approached the homes where the gang members were congregating, one walked up to me and my research assistants, asking, "What are you guys doing?"

"We're conducting surveys of neighborhood youth in Little Village. Are you between fourteen and eighteen years old?"

"Nah," said the Latin King, "but my guy has some kids that age. Come over here."

We followed the gang member to the house, and a six-foot-four-inch-tall man with a teardrop tattoo on his face came out to greet us. "What's up? I'm Jake," he said.

After I explained the study, Jake brought out his two teenage daughters, who agreed to take the survey. He and I spoke as the research assistants administered the surveys to the girls.

"Let me get this straight," Jake said, shaking his head. "You're walking around with iPods and cash to do surveys. In this neighborhood?"

"Yes," I said.

"You must be crazy," Jake said, laughing.

"You know, it hasn't been so bad. People have been really nice."

"Yeah, well, there was a shooting exactly where you're standing twenty-four hours ago. We were chilling here and some Two Six came by and shot at us. We hit them up yesterday, and we're waiting for them to come back." As Jake spoke, I moved a few feet to my left to take cover from the street behind a tree.

"You guys aren't afraid standing out here?" I asked.

"Nah, we're ready for them." Before Jake could continue, we were interrupted by a car pulling up. All the gang members stared intently but let their guard down after seeing that the car was driven by Tony, a violence prevention worker for the PCG. Tony was a former member of the Latin Kings who got out of the gang life and made a new living as a community organizer working to reduce violence. He was forty-five, had served time in prison, and walked with a limp as the result of having been shot in the leg years ago.

"What's up, guys?" Tony asked from the driver's seat of his rusty sedan.

"What up," Jake and the other gang members replied.

"Hey, the roof of my brother's garage came down this morning. I need a bunch of guys to help with the cleanup. Can you guys help me out?" Tony asked.

"I don't know, man, things are pretty hot right now. I need some guys on this corner," Jake replied.

"Come on, man, help a brother out," Tony persisted.

"All right," Jake answered, and nodded to the group standing on the corner. Eight gang members piled into Tony's car and drove off. The three gang members left on the corner walked away, and after Jake's daughters completed the surveys, we quickly left the area as well.

Though I didn't realize it at the time, Tony was not interested in getting gang members to help his brother. Rather he was trying to prevent violence on the block by getting the gang members off the street. A few weeks later I ran into Tony at PCG headquarters and asked, "Did you get your brother's garage fixed?"

"Ha," Tony answered, "I wasn't trying to get a garage fixed, I was trying to get those dudes off the corner before the Two Six came and they shot up the block." By asking the group of gang members for help, Tony managed to get them off the block's public space, where they were prime targets for a retaliatory shooting. When I entered the block, twelve gang members were standing on the sidewalk waiting for a shootout with the Two Six. By the time I left, the streets and sidewalks were clear. With the timely help of a PCG violence prevention worker, the block went from hot to cold.

Though shootings and homicides still plagued this area, nonprofit organizations like the PCG worked incessantly to prevent small gang beefs or conflicts from spiraling into retaliatory shootings. Violence prevention workers like Tony were always on call whenever trouble between gangs started to heat up. They would go to the scene of an altercation or shooting and work to get gang members off the streets to prevent them from being targets or distract them from retaliating.

In addition to violence prevention, the PCG hosted several mentoring programs for neighborhood youth that kept kids off the streets. On 2700 South Booker Street, a block in Two Six territory in the westside borderlands, a group of youth riding their bikes explained that very little happened on this block because of the PCG. "We all go to the PCG. It's where you go to talk about your problems," said Daniel, a fifteen-year-old resident on the block.

"What do you mean?" I asked.

"It's a place where you can relax, not worry about being unsafe. The people there are nice. I know Howard over there, he's a really cool guy."

"Yeah, the organizers there care about you a lot more than the teachers at my school," added Mike, perched on his bike.

The PCG headquarters had recreation rooms where youth played video games, exercised, or watched TV. It was a place that attracted dozens of young people away from the streets, even when tension ran high among gangs in the area. Alderman Muñoz also directly helped residents in the westside border-lands. Barbara, a fifty-year-old resident on 27th and Booker, explained that the alderman helped her shut down a liquor store that attracted gang members: "The liquor store was trying to get a permit to renovate, but I convinced the alderman to refuse them. How can you have a liquor store so close to a school?"

Not all blocks in the westside borderlands were successful at keeping gang members off the streets. This was the case on 2700 South Bell Avenue. The block was like an island. To the north and south were some of the most aesthetically beautiful homes in the neighborhood, with well-maintained front lawns and residents holding yard sales on the weekends. When I stepped onto 2700 South Bell, however, I was surprised to see no children or adults outside, and no one answered the door when we knocked. After an hour canvassing, a resident at the end of the block finally opened her door. Karina greeted me cautiously. As we spoke in her living room, she peered through a small opening in the door to carefully watch the cars driving by. I could tell she was worried about drive-by shootings. After allowing her son to take the survey, Karina encouraged us to move to the backyard.

Karina's son Tomas, who walked with a cane, met us at the back door. Tomas thanked us for getting away from the front porch because he was concerned about drive-by shootings on the block. "A lot of shootings happen right here on this corner," he said. Pointing to the scar on his right knee with his cane, Tomas told us that a stray bullet struck him in the leg, breaking several bones. "I wasn't the intended target," he said. According to Tomas, one house near the corner belonged to members of the Two Six gang who routinely hung out on the front steps and were the targets of drive-by shootings from Latin Kings.

"Is that why people pay close attention to the cars passing through the block?" I asked.

"Yeah," Tomas answered. "On this block you always want to see who is in the driver's seat. If you see tinted windows, you know to duck for cover."

Ridgeway Avenue, the street marking the boundary between the Latin Kings and Two Six gang territories, was one block over from Bell Avenue and close enough to a busy street that drive-by shooters could escape easily.[7] To make matters worse, Bell was a one-way street with no speed bumps and traffic flowing toward the busy street, factors that made for an even easier getaway by car. Several youth I interviewed in the westside borderlands described 2700 Bell as one of the most dangerous blocks in the neighborhood.

"I normally avoid 27th and Bell," said Bernie, a sixteen-year-old, "but when I have to drive by it, I always ignore the stop signs. You don't want to be there very long."

"I don't ever go near 27th and Bell," said Maurice, a thirty-year-old resident. "Not even when I'm driving."

To my surprise, a small corner grocery store operated on the corner of 27th and Bell. As I walked through the doors, a buzzer sounded to alert the clerk of a customer. A dark-haired middle-aged woman named Sara emerged from behind the counter. She was the store owner. I asked what she thought about the violence on the block.

"It's bad. Thank god, I live in Cicero, but when my daughter is here to help me out in the summer time, I never let her go outside. Never!"

"Yeah, I've heard from a lot of residents that it has gotten really bad on this corner."

"I really want a police camera on this corner," Sara said, "because the gang activity has caused my store to be very slow in the summer time."

"Have you tried to do anything about it?"

"Yeah, six months ago I went with six other residents to the alderman's office to request they put cameras in the corner because we've had four kids get shot in the past year. Three of them were gangbangers and one of them was just riding his bike and got shot in the leg. We were told by the alderman's assistant that they could not install cameras because the ward had no money to do that. He [the alderman] doesn't have money for a camera, but he has money for cameras in other parts of the neighborhood!"

Sara was referring to the surveillance cameras along 31st Street. The presence of cameras in other parts of the neighborhood led some residents to believe the alderman favored certain residents over others. In reality, the surveillance cameras on 31st Street were paid for by a state legislator; these cameras were too expensive to install and operate solely on the ward's budget. According to the Urban Institute, surveillance cameras help reduce crime but cost $190,000 per month to operate, or over $1 million per year.[8] The cash-strapped ward simply does not have the budget to continue adding cameras, but this was understandably upsetting to residents on blocks like 2700 Bell.

"Have you or the residents ever tried to confront the gangs themselves?" I asked.

"I did once. I told them to walk away from the front of my store because they were scaring away customers, and they told me, 'We don't care. Fuck you. Go inside.' The cops can't do any-thing about the gangbangers hanging out here because they're just standing there and not committing a crime. But the real problem ain't these gangbangers on our block. It's the ones from the other side that come here and shoot up the block."

Sara was right about the police's limited power to move gang members off sidewalks and street corners. In 1992, the Chicago city council passed an antiloitering law that permitted police to arrest individuals "loitering with no apparent purpose," but the U.S. Supreme Court ruled the ordinance unconstitutional.[9] With no surveillance cameras or help from the police, the store owner, in the words of Chicago school urban sociologists, tried "inter-vening on behalf of the common good" to get the gang members off the streets but was promptly dismissed with a "Fuck you."

Renee, a forty-five-year-old resident on the block, explained that the police did not help her clear the gang members from the street in front of her home; instead the police treated her like an enemy. She said, "I don't know what makes the gang members feel entitled to sit on my front steps, but they do it all the time.... It's scary to stand up to them." A few weeks before our conversation, someone called the police to report that the gang was selling drugs in front of Renee's house. When the police responded, they knocked on Renee's door and berated her. "They told me I was going to go to jail if I continued to let the gang members stand in front of my house!" she exclaimed. "I got into it with [the police]. I told them I wasn't going to put up with threats from them too." Pointing to an indentation on her porch left by a stray bullet, she said, "Do the police really think I want this shit?"

Sara's and Renee's experiences show how difficult it is for some residents to address the gangs on their blocks.[10] Though public officials like Mayor Emanuel and President Obama em-phasize the need for "community" to deal with violence in Chicago, residents on blocks like 27th and Bell were active community members. Yet, their efforts to contact the police or alderman, or to confront gang members directly, were not enough to reduce the threat of shootings in their block. Talking back to gang members on a street corner or taking back control of public space from gangs is not as simple as many believe. Successfully moving gang members away from public spaces requires institutional support, or what criminologists call systemic social organization or new parochialism.[11] As the stories of residents in the burbs and 2800 Shedd exemplify, blocks with ties to nonprofits and neighborhood political leaders were better equipped to socially control the gang members on their streets. Residents without these relationships were at a greater disadvantage.

At the end of our conversation Sara gave me the names and addresses of six neighbors she asked to join her in lobbying the alderman for a camera, and after leaving her store I encountered one of her collaborators: Maria, a sixty-five-year-old grandmother. She stood outside the store with one hand on her hip and the other shielding her eyes from the sun while she closely monitored five Two Six gang members standing on the corner.

"Worried about the gangbangers?" I asked.

"Yeah," Maria replied. "Four kids have been shot on that corner in the past year, and the three who were killed didn't even live on the block." We continued our conversation in her front yard as she kept a close eye on the gang members. She explained how residents on the block and the storeowner came together to approach the alderman: "[Alderman Muñoz] comes through the block with volunteers asking for signatures and asking if we would like to have a block party. Why do I want a block party when there are gang members shooting up the neighborhood? I don't want a block party. I want a camera put on the corner here where all the fights and shootings happen. I asked the alderman this when he knocked on my door, and he says, 'But I don't want the area to look like a neighborhood of delinquents.'"

After talking to Maria, I knocked on the door of Miguel, a forty-six-year-old resident who came up with an alternative plan to rid the block of gang members. Considered by his neighbors as the block group's leader, Miguel told me, "The gangbangers on the block live in two homes next to each other and have four kids who are all lookouts for the drug dealing they do inside. The police know what they are doing, but they don't come, and when I complain to [the police], they just tell me to call them when I see anything. A couple of neighbors and I, as well as the owner of the corner store, went to the police captain after the alderman kept canceling on us. And the captain told us that people will think that the neighborhood is bad if we put a camera up there."

"Does the alderman come by here?" I asked.

"Not really, he only comes during election years when he tries to give people block parties in exchange for their votes. But when it's not campaign season, he's not around. In the past, when Harold Washington was mayor, the previous alderman, Jesus Garcia, would always come here, knock on people's doors, get to know people. When Garcia was alderman, we convinced him to put a stop sign on this corner because cars were coming close to hitting kids. He listened and put up a stop sign, but with Muñoz, you can't go to him for anything."

Miguel's frustration with the alderman was a startling contrast to the approval of residents on blocks in the burbs. Though the political and nonprofit leaders in the 22nd ward did their best to address the violence, they had limited resources to do so. In Chicago, each alderman received $1.32 million in discretionary funds to serve the ward, and though that number appeared high to residents, it was not enough to operate more than one surveillance camera. Because of this, Alderman Muñoz explained (to a news reporter), "You can't put a camera on every corner, yet everyone wants one. This is 236 residential blocks. We are focusing cameras around schools and parks to prevent crime where children congregate."[12]

The residents on 27th and Bell bore the brunt of the ward's lack of resources. Worn out by their failed efforts to keep gang

members off the streets and limit the number of drive-by shootings, residents redirected their efforts to lobbying the landlords
who leased apartments to the gang members. Miguel explained,
"We talked to the owners of the homes that the Two Sixers were
renting, and we succeeded in getting one owner to not renew the
lease of one of the two families, but the other owner refused."

"Really?" I replied. "How did you do that?"

"A lot of the homes here are for rent by owner, and the
phone numbers of the owners are usually posted on the 'for rent'
signs. The Two Six gang members don't really take care of the
property, so they have never taken the 'for rent' sign off their
window, and so I called the number and managed to get ahold
of the owners. One was sympathetic and didn't renew their
lease, while the others simply refused because of the possibility
of a housing discrimination lawsuit."

"And with the one family that has remained, what have you
tried to do with them? Have you tried to reach out to them?"

"You know, in the past, my wife knew many of the gang
members because she taught them in elementary school. She
would tell them, '*Mijo* [son], get out of the front of my house, I
don't want anyone shooting at my house.' And they would listen.
She even convinced some of them to stay in school, and some of
them would even graduate. But the gang members living here
now don't know us because they just recently moved in and don't
want to talk to anybody. When she tries to talk to them, they just
call her a bitch. But even if we did have relationships, we have no
control over the gang from the other side of the neighborhood,
the Latin Kings, who come here and shoot at these guys."

In contrast to the public perception that residents on
violence-plagued blocks do nothing to address the problem,
Miguel's stories show that residents go to great lengths to fix the
problem. Without the luxury of a responsive police force or
flexible budget, residents like Miguel had to do more work with
fewer resources. "I went door to door to every house on this

block telling people to tell their landlords not to put 'for rent' signs on the windows of their properties," said Miguel. "I also told the landlords we would use our personal contacts to find good [non-gang-affiliated] tenants."

Miguel succeeded at getting one gang family evicted, but the other remained, and after running out of options to deal with that gang, he, Sara, Maria, and the other residents resorted to staying in their homes to avoid the violence. The block group dissipated shortly afterward. "We still look out for each other," said Miguel, "but we haven't met to try and do something about the violence in over a year. What else could we do?" Despite displaying all of the characteristics of a group with collective efficacy, these residents could not change the dynamics of violence on their block without the resources and support of public officials and nonprofit institutions.

PCG organizers acknowledged their inability to address the needs of all residents, especially those on blocks like 27th and Bell. Steve explained, "A lot of times, residents jump to the conclusion that we must be corrupt or not care about the community if we don't meet their need. What they don't know is that time and resources are limited. For example, every year there is only so much money to pave a certain number of streets, and that certain streets have to be prioritized for whatever reason, like traffic density. Another example is surveillance cameras. They might be where they are because there is a school across the street, or that intersection was deemed a hot spot by the police. People don't know the background of decisions, and they just assume the worst. And when you have an office that doesn't return phone calls or is not the most hospitable, which is a big thing we've struggled with, then you just fuel that sentiment among residents. When you don't have good customer service, people automatically assume something shady is going on."

"Does it concern you that your lack of response might be eroding residents' desire to improve the neighborhood?"

"Not anymore," said Steve. "It's just a reality. In the past it would bother me, but in this line of work you have to pick and choose your battles."

Nonprofits like the PCG operated on shoestring budgets and were often left scrambling when funding from the state legislature for violence prevention dried up. Though neighborhood leaders' victories in their political turf wars with the Democratic Party helped funnel resources to the 22nd ward, it was not enough to deal completely with all the pockets of gang violence in Little Village's westside borderlands. As Alderman Muñoz explained, surveillance cameras were too costly to install on many residential blocks, so the city and state prioritized their placement near parks and schools as well as near Cook County Jail (see figure 3.3).

THE EASTSIDE BORDERLANDS

On 2800 South Pitt Street in the east side, gangs had more control over blocks than residents. On this block, gangs' complaints about police outnumbered residents' complaints about the gangs. "The biggest problem on the block is the police," said Ramiro, a twenty-three-year-old member of the Latin Kings who spoke to us on his bicycle. "They're never around when something happens. They just arrest dudes." As we spoke, a police car pulled up at the end of the block and the officer looked at us from a distance. "See, they're going to come over and arrest the both of us now."

After a few minutes the police car drove away.

Just as we were about to continue our conversation, a white sports utility vehicle pulled up in front of us and called over Ramiro, who approached the driver, whispered something to him, and walked back to me as the vehicle drove off.

"Like I was saying," Ramiro continued, "if we had a park, I wouldn't be trying to be gangbanging, I'd be at the park playing ball. I'm a hooper." Ramiro was a huge basketball fan and loved playing whenever he had a chance, but aside from the green lawns on Marshall Boulevard, the east side of Little Village was starved of green space and public parks.[13]

The Latin Kings dominated 2800 Pitt and the surrounding blocks. Many of the women I saw there were the wives of Latin Kings who, adorned with the gang's tattoos and gold jackets, pushed their babies in matching black and gold strollers (the gang's colors). At another home on the block, an eighteen-year-old gang member answered the door and agreed to take the survey. He had just gotten the gang's name tattooed on his chest and proudly conducted the interview without a shirt. After knocking on a few more doors we found a home where the youth were not gang members.

"The block can get pretty bad with the shootings," said Cindy, a forty-eight-year-old mother of two daughters, "but the gangbangers don't mess with you if they know you. Like, I know these guys, they know my daughters, and as long as I leave them alone, they leave me alone."

With no nonprofit infrastructure, little help from police, and no attention from leaders of the 24th ward, where Little Village blocks accounted for less than 5 percent of the ward's constituency, east side residents rarely tried to get gang members off their blocks. Instead, they engaged in direct negotiations with gang members to protect themselves.

"We've never considered moving [out of Little Village] because if we did, it's the same [violence,] only with different gangs, except you have to start all over getting to know everyone on your block," said Janet, a thirty-eight-year-old mother of two sons. She continued as we sat on her front porch, "The gangs get you when they don't know you, so you put yourself out of danger by getting to know them."

Residents on Pitt and Sword Streets explained that in response to the lack of institutional support, they formed mutually beneficial relationships with gang members to be left alone. "The gangs on the block shot at my car with me and my daughters inside," said Janet. "Because my car is beat up like a lot of the cars driven by gangbangers, they mistaked me for a rival gangbanger. I got so mad because I tell my kids to never talk to police and never snitch on anybody in the neighborhood, and they still shoot at me.... So I walked with my kids to the house of one of the gangbangers. I told them, 'Look, we don't call the cops on y'all, and y'all shot at my kids. Leave us alone, and we'll leave you alone.' They apologized and promised to leave us be, and we haven't been bothered by them since."

With less institutional support to socially control the gangs than on the west side, eastside residents were less concerned about rival gangs committing drive-by shootings and more worried about being mistaken as a rival to the Latin Kings on their own block. In exchange for gang members leaving her children alone, Janet agreed not to report the gang's activities to the police.

Alicia, a thirty-two-year-old mother of three little girls, lived near a nightclub on Pitt Street that attracted loitering gang members and drive-by shootings. At first, she sought to pressure the 24th ward alderman Michael Chandler into closing the nightclub. "We went to every house on the block collecting signatures to get the club closed because it was bringing in all this trouble," she said. "We tried giving it [the petition] to the alderman, but we couldn't meet with him, so we gave it to his assistant and they didn't do anything about it."

"What ended up happening after that?"

"We just stopped. My neighbor Rocio stopped hosting meetings at her home, and then we just lost touch with each other."

The alderman's inaction and the ever-present threat of shootings on the block led Alicia to reach out to the gang to protect her children. She explained, "One of their female gang members who was a lesbian began threatening my daughter because they had all been going to a swimming pool and she [the gangbanger] thought my daughter was staring at her girlfriend. This gangbanger came by the front of our house yelling that she was gonna kick my daughter's ass, and that we were gonna hurt bad and this and that. So I got out, and yelled back, 'You are not going to hurt my daughter. Who is your block chief? Let me talk to them right now.' I really wanted to go out there and just plant her, but I knew if I did anything, they [the gang] would come after my daughter first. I didn't want any trouble, so I went to the block chief, told him what happened, and he said I didn't have to worry about it, and that my daughter would be left alone."

A "block chief" is the gang leader in charge of lower ranking gang members on the block. In the case of Alicia's conflict with the female gang member, reaching out to the block chief granted her daughter protection from the gang's aggression.

"So what did you say to the block chief to get him to listen to you?" I asked.

"I told him they wouldn't get any trouble from me calling the cops," Alicia answered. Like Janet, Alicia developed mutually beneficial relations with the gang, but only after failing to receive institutional support from her alderman.

On 2500 South Sword, in 22 Boys territory, Mateo, a forty-seven-year-old resident, claimed that he was robbed at 4:00 a.m. on his way to work. "The gang operates a drug house on the block, and they shot out all the street lights here so it's really dark at night. We've been trying to pressure the alderman [of the 28th ward] to fix the lights."

"I went to [Alderman Chandler's] office up north [in the Garfield Park neighborhood]," said Elena, Mateo's wife, "and he was there when I was there, but I only got to see his secretary, who said they would look into it. It's been months and nothing has happened. They [city officials] just don't care about us here."

To keep their teenage children safe, Mateo and Elena did not let them leave the house at night.

The last strategy residents took to protect themselves was to engage in their own acts of violence and aggression toward gang members. This was especially the case among men. Ben, a tall and athletic thirty-five-year-old father of three who lived on Pitt Street, described the violent encounter he had with a gang member who had stolen from him: "Every September, during Mexican Independence Day, I would always hang this big Mexican flag out on my front steps. And this past year, I saw this punk kid steal my flag! So I ran after him and lost him. I came across some kids in the alley and asked if they had seen a kid carrying a Mexican flag, and they said, 'Yeah, Cesar is right down there.' So I ran after him and asked why he stole it. He said he didn't, that he found it in the alley. So I beat the crap out of this kid. Apparently he was a member of the Latin Kings, and I learned that the gang put a bounty on my head. So instead of going to the police, I went straight to the block chief and told them that I had to beat this kid up, and that I wouldn't be a man if I didn't. This kid disrespected my family and my home by stealing the flag. The gang leader understood my point, called off the bounty, and made sure we weren't bothered again."

This form of vigilante justice in the eastside borderlands was based on masculine notions that men should protect their honor, home, and family. Like men in the urban ethnographies of Elijah Anderson and Ruth Horowitz, Ben adhered to these informal street codes to protect his home from the gang.[14]

A few houses down from Ben, a male resident in his early sixties relied on displays of aggression to keep gang members away from his house. One late afternoon, I was walking on the sidewalk toward my car. Simultaneously, a Latin Kings gang member exited his home across the street from me and greeted a friend with the gang's signature handshake. The two were standing in the middle of the street when the old man got out of his chair, picked up a hammer with one hand and a thick metal spatula with the other, and began crashing the two tools together to produce an excruciatingly high-pitched sound. Clank! Clank! Clank! This got the attention of the gang members standing on the street. The old man continued pounding the hammer and spatula together. Clank! Clank! Clank! One of the gang members flashed a gang sign at the old man, who responded by screaming at the top of his lungs, "Fuck you!" The older man aggressively stared down the gang members as they walked away. When I drove away, the old man was still clanking the tools in an aggressive display to get the gang members off the street.

Without institutional support from nonprofits or public officials, the only effective way residents could socially control gangs was by threatening to call the police, approaching gang leaders, or behaving aggressively toward lower-level gang members. None of these protective strategies seemed to break the cycle of violence in the east side. As one resident described it, "The block is like Mexico, where we settle everything ourselves instead of going to police."

* * *

Urban ethnographies have documented dynamics similar to the ones I observed on these Little Village blocks.[15] But by comparing residents' stories across randomly selected blocks of a neighborhood, we can see that residents' inability to address violence on their block did not emerge from their apathy or lack of will. Instead, they stemmed from the blocks' disconnection from an effective nonprofit and political structure. This disconnection was geographically concentrated in the gerrymandered areas of Little Village's east side where political turf wars between the Democratic machine and local independents stranded residents on islands of gang-controlled blocks with little institutional support to prevent violence. Little Village's geography of violence was rooted in political turf wars that fragmented the east side into various wards, rendering residents much less capable of changing blocks' physical landscape and controlling gangs' use of space than their counterparts on the west side.

Research on urban violence emphasizes the importance of factors like broken windows, collective efficacy, and ecological disadvantage to explain why some areas have more violence than others. Based on this research, programs designed to reduce violence focus on cleaning up streets or mobilizing residents into block groups. Missing from these explanations, however, is the role that political relationships play in connecting blocks with nonprofits and public officials who broker violence prevention resources while leaving other blocks devoid of such resources. The stories of residents in Little Village's burbs, westside borderlands, and eastside borderlands show the importance of the heterogeneous political spaces within neighborhoods for the concentration of violence within a neighborhood.[16] Residents in the burbs and in pockets of the westside borderlands were able to alter their blocks' physical environment using resources from ward officials. But in eastside areas gerrymandered by political turf wars, residents' efforts to control gangs were not met with support from local aldermen. Lacking institutional support, these residents had little choice but to cooperate with gangs or respond with aggression to ensure the safety of their homes and children. By paying attention to the political turf, as well as the gang turf of neighborhoods, it may be possible to better understand why some blocks have a stronger capacity to prevent violence than others.

4

Transforming Violent Streets on the Westside

"I'M SCARED TO WALK TO SCHOOL," said James Rodriguez, a seventeen-year-old student at Farragut High School in Little Village. Speaking to me in the entryway of his home, James continued, "I was dressed in my [school] uniform, and a gangbanger asked if he could use my phone. I said no. Then he pulled a gun out and told me to give him the phone. I gave it to him and he walked away. I ran toward school and flagged down a police car who gave me a ride home. I don't walk by myself anymore. I usually walk with friends or get a ride from my parents now."

Stories like James's were far too common among the 710 residents I interviewed in Little Village. The streets surrounding Farragut were among the most dangerous in all of Chicago. Farragut is located on the edge of the 22nd ward in Little Village's west side (see figure 4.1), sitting squarely in Latin Kings territory. For many Farragut students, this meant that they had to cross rival gang boundaries to get to and from school each day.

Farragut enrolls predominantly Latino students who live in Latin Kings territory, African American students from the adjacent North Lawndale neighborhood (territory of the Gangster Disciples street gang), and Latino students residing in Two Six gang territory (the main rival of the Latin Kings). With members of rival gangs—or even just residents from rival turf—regularly entering Latin Kings territory, the gang routinely engaged in

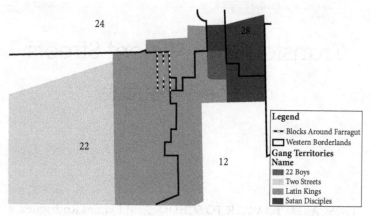

FIGURE 4.1 Gang territories, wards, and blocks near Farragut High School.
Source: Map produced by author.

violence to demonstrate its power over the streets surrounding the school.

"I wake up every day at 6:00 a.m. to walk to school before all the gangbangers wake up," said Iliana, a sixteen-year-old Farragut student. Iliana lived in Two Six gang territory and had to cross the gang boundary to attend classes. She first learned the meaning of the gang boundaries at age fourteen, when she crossed to play soccer with friends who lived in Latin Kings territory. "They [Latin Kings] saw me cross the street and they surrounded me. They told me I shouldn't be in this block because I'm from the other side. So I just ran away."

The violence around Farragut accounts for a large share of the overall violence in Little Village. From 2001 to 2015, the eight residential blocks surrounding Farragut accounted for 4.5 percent of all aggravated batteries (incidents of violence involving a weapon that leads to a victim's hospitalization) in Little Village. That number is staggering considering that the average block in Little Village accounted for 0.2 percent of batteries in the neighborhood. The blocks surrounding Farragut were the largest violent hot spot in Little Village's west side.

All of that began to change on a day in September 2009. Derrion Albert, a student at Fenger High School in Chicago's Roseland neighborhood, was walking home after school when he got caught in the middle of a fight between two groups of students. The large fight, recorded by students' cell phones, involved hand-to-hand combat and the use of makeshift weapons. In the chaos, Albert was struck in the head with a railroad tie and died soon after. The amateur video recording of Albert's murder was broadcast on the news and social media to the horror of millions across the nation. Major television networks like CNN and NBC devoted large portions of their news broadcasts to the topic of youth violence in Chicago. The national media coverage brought attention to the fact that a record high thirty-six Chicago Public School students were killed as a result of street violence in the 2008–9 academic year.[1]

In October 2009, the shock wave created by the tragedy reached the White House, where President Obama sent Education Secretary Arne Duncan and U.S. Attorney General Eric Holder to Chicago to meet with Anjanette Albert, Derrion's mother. "Youth violence is not a Chicago problem, any more than it is a black problem, a white problem, or a Hispanic problem," Holder said to the media. "It is an American problem."[2] Months later Chicago Public Schools (CPS) received $260 million from President Obama's federal stimulus legislation, of which $40 million was allocated to create one of the largest and most expensive violence reduction initiatives in the city's history: the Culture of Calm.[3] Six of the most violent high schools in the city were selected as pilot sites for the intervention, and Farragut was among them.

The Culture of Calm established a mentoring program and a crossing guard program called Street Watchers. The mentoring program sought to increase the attendance and grade point average of fifty students chosen by a CPS formula to be the most at risk of falling victim to violence. The ultimate objective of the mentoring program was to simply prevent the physical harm of these "at-risk youth." Street Watchers sought to decrease violence during school hours by distributing fifty crossing guards wearing bright yellow vests across all street corners surrounding the school to deter violence simply by their highly visible presence. In Little Village, a call for grant proposals circulated among neighborhood nonprofits for a portion of the $2 million in available contracts to implement the programs, and the PCG secured the contract.

The influx of federal funds to these distressed blocks of Little Village significantly decreased violence on the streets around Farragut. Figure 4.2 shows annual violent crime trends in the eight blocks surrounding the school. This analysis includes only homicides and aggravated batteries. From 2001 to 2010 levels of violence fluctuated greatly, but when the program began in 2010, violence was on the upswing, poised to reach the high levels of 2003 and 2006. Instead violence declined slightly in 2010–11 and dramatically declined in 2012–15. The worst years before Culture of Calm saw two homicides near school grounds and an average of one extremely violent incident *per month*. Since the implementation of Culture of Calm, no homicides have occurred in the blocks surrounding Farragut High School, and between 2012 and 2015 these once violent streets averaged just one violent incident *per year*.

The large decline in violence around Farragut demonstrates the west side's capacity to prevent violence, highlighting the importance of political independents' victories over the mainstream Democratic Party in the turf war for the 22nd ward. While gerrymandering in the east side of Little Village stunted the development of an organizational infrastructure for addressing violence, the 22nd ward's high level of political organization helped build a nonprofit infrastructure to acquire and effectively implement violence prevention programs. Through the community's struggle to build a new high school, the PCG grew into an organization

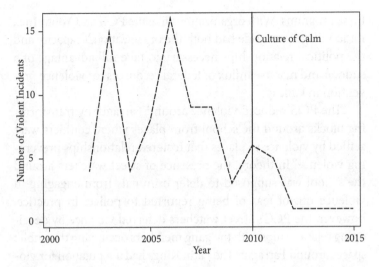

FIGURE 4.2 Violent crimes on blocks surrounding Farragut High School before and after Culture of Calm implementation.
Source: City of Chicago 2015.

with the capacity to implement large violence prevention initiatives like Culture of Calm. The PCG also collaborated with Youth Inc., a violence prevention organization that had been working with gangs in Little Village since Professor Irving Spergel's intervention in the 1990s to socially control the Latin Kings. A vast network of relationships that included residents, gang members, nonprofits, school faculty and staff, city administration, and the federal government transformed the violence in the blocks surrounding Farragut.

This successful intervention would not have been possible without the election of Barack Obama, a Chicagoan and former Illinois senator, who as president shone a national spotlight on Chicago. The media attention on violence in the president's hometown fomented national concern over violence, and the President's personal concern for the city's young victims helped Chicago Public Schools acquire the federal resources to design and implement these programs. With organizations like the PCG and Youth Inc., Little Village's west side had both the organizational capacity and the political relationships necessary to take full advantage of a sudden and massive influx of federal resources for violence prevention in Chicago.

The PCG reduced violence around Farragut by transforming blocks around the school from places where conflicts were settled by violence to places that fostered relationships preventing violence. In theory, the presence of street watchers around the school was supposed to deter criminals from engaging in violence out of fear of being reported to police. In practice, however, the PCG's street watchers deterred violence by developing relationships with the gang members occupying the public spaces around Farragut. The Latin Kings had a reputation for violently retaliating against residents who reported the gang's crimes to police, so the PCG had to find alternative ways to prevent violence. Instead of using police as a first line of defense, Tony, the supervisor of the Street Watchers program, regularly communicated with gang leaders to build a new social order around Farragut. This communication protected street watchers from gang reprisal, reduced gang activity at the school, and prevented violence from breaking out. The PCG's direct work with gang members was the last link in a chain of relationships from the White House to Chicago Public Schools to the the 22nd ward that enabled the influx of government resources to transform violent streets around Farragut. The following stories relate how the PCG overcame several barriers to accomplish this feat.

TRAINING DAYS

Tony, the director of the Culture of Calm program at the PCG, spent much of the summer prior to the program's launch advertising job openings for street watchers. Recruitment was challenging; the job involved waking up early in the morning to stand on the corners of some of the most violent blocks in the neighborhood between 6:00 and 10:00 a.m. and again between 2:00 and 5:00 p.m. Street watchers were paid only minimum wage to do this outdoor work through the brutal Chicago winter. It was not an easy job.

Tony posted flyers at churches, community buildings, and schools throughout the neighborhood, but he also took a less conventional approach to recruitment, advertising at the basketball league organized for gang members. As players huddled near a fan to cool off in the gym, which lacked air-conditioning, Tony handed out flyers, saying, "Anybody want a job? We're hiring. You hear that? We're hiring!" During a break between games he approached Alonzo, a Latin King, as he was walking off the court: "Hey, if you're looking for a job, I'm hiring people for this program at Farragut High School."

"But I've got a record, man," Alonzo responded.

"That's cool," Tony answered, "as long as you don't have no Class X felonies, you're straight." Tony handed Alonzo more flyers. "Here, hand some more of these out to your people, and make sure to tell them they can apply with a rap sheet, but no Class X felonies." Class X felonies include aggravated kidnapping, aggravated battery, home invasion, aggravated criminal sexual assault, armed robbery, aggravated vehicular hijacking, aggravated arson, and possession of 14 to 100 grams of a controlled substance.[4]

Tony believed that hiring gang members for the Street Watchers program was essential for obtaining the cooperation of the Latin Kings, who were responsible for most of the violence occurring around Farragut. "I have to let [the Latin Kings] know we're not trying to target them," said Tony, "that we're only out here to make sure no kids get hurt." By hiring just a few Latin Kings, Tony hoped to convince the gang that it was policing itself.

Tony added, "I don't want to bring in just any gang member. I want to bring in guys fresh out of prison who are trying to get a fresh start. Plus, these guys need jobs. Who else is going to hire them?" By hiring gang members recently released from prison, Tony hoped to find men with a strong incentive to refrain from engaging in violence. Breaking the rules could cost more than their jobs; it could send them back to prison.

After weeks of deliberation, Tony hired three gang members. Of the three, Sam was the most important. He was a midlevel leader who had just returned to the neighborhood from prison. "Sam was a guy with a lot of juice," said Tony. "He grew up around the school, and he was respected enough by the young guys that they would actually listen to him." Because street watchers were supposed to report crimes to police, Tony needed to maintain an open communication channel with a gang leader to prevent the gang from retaliating against his employees.

"The gang has guns. My employees don't," said Tony. "So we can't be authoritarian with the gang. But at the same time, I'm not going to give the gang more power than they really have." Tony made the gang members he hired aware that assaulting a street watcher on school grounds would not be charged as a normal aggravated battery. Instead, according to Illinois law, the crime would carry an additional ten to fifteen years. "It's a special battery," Tony told the gang leaders. "Your boys would be locked up for a long time."

The Street Watchers program hired fifty people, but the mentoring program was much smaller, with just ten mentors. Their objectives were also more challenging: (1) raise the GPA of the selected students by half a point each semester, (2) increase their attendance by 50 percent, (3) decrease their rate of suspension or disciplinary problems, and most important, (4) make sure mentees were never victimized by violence. Nilda Hernandez, supervisor of the mentorship program, hired mostly college-educated young adults to be mentors. Each mentor had prior experience as a social worker, youth group organizer, or mentor for other programs.

Two weeks before the start of the school year, the PCG held a full day of training for mentors and street watchers at a church. I arrived at 6:00 a.m. and helped Tony deliver boxes of donuts and coffee to the conference room as the sun rose and roosters crowed from the yards of nearby homes. We unfolded dozens of chairs to form a large circle. By 8:00 a.m., the seats were filled with street watchers and mentors, a motley crew of characters: a mix of former gang members adorned with tattoos, college-educated young adults dressed in business casual attire, older people with strong Spanish accents, and middle-aged working-class men in track suits with slicked-back hair. Mentors were required to have a college degree, but anyone without a Class X felony on their record could be a street watcher. Approximately 20 percent of the new hires were African American, and the remaining 80 percent were Latino.

"Hi everyone," said Tony to begin the training. "We're here today to make sure that you have all the tools you need to serve the kids. You are going to be hearing from people from a variety of organizations who can help refer services to the kids you get to know." The first few hours of the training consisted of thirty-minute sessions with staff from a variety of organizations who provided services related to violence prevention. Presenters explained their organization's services and how they could assist young people in difficult life situations. Diana, a representative from Job Corps, told the group, "If you want to help a kid find a job, I have contacts at the University of Illinois–Chicago's urban health program and Hispanic Center for Excellence that can help." José, a lawyer from an organization called Community Alliance told the group, "If any of your students need a lawyer, call me because I have contacts with several law firms that do pro bono work. We are willing to help students with whatever issue they have, whether it's related to violence, being foreclosed, or police." At the end of his session José handed out a pamphlet detailing important facts to know when talking to police; these include the right to ask if you are being charged with a crime, the right to video-record police, and the right to an attorney.

Susan, a staff member at Cook County Hospital, explained, "If your kid needs medical care and doesn't have insurance, go to the county hospital but expect to be treated rudely. That's just how they are." She pulled a card out of her pocket. "Here is a phone number that will get you directly in touch with a doctor at the county hospital. This way you don't have to navigate the long and complicated menu when you call the general hospital number."

"What if the kid I'm bringing to the hospital is a gang member?" asked a street watcher.

"Prepare to be questioned and treated like shit by both the hospital staff and police. The hospital staff let cops in to harass kids, but they are not, I repeat, they are not allowed to do that! If you see that, take the names of the staff and tell the kids they don't have to talk to the police."

The PCG's training armed mentors and street watchers with a variety of resources to assist the youth they would encounter on the streets, whether they were students or gang members or both. This training prepared mentors and street watchers to not simply deter violence but also to broker resources for finding medical care, a job, or legal assistance. "We want kids to know that they can solve their problems without violence through these other resources," Tony said just before the group broke for lunch.

As we sat eating sandwiches, mentors and street watchers exchanged tips about how to handle violent situations. Al, a mentor, told a group of street watchers, "You need to let these kids know that when they threaten someone [verbally], that can be considered aggravated assault. That's why I always try to tell my students to never curse."

The second half of the day focused on teaching everyone how to quell a violent situation. Dr. Jim Donahue, a psychologist from a neighborhood health clinic, stepped to the center of the circle of chairs and addressed the group. "The first step with getting help is to know how to get help. Never just tell your student to come to my clinic. If they do a walk-in, they will have to wait at least one hour, and 99 percent of the time they're going to walk out because of the wait. You need to set up an appointment for them."

He continued, "Now, before you try intervening in anything, you have to get to know as many of these kids as possible first, and you need to teach them how to communicate their emotions. The urge to commit violence is an emotion that they just have to quell, and it takes time to get there. If you can't get them to communicate, then you at least need to try and physically get them out of the situation. Insist on giving them a ride home."

Freddy and Santino, violence prevention workers from Youth Inc., followed Donahue's presentation. Men in their forties with streaks of gray hair, Freddy and Santino each had twelve years of experience working in violence prevention. They grew up in Little Village and were former gang members—Freddy in the Two Sixers and Santino in the Latin Kings. Few violence prevention workers had more experience working directly with gang members.

"This is not a nine-to-five job," said Freddy. "We're on call twenty-four-seven. When a kid gets shot, we go to the hospital. When a kid dies, we help the mother cope. I can tell you, nothing beats knowing the friends and family of the person you are trying to mentor."

"You need to find a way to connect with them," Santino added, "whether it's through sports, recreational activities, healing circles, tutoring, art, whatever. You just need to find a hook to get them in."

"You also can't fear them," said Freddy. "They can sense that. How can you expect them to be helped if you make them feel feared? Show no fear and keep your promises. Think of all the people who have let these kids down. You can't be added to that list."

Nodding his head in agreement, Santino said, "And be your authentic self. Don't out-thug them, don't out-dress them. Find your own style."

A street watcher stood up and asked, "Well if we're out on the streets, what do we do if we actually see a fight break out? Do we call the cops? If we call, I know we're going to get in trouble with the gang."

"Just take out a pen and paper and jot down notes on what you saw," said Santino. "And give the notes to Tony, who will then give that to the police. Do not use your phone, do not say anything to anyone on the street." Santino's advice helped put street watchers out of danger and made Tony primarily responsible for reporting crimes to police. Tony's training positioned him as the key mediator between the Latin Kings and the police.

OVERCOMING A ROUGH START

Though the mentors and street watchers were trained to forge relationships and broker resources, the Culture of Calm got off to a rocky start when Principal Valdez of Farragut initially refused to assist the PCG. The principal looked negatively on the organization because it hired former gang members. So Tony's first hurdle was to mend the PCG's relationship with the principal. Things did not start smoothly. One month into the program, Valdez was still skeptical about the PCG: "The programs they run have a reputation for corruption. I know violence prevention programs are supposed to hire guys who were ex-gang members, but some of the people [the PCG] hire are the worst of the worst. It's like being an alcoholic. You don't want to be in a bar if you're a recovering alcoholic. Some of these guys in these programs are still gangbanging. And the guys they chose for the street watchers program.... You can't have guys with their pants all baggy and [tattooed] because they look like gangbangers when they're out there."

Valdez was critical of the PCG because of the risks associated with hiring former gang members. She worried that a violence prevention worker might get caught dealing drugs or engaging in violence. A slip-up by the PCG could damage her reputation in CPS or even get her fired. The principal was more comfortable working with Freddy and Santino of Youth Inc. because Santino had been a student of hers decades ago when she was a teacher. Her preference was worrisome to Tony, who explained, "The contract [to implement Culture of Calm] is up for renewal every year, and if you're not doing a good job, then CPS can give the grant to somebody else." Knowing this, he suspected that Valdez was setting up barriers to sabotage the PCG's implementation of the Culture of Calm programs in the hope that the contract would be awarded to Youth Inc. the following school year.

Tony's suspicions were confirmed by my interviews with organizers at Youth Inc. Although the PCG and Youth Inc. collaborated at times, they also shared some bad blood over the need to compete for funding to implement violence prevention programs. After the PCG won a number of key grants, Youth Inc. staff grew resentful. At Youth Inc. headquarters one day, Freddy said to the other staffers, "I'm tired of the PCG winning these grants all the time."

"Forget the PCG," Santino responded. "Why don't we go straight to Chicago Public Schools at the contract renewal time and gangster [steal] the grant from them?"

Freddy leaned back in his chair, crossed his arms, and looked at the ceiling as he thought about Santino's words.

"You know that's how CPS works," Santino continued. "You know if organizations don't do what CPS wants, then they can give the contract to somebody else. We should just talk to Principal Valdez and see if we can gangster it. Bring her on board with us and get that contract."

"Nah," Freddy finally replied, "we can't do that."

Though Freddy chose not to undermine the PCG, Valdez indeed favored Youth Inc. and set up barriers for Tony and his street watchers. During the school lunch hour one day, she peeked out her office door, greeted Tony, and said, "You know, I respect what you do, but I don't like some of the people you hired as street watchers. The other day I went for lunch and saw some that straight up looked like gangbangers with baggy pants, and I swear, one of them is a Latin King."

"I understand your concern," Tony replied with a half-smile. He sighed, looked the principal in the eye, and continued, "But the reality is that the police don't run the streets. These street organizations do, and for us to be cool with the gangs, we have to have some people like that in the program." The interaction ended peacefully but did not resolve the tension.

The conflict deteriorated further when Tony, sitting across from me at a table in a neighborhood restaurant, received a call from the police commander reporting teacher and resident complaints about some of the street watchers. Even sitting a few feet away, I could hear the commander's voice screaming through the cell phone. Tony held the phone several inches from his ear to spare himself the pain of the shouting. When the call ended, Tony said, "Apparently, during lunch hours, Principal Valdez drives her car around the school and calls police on street watchers smoking or using their cell phones on the job." Because Culture of Calm funds came through CPS, the street watchers had to follow CPS rules, which prohibited cell phone use on duty and smoking on school grounds. After three offenses Tony was required to fire and replace street watchers. To enforce these rules, Valdez drove around the school campus in her red sedan and took notes. On three occasions, while shadowing some of the street watchers, I observed her driving around the neighborhood during school hours, not lunch breaks.

Valdez's efforts led to the firing of ten street watchers. Two months into the school year, the Thanksgiving holiday party at the PCG was supposed to reward staff with free food and a day off work, but Tony had little time to relax. He was on his phone frantically calling everyone he knew to find replacements. He was not oblivious to Valdez's motivations. Sitting in the stairwell of the PCG office while taking a break from his phone calls, he lamented, "The principal of that school hates us! She is giving us a hard time so that next year, when the contract is up for renewal, she can try and convince CPS to give it to Youth Inc."

The principal's actions also constrained the mentors, who, on the first day of school, learned they were not permitted to enter the school. "I tried walking in through security, and they let me into the waiting room, but I was not allowed to enter the hallways or lunch areas of the school. How in the hell am I supposed to find these kids [mentees]?" asked Richard, a PCG mentor. "They [the school staff] told us we had to wait for our students in the waiting room after school finished, but most of these kids ditch school early." This made it extremely difficult for mentors to find their mentees and arrange times to meet. Teenagers often forgot or ignored appointments, so face-to-face contact was critical. Mentors had to wait at the school door, hoping to catch their mentees leaving school, or look for them at home.

In the rare event that a mentor tracked down a student, he or she was further hampered by Principal Valdez, who did not allow mentors to use school space for one-on-one sessions. John, a PCG mentor, shared, "I have fifteen kids that I have to mentor, and the school doesn't provide me the space to do that. They don't let me even enter the building and do the mentoring sessions inside the school! They claim they have no space for me to meet the students, and so I meet with them at a nearby taco restaurant."

Even more constraining was the fact that PCG mentors were required to obtain the consent of their mentees' parents before beginning any one-on-one sessions or interventions. With no help from the school to contact parents, Santiago, a PCG mentor, explained, "Most of my work in the first few months wasn't even working with the kids, but trying to track down these parents and getting the forms back from them, and the school doesn't help with getting any of this done."

Frustrated with the process, about half of the mentors quit by the end of the fall semester, sending Nilda into a scramble to find qualified replacements, just as Tony had for the street watchers program. "I had no clue that this was going to be such a difficult process," said Nilda. "It's almost as if Principal Valdez wants us to fail." Nilda was unaware of the principal's distrust of the PCG, but she still sensed the principal was sabotaging her efforts.

Nilda's intuition was supported by the principal's preferential treatment for workers from Youth Inc., who were given unfettered access to the school even as PCG mentors were excluded. Freddy of Youth Inc. explained. "Principal Valdez has been at Farragut a long time. She was my GED teacher back in the day. She has a relationship with my mother-in-law and was actually trying to hire me to be security at the school because of my connections with the Latin Kings, but Youth Inc. offered me a job. So instead she has given us free rein on the building and knows the work we do. I don't even have to sign in to enter the school, and I can go and pull somebody out of class when we need to."

"She's a dictator," Nilda said. "She could do what she wants and she doesn't have to explain anything to us."

The situation reached a boiling point after Tony attended parent-teacher conferences. "Parents were telling me they heard the principal say street watchers were getting paid ten dollars an hour to do nothing," he said. "I'm done with all this. I have to talk with Freddy to get this straightened out." He asked Freddy, "Could you call Principal Valdez to make her see that even though I work for the PCG, that I'm still a good guy?" Freddy agreed to see what he could do.

"This beef between the PCG and the Farragut principal is deep," Tony lamented. "I don't know what else to do."

The following week Principal Valdez and Tony had no choice but to work together when *NBC Nightly News* decided to film a story about the Culture of Calm program at Farragut. The segment included interviews with the president of CPS, Principal

Valdez, and various students, all filmed on site at Farragut. With the spotlight of the national news media looming, Valdez's sabotage ceased. In fact, she held a meeting with the street watchers for the first time and approached them as partners.

"Principal Valdez actually told us she was happy with our work so far!" Tony exclaimed to Freddy as they crossed paths near school grounds.

"Ha!" Freddy yelled back. "See, I told you she was going to be cool after I talked to her." It appeared as though a combination of Freddy's influence and the national media attention got the principal to change her attitude toward Tony and the street watchers.

"We need you on your best behavior," Valdez told the street watchers at a meeting in preparation for the arrival of the news film crew. "And whatever you do, do not talk to the media. Leave that to us." The filming of the news segment went off without a hitch and was broadcast to the nation as part of a series of stories covering programs that "make a difference."

With patience, relationships with other organizations, and persistence, PCG staff were able to weather the storm of the principal's resistance. In their evaluation of the Culture of Calm program, the University of Chicago Consortium on School Research found that a lack of support from school principals, lack of space within schools, and delays were common implementation barriers at all schools, not just Farragut.[5] But navigating administrative politics was only half the battle for the PCG. Even after overcoming this problem, they still had to do the work of transforming the streets around the school.

TRANSFORMING VIOLENT STREETS

The Culture of Calm program transformed the streets around Farragut from places where gang conflicts were settled through violence to places where relationships were brokered or mended to prevent violence from occurring. Street watchers in fluorescent yellow vests worked not just to monitor gang activity but also to get to know the youth at Farragut.

"I love these kids," said Chuck, a forty-year-old African American street watcher, as he stood on a street corner. "They're so young and they try to act so hard, to be so gangster, and you just gotta get them to understand they don't have to be that way all the time." Chuck provided an example of how he built relationships with youth on his street corner: "This kid must have been sixteen years old. I see him every day walking to the school boxing gym with boxing tape around his hands, so I started calling him Little Boxer. And I think it rubbed him the wrong way because he started staring me down every time I called him that. Then he started coming with his other sixteen-year-old friends, and they all started staring me down. So I stared them back! And after a couple days I approached the kid and told him I was calling him Little Boxer because of the tape on his fingers, and that I didn't mean anything bad by it. He laughed and thought that was cool. Now we're friends, and he even gives me a heads up when trouble might be brewing with certain kids."

Chuck's successful attempt to build a relationship with Little Boxer exemplified some of the lessons Santino taught street watchers at the training. In his interactions, Chuck did not show fear, nor did he try to "out-thug" the kids by threatening them back. He stood his ground and then reached out to the boy. His efforts resulted in a friendship that also provided key information for violence prevention.

Applying the lessons she learned from the psychologist at the training, Rebecca, a forty-two-year-old street watcher, talked about the importance of getting kids to reflect on their emotions to ease a conflict: "When these kids are fighting, it's all this emotion that's coming out, and they fight without thinking, so when you get them to think about the consequences, the battle is over for most of these guys."

Rebecca put this lesson to practice on a snowy afternoon when she caught two students cursing at one another. "Hey, there's no need to say that," she told them.

"I'll whoop your ass," one young man said to the other.

"No you're not," Rebecca said. "Think about it. Is this guy worth it? Worth getting suspended from school? Going to jail?"

The young men kept quiet and stared at each other before slowly walking in opposite directions.

"There we go," Rebecca said before turning to the small crowd of students who had gathered around them. "That's it. Let's just go home, everyone. There's nothing to see here, people." After a few minutes the kids dispersed.

Following Freddy and Santino's advice, street watchers found creative ways to build relationships with the kids they saw every day to prevent violence from breaking out. "Oh, I love that song," Blake, a street watcher, said to a group of kids listening to music on the way to school. He danced and sang the song out loud in his cracked voice, much to the delight of the kids walking by. These small exchanges built a bond between the street watchers and the students that would be helpful for addressing conflicts in the future. "A lot of these kids fight because they feel they have to," said Blake. "It's that pressure of not wanting to look like a punk. They don't want to fight, but if there's no way out, they have to. And we [the street watchers] give them a way out."

Previously the street corners around Farragut had been places where disputes were settled by violence, but relationships between street watchers and youth prevented conflicts from reaching that point. The street watchers mended relationships among youths and kept warring parties apart.

Sam, the Latin Kings gang leader on the street watcher staff, helped the program gain the legitimacy it needed to influence gang members' behavior on the streets. After school one day Tony, Sam, and I were standing on a street corner just outside the school's front doors when two Latin Kings came riding past us on bicycles carrying lead pipes. Seeing this, Sam shouted, "Hey, Shorty! Where you going with that pipe?" The two immediately turned around and came back to us. They looked like they were twelve or thirteen, but their arms were adorned with tattoos of the gang's letters and symbols.

"What are you guys up to?" Sam asked.

"Just doing the rounds," one answered.

"Y'all can't be doing that right now, not around here at least," Sam said. "And keep the damn lead pipe under your jacket or some shit. You can't be starting shit around the school, got it?" The kids nodded, put the pipes underneath their baggy hoodies, and rode away.

"Sam has a lot of juice with the young Kings," Tony said as we walked to another street corner. "The Kings have their younger guys ride around the neighborhood like a patrol to alert the gang of police or a rival entering their turf, but Sam is changing all that. He can go to any one of these guys, pull them aside, and say 'You need to chill out,' and they'll listen."

"Why do you think they listen?"

"Well, first, because they know they might get their ass beat if they don't," Tony answered. "But most of them aren't scared of that. It's more like, these kids know Sam just got out of jail, they know his livelihood is at stake with this program. If they fuck it up, they know they might cost Sam his job."

Sam's participation in the Street Watchers program provided the rest of the workers with the legitimacy to tell younger gang members to take their activities elsewhere. This legitimacy enabled street watchers to stop physical fights from escalating into more serious violence. One rainy day Sean, a street watcher, returned to PCG headquarters at the end of his shift with a story for Tony: "I saw a King tuck a pistol into his pants and walk down Sword Street. I knew him because he walks by a lot. I just told him, 'Look, man, I don't know what you're up to, but you're putting me in a bad spot. If you're going to walk with that thing, could you walk in the alley or something, because if something happens you're going to get me in serious trouble.' "

"What did he do?" Tony asked.

"He was like 'All right, cool,' and he just turned and walked down the alley away from the school."

"Okay, good." Tony said. "I'll tell Freddy and Santino to keep an eye out for this guy."

The relationships that developed on the street corners built a sense of mutual obligation between street watchers and gang members. The street watchers looked after the gang members, and the gang members avoided doing anything that could cost a street watcher his or her job. "I try to tell them about my kids," said Sean, "to let them know I'm feeding a family with this job and so I really need to keep it."

Though the goal of the Street Watchers program was visibility, it was more than the simple presence of watchers that deterred violence around Farragut. The *relationships* forged between street watchers and gang members helped ease tensions and protect the blocks. As evidence of this effect, during the week that Sean saw the Latin Kings member with the pistol, police records indicate that no violent crime occurred near the school.

The street watchers were also critical for reducing violence between African American and Mexican gang members around the school. "Before there was black and brown tension at the high school, where black security guards would back up the black students and Mexican security guards would back up the Mexican students," said Tony. "It was bad." But by hiring a mix of black and Mexican street watchers, Tony helped ease the racial tensions triggering violence between the African American Gangster Disciples and the Mexican Latin Kings during afterschool hours.

"We have this system," Tony explained, "where the black street watchers would distract the GDs [Gangster Disciples] as they walked home and the Mexican street watchers would distract the Latin Kings."

"How would they distract them?"

"Just putting your arm around them, asking them how they're day is going, making sure they just keep walking home and don't stick around."

One afternoon Tony got word of rising tensions between a member of the Gangster Disciples and a member of the Latin Kings. In response, he had Chuck and Sam stand outside the school doors, ready to intercept the teens as soon as they left for the afternoon. "Nah, Chuck, I'm going to mess this kid up," said the young Gangster Disciple as he walked out of the school.

"Hey, Stan, we ain't doing that, Stan, we ain't doing that!" Chuck replied, putting his arm around the kid and walking him toward home. At first the youth resisted, but Chuck, a tall and heavy man, proved too strong to push away.

"Come on now, Stan, don't get me trouble man," Chuck said. "Let's go, let's just go home."

When Chuck and Stan were a block down the street, Sam snagged the young Latin King as he walked out the door. "Hey, not today, little man. Not today," said Sam.

"What the fuck, man? This GD was talking shit."

"I said I don't care, man, not today," Sam insisted as he grabbed the kid by his hoodie with one hand and walked him away. "You know you can't be doing this. Let's go."

Easing racial tension was not always easy, however. In the middle of the year, Tony replaced a Mexican street watcher who had been fired with an African American street watcher on the corner of a block where a Latin Kings gang leader lived. This did not go over well with the gang leader. He approached the street watcher to ask where he was from. Feeling nervous for his safety, the new street watcher called the police.

"I had to play dumb to the cops," Tony said. "I wasn't about to call the cops on one of the Kings' leaders." Instead Tony walked to the gang leader's home and explained, "Look, I don't mean no disrespect, but we got to have guys out on these street corners. It's part of the school's program to keep the area safe."

"But your guy was wearing a blue hat on my block," said the gang leader. "I can't let that happen." Blue was the color of the gang's rivals to the east, the 22 Boys.

"Hey, this guy didn't know that, all right? He's just from another neighborhood," Tony said. "How about this: I'll put somebody who you could trust on your corner. Just make sure nothing happens to him, all right? You know if you guys run on [violently retaliate] any one of these street watchers, it's a special battery. The cops are going to lock you up for a lot longer."

"All right, that's fine. Just get this guy out," the gang leader responded.

Although this conversation helped dispel the street watcher's conflict with the gang leader, Tony still had to find a replacement for that corner. He chose Grace, a sixty-two-year-old grandmother. "The Kings know what will happen if they go after one of our guys," said Tony, "and I know for a fact that none of them would run on a grandma." He was right. There was no gang activity with Grace on the street corner. In fact, during the entire year no street watcher was ever harmed for reporting a crime or conflict to the police. "Of course, some threats were made," said Tony, "but nobody ever got retaliated against for talking to police."

On most occasions, however, street watchers prevented conflicts from ever escalating into acts of serious violence that required police intervention. "I think we were successful because we always tried to squash beefs before they got bad," said Tony. "We used the police as a last resort. I think the gangbangers respected that, and listened to us for that reason. They knew we didn't want to call the cops as much as them because then we both look bad. They get locked up, and we get in trouble for not doing our jobs." The relationships formed through the everyday interactions between the street watchers and the gang members built a social order in which each felt a mutual obligation to help the other.

* * *

The PCG's successful implementation of the Street Watchers program followed a long history of innovative alternative violence prevention programs implemented in the 22nd ward of Little Village dating back to the early 1990s.[6] The resources and organizational infrastructure employed by the PCG to support the Culture of Calm came from politically independent groups' victory in the political turf war against the Democratic machine. After gaining political representation, social services, and a new high school, the PCG and Youth Inc. were well equipped to communicate directly with funders, police, and local gang leaders. Most of the city's aldermen are beholden to the mayor's "tough on crime" agenda, which emphasized punishment and arrests. In contrast, 22nd ward alderman Ricardo Muñoz supported alternative approaches that incorporated relationship building and service provision, not just suppression.

By keeping an open communication channel with both the police and the Latin Kings, Tony and the street watchers significantly reduced violence around Farragut. The Street Watchers program in Little Village supports the findings of other urban ethnographies showing the importance of third parties, like the PCG, for creating informal social order in high-crime areas.[7] Church leaders and nonprofits have played crucial roles in brokering peace between gangs, yet these ethnographies do not explain why mediators are present in some areas of a neighborhood but not others. In Little Village, the neighborhood's west side had a deeper and more extensive form of systemic social organization than the east.[8] The blocks around Farragut benefited from nonprofit violence prevention organizations' social ties to actors as diverse as the Latin Kings, Chicago Public Schools, and the 22nd ward alderman. These ties allowed them to capitalize on the funds produced by another key relationship, that between the mayor's office and President Obama. Federal funds helped pay for the Culture of Calm, enabling the PCG to hire, train, and supervise street watchers in ways that prevented disputes among gang members from turning violent. Just a few blocks east of Farragut, the street dynamics could not have been any more different. In the absence of an organizational infrastructure and responsive political leadership, the streets remained a battleground for street turf wars involving gangs and police that triggered violence.

PART TWO

STREET TURF

5

Silence and the Art of Arson

WHEN EASTSIDE RESIDENTS PROMISED NOT to call the police in return for gang protection, they abided by what locals in Chicago call the "code of silence," which many political and law enforcement leaders consider one of the most powerful forces sustaining neighborhood violence. The code drives a wedge between police and residents, allowing street violence to persist without the threat of repercussion from the legal system. To combat the code, the city of Chicago created a public campaign to raise awareness of the consequences of protecting violent criminals. The campaign, called Silence Kills, included television and print public service announcements in which family members shared stories of losing a loved one to violence. Their stories were accompanied by the tagline "Stop the violence, stop the silence, silence kills."[1]

"If you know about a crime, report it," Mayor Daley said at a news conference announcing the campaign in 2010. "Something as simple as using a cell phone to report a crime can solve a crime. And there are many ways people can safely and anonymously report crimes and criminals." In the campaign's logic, violent crime rates would drop if residents in violence-plagued neighborhoods could be convinced to call police. But the mayor and proponents of the Silence Kills campaign did not fully understand the context driving residents' silence. While canvassing in

Little Village, I found that residents followed the code not because of a lack of sympathy for victims but because of fear—of both gangs and police.

"What do you think about the police in the neighborhood?" I asked Rachel, a thirty-five-year-old resident, as we sat in her backyard.

"They're terrible," she answered. "We don't call them because they tell the gangbangers who calls."

"What do you mean?" I asked in disbelief.

"The cops tell the gangbangers who is calling," Rachel repeated, rolling her eyes to indicate that I was asking a question with an obvious answer. "A lot of people know that around here."

After hearing Rachel's and others' stories of apparent police collusion with gangs, I investigated these claims through fieldwork with the Latin Kings, who had ties with Youth Inc., the violence prevention organization where I volunteered.

On the way to an event with Freddy, the Youth Inc. organizer, his van got a flat tire. "How is your research going?" Freddy asked as we changed the tire.

"It's going well," I answered. "You know, I was surprised at how many residents have said that they don't bother calling police because the police reveal informants to the gang."

Freddy paused for a second, looked around to make sure no one was nearby, and told me to come closer to him as he whispered, "You got to understand. Some of the Latin Kings have police scanners. Not just any scanner, but the *actual* police scanner. So when the cops make the call, they hear [imitating a cop's voice while pretending to hold a scanner] 'Ten-twenty, can you go respond to Blake Street and Twenty-fifth? The neighbor at 2530 just called saying the gangs have been dealing drugs every day, and these folks have called more than once or twice so we should really get out there.'"

My later fieldwork confirmed what Freddy suggested that evening. To coerce residents into following the code, the Latin

Kings conducted covert surveillance of police to identify informants, violently retaliated against residents, and misled residents into believing it was police who revealed their identity. The code of silence persisted not because of a character flaw of Little Village residents, but as a result of a turf war over residents' cooperation between the Latin Kings and police. The Latin Kings depended on the code of silence to support their illicit economic activities. If residents routinely reported their crimes to police, it would become difficult for the gang to survive.[2] Aware of this, gangs often try to win over residents through bribes or the threat of violent retaliation. Like gangs, police also depended on relations with residents to support their activities. Without residents reporting crimes, identifying criminals, and testifying in court, the police could not do their jobs.[3] Policing neighborhoods with organized criminal groups requires careful work to protect informant identities. This is one reason why law enforcement agencies combat the code of silence through anonymous tip hotlines.

When police inadvertently disclosed informant identities, this triggered conflict between gangs and residents, resulting in the gang enforcing the code with violence. The gang's weapon of choice was the Molotov cocktail. This violent crime is legally categorized as aggravated arson, which the Chicago Police define as "malicious burning of a dwelling of another when the offender foresees or anticipates that one or more persons will be in or near the property being burned."[4] Between 2007 and 2012, 74 percent of all aggravated arsons took place in the far eastern section of Latin Kings territory in Little Village. The Latin Kings were so adept at enforcing the code that Little Village's east side became an aggravated arson hot spot.

Survey results indicated that the majority of Little Village youth following the code of silence resided in Latin Kings territory. Respondents were asked, "If you spotted a gang member committing a crime, would you call the police?" Figure 5.1 maps the location of residents who followed the code by census tract.

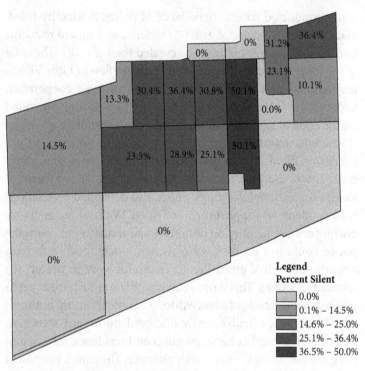

FIGURE 5.1 Percentage of surveyed residents who followed the code of silence by census.
Source: Data and map produced by author.

Interestingly, most Little Village residents did not follow the code of silence. In the two tracts of the burbs, not a single respondent followed the code of silence. In the far western side and small pockets of the east, only 15 percent claimed to follow the code of silence, in contrast to 50 percent in the eastern section.[5] Figure 5.1 shows that aggravated arson and adherence to the code of silence were both concentrated in similar parts of Latin Kings territory on the neighborhood's east side.

In contrast to the west side, where relations between the PCG and the Latin Kings enabled street watchers to report gang crimes to the police, the east side had no intermediaries to prevent retaliation against residents who broke the code of silence. Youth Inc. was the only organization with that capacity, but with a budget in the hundreds of thousands and a staff of just two organizers (Freddy and Santino) working the streets, the east side simply did not have the personnel or resources to prevent violence on a large scale. In contrast, the PCG's violence prevention budget was in the millions, enabling them to hire dozens of personnel.

The stories that follow show how the turf war between police and the Latin Kings concentrated arson and residents' adherence to the code on the east side. The city's Silence Kills campaign proposed that residing in a violent neighborhood renders some individuals more likely to follow the code than others, and that eliminating the code requires persuading individuals to cooperate with police. By contrast, this chapter takes a relational perspective, showing that the code of silence is the outcome of competition between police and gangs for residents' cooperation. Tackling the code requires turning the tide of this competitive turf war, a war that the Latin Kings were winning. To prevent further erosion of residents' trust in law enforcement and to avoid inflating gangs' reputation as powerful street organizations, police needed to learn that gangs closely monitored and subverted them.

THE LATIN KINGS

The Latin Kings were what many would call a "supergang" or a corporatized gang.[6] They were one of the city's largest wholesale drug dealers (selling to drug dealers, not drug consumers) of heroin, cocaine, and methamphetamine, as well as sellers of fake IDs and social security numbers.[7] According to law enforcement intelligence reports, the Latin Kings had a bureaucratic structure comprising a president and midlevel block leaders (known as block chiefs) who supervised the gang's lowest-ranking members, called soldiers.[8] Much of the Latin Kings' illegal activity in public spaces consisted of soldiers selling fake IDs and patrolling the neighborhood with a firearm to fight off rival gangs or drug dealers. Maintaining a code of silence with community members was necessary to protect the gang's illicit businesses.

The Latin Kings' relationship with police had been hostile and adversarial throughout its history. Since the 1980s, when the gang grew into a large and corporatized street gang, law enforcement had resorted exclusively to suppression strategies of arrest and creating stiffer sentences for organized criminal activity. During the 1990s, Irving Spergel embarked on his gang violence reduction project in Little Village, which incorporated gang members into violence prevention work, but he was unable to attain support from police or city officials. Spergel wrote, "The reality of project achievement did not make sense in Chicago's political, criminal justice, and social-agency climate between 1992 and 1997, and perhaps still does not today.... The key leaders of the city were not aware of or willing to address the systemic and complex nature of the youth gang problem in Chicago in inter-institutional and balanced strategic terms, involving social intervention and job and educational opportunities, as well as suppression targeted to gang youth." During the 1995 aldermanic elections in Little Village, Spergel documented that only suppression-based strategies were discussed as solutions to the problem of gang violence during candidate debates.[9]

The turf wars continued through the 2000s as law enforcement agencies conducted several raids on the gang's leadership. In 2006, the U.S. Bureau of Alcohol, Tobacco, and Firearms arrested the gang's highest ranking leader in Operation Broken Crown.[10] This operation was so well publicized that it was featured in an episode of *Gangland*, a popular cable television program.

In 2008, the Federal Bureau of Investigation conducted Operation Pesadilla (nightmare), which resulted in the arrest of over forty Latin Kings.[11] In 2009, the FBI conducted Operation Augustin Zambrano, which resulted in the arrest of the man who stepped into the role of the gang's leader after 2009, as well as eighteen midlevel associates.[12]

Though the PCG used programs like Ceasefire and Street Watchers to prevent violence, it saw little opportunity to convince the police to ease up on their war against gangs. "The police have never been the most responsive," said Howard, a PCG staff member. "I remember meeting with the commander and asking him to tell officers to be more careful with protecting informant identities. But change ultimately comes down to the culture of the police. And when you have to pick and choose your battles with the city, the police simply are not going to change. We're better off leaving them alone."

Constrained by battles with city officials over resources in Little Village, the leaders of the 22nd ward were not able to advocate for serious changes in policing strategies. When Youth Inc. managed to build a relationship with the local district police chief on the east side, their efforts were undermined by leadership turnover within the police. "We had a good relationship with one commander who approached us to have workshops on cultural sensitivity with youth," said Freddy, "but then the commander left and we lost that. Then we had to start a relationship with the new guy. Then the new guy left and we had to start over with the new new guy."

The combination of political constraints and police leadership turnover left police outside the circle of violence prevention programming in Little Village. This kept law enforcement agencies locked in an adversarial turf war with the Latin Kings.

The centrality of suppression to the city's gang control strategy was exemplified by the political response to a secret meeting between Chicago Police Chief Jody Weis and leaders of the Four Corner Hustlers street gang in Garfield Park.[13] With homicide rates rising and a spike in the number of police officers killed in the line of duty that year, the chief offered the gang leaders in the neighborhood an ultimatum. "[We told] these guys: You got to cut the violence—or else," said a police officer. "The first gang that kills somebody, we will go full barrel after your whole gang."[14] If the gang became involved in a murder, "authorities [planned] to make their leaders' lives miserable, doing everything from towing their cars for parking violations, to ramping up parole visits, to pulling them over repeatedly for traffic stops."[15] This strategy of sitting down with gang leaders was informed by the success of efforts to decrease violence in Boston by communicating directly with gangs.[16]

After the meeting came to light, city and state elected officials sought to score political points by criticizing Chief Weis and calling for greater gang suppression. Alderman Bob Fioretti stated that Weis was "negotiating with urban terrorists," and Alderman Joe Moore said, "We ought to be working hard with the feds and U.S. Attorney's office to start applying these RICO statutes [laws against organized crime] now instead of giving [the gang leaders] a warning."[17] U.S. Attorney Patrick Fitzgerald said that he had no interest in bargaining with gang members but instead wanted to send the gangs "a message that...the more violent they are, the more of a target they are."[18] Even Governor Pat Quinn criticized Weis's strategy, saying, "In my opinion, I don't think that's the way to go. I think a better way to go is to take on the assault weapons used by gangs to terrorize neighborhoods."[19] Despite Mayor Daley's publicly defending the strategy, and evaluations showing that the meeting contributed to a 40 percent decrease in homicides in Garfield Park, all of the candidates for mayor in 2010 disapproved and promised to fire Weis upon taking office.[20] The city's attempt to implement an alternative gang control strategy was attacked by government leaders who insisted on prolonging the turf war.

This was the state of relations between police and gangs when I embarked on fieldwork with the Latin Kings by volunteering at Youth Inc.

"Do you play basketball?" Tony asked me as we sat in Youth Inc. headquarters.

"Yeah," I said. "I played in high school and still do every now and then."

"Great, because I need some young guys for my team. You want to play in a league? We play on Thursday evenings at Johnson Elementary School."

I accepted Tony's invitation. When I walked through the gym doors for my first game, all of the players warming up had Latin Kings tattoos and colors. "Am I in the right place?" I asked myself.

The league was composed entirely of gang members from the Latin Kings and violence prevention workers. Organized by Youth Inc., the league served several important functions. Besides getting gang members off the streets, it enabled Freddy and Santino to build trust with them. Friendships formed on the basketball court would prove critical when Freddy or Santino needed to suppress a conflict or stop the gang from retaliating. Organizers also used the league to share information to help gang members find a job, access social services, or get a criminal record expunged. The league had twelve teams, one with violence prevention workers and the rest representing different block sections of the Latin Kings. The names of the teams referenced their particular block; for example, the basketball team from 7700 South Cutler Street was the Cutler 77s. The games were held on Thursday nights in a local elementary school gym from 7:00 to 11:00, with a new game starting at the beginning of every hour, so there was plenty of down time for players to talk in the stands.

When I joined the league, I did not have to introduce myself because the Latin Kings already knew me as "the survey guy" who canvassed their blocks. Two additional factors helped me establish rapport with gang members. First, the basketball team I played on was by far the least talented; we did not win a game all season. But because I played organized basketball in high school, the Latin Kings respected my skills. Second, because I wore glasses, always had a notebook on hand, and was often dressed formally when I arrived at games, gang members routinely teased me, calling me "the Mexican Clark Kent." Their respect for my basketball skills and trash talking helped establish trusting relationships. Through this trust I was able to ask gang members about the code of silence as we sat in the stands between games.

IDENTIFYING INFORMANTS

"You should have joined our team when you had the chance!" yelled Vinny, coach and leader of the Cutler 77s, who just finished beating my team by 40 points.

"We would have helped you get as many surveys as you needed!" Stylo, a twenty-four-year-old gang member, shouted, and the rest of the team laughed. With the game over, both teams walked to the hot dog stand. I told Stylo I could use some of his help for my research and asked whether gangs in general used police scanners to get a heads-up on police.

"Yeah," he answered, "and we got a few of our own too."

"Yeah, right, man. Stop playing," I replied. But Stylo was insistent and went on to describe how the Latin Kings acquired one of the police scanners.

"A cop spotted one of us hopping over a fence and running away," he said, "and he's in a rush to get over that fence and chase us, and his scanner fell out of his jacket. One of our boys saw this from his house, walked by like nothing happened, and snatched it up." As Stylo recalled the story, he laughed loudly and drew attention from a few Latin Kings sitting nearby. They laughed along and told me that they acquired another police scanner when a police officer set off on a foot chase with his car door open. Kyrie simply grabbed the scanner off the car seat.

Having a police-issue scanner made it easier for the Latin Kings to listen in on police communications. They could find police frequencies on ordinary radio scanners or websites, but extensive effort was required to determine local beat officers' exact frequency. The police-issue scanner was already programmed to the local channels, making it easier for the Latin Kings to monitor police activity in their territory. This allowed the gang to engage in covert surveillance of police without bribing officers, as residents were led to believe.[21]

Vinny later confirmed the gang's use of the scanner when I encountered him while canvassing the 2700 block of South Blackrock Avenue. Just as I was about to ring the doorbell of another house, I heard a voice calling my name. It was Vinny, drinking beer with his friend Sal on Sal's front porch. I walked across the street to join them, and we sat around a table where a police scanner lay amid several empty beer cans. The scanner was surprisingly large and looked like a 1980s mobile phone. I asked, "What is that?"

"Oh, we use this to listen in on what the cops are up to," Vinny responded.

"You know, that's really smart. Can you guys figure out who is calling the cops sometimes?" I asked.

"Yeah," Vinny answered, laughing, "and we tell them [residents] it was the cops who told us to scare the shit out of them."

Although I did not observe gang members in the act of identifying informants, I did listen to police communication within Latin Kings territory using a cell phone application that cost just 99 cents to download. After listening for an hour, I was able to discern the location of two informants.[22] Below is a transcript of two exchanges between dispatchers and officers disclosing informant addresses in Little Village. They were recorded on a Friday evening in the summer of 2011.

DISPATCHER: Report of a male wearing a tan hat, black jacket, with a bottle in his hand, spraying graffiti on a garage at 2545 South Sword.

OFFICER: Okay, ten-four.

[Eleven minutes pass.]

OFFICER: At 2545 South Sword, property is abandoned, no one here. Do you have any info on the caller?

DISPATCHER: Woman called from her backyard, spotted the male spraying graffiti on garage door. Check the home across the alley from the garage.

OFFICER: Ten-four.

[Ten minutes pass.]

OFFICER: Got it. Speaking to her now.

In this exchange the officer and dispatcher disclosed the informant's approximate location ("the property across the alley"). If the Latin Kings were listening, they could have easily located the informant.

The second exchange involved the report of an aggravated battery in progress.

DISPATCHER: Reported battery in progress at 2642 South May. Two young males fighting on the street. One male black wearing red shorts and blue hat, another male wearing black pants white shirt.

OFFICER: Okay, ten-four.

[Ten minutes pass.]

DISPATCHER: Shots fired, only heard, nothing seen.

OFFICER: Ten-four.
                [Five minutes pass.]
OFFICER: Area is clear. I knocked on 2642 South May,
                but nobody is saying they made the call. Do
                you have an address on the caller?
DISPATCHER: Sure, stand by.
                [Two minutes pass.]
DISPATCHER: Yes, 2648 South May.
OFFICER: All right. Thank you.

It is difficult to discern how frequently these inadvertent disclosures of informant addresses took place in Little Village. However, it was clear from listening to police radio communications that many residents were savvy enough to not provide identifiable information when reporting crimes. On four other calls in the recording, police officers asked the dispatcher for details on the resident reporting the crime, only to have the dispatcher reply, "Nothing, anonymous caller." The high percentage of residents willing to report gang crimes in Little Village likely reflects residents' ability to use anonymous tip lines or their refusal to disclose personal information to 911 dispatchers.

Identifying informant addresses by listening to police radio communication was tedious and difficult. The audio was not always clear, the volume increased and decreased uncontrollably, and the words were sometimes difficult to make out. Gang members most likely listened to police communication only while engaging in high-stakes activities like transporting drugs or targeting a rival gang member. The gang could not, nor would they desire to, monitor police communication twenty-four hours a day, but they could for moments at a time.

The Latin Kings used their access to police communications to enforce the code of silence. They used the information they gained to both retaliate against the informants and to claim that police had voluntarily provided the information. Previous research shows that gangs can inflict violence upon residents to maintain power, often in response to a failure to live up to a business agreement, but such acts are considered rare because the threat of violence might scare residents into cooperating with police.[23] But the Latin Kings maintained their power over residents in part by damaging the police's reputation and making residents fear corrupt police. As the gang eroded residents' faith in police integrity, the residents were faced with the choice of either cooperating with the gang or moving out of the neighborhood. Of the ten residents I identified who experienced gang retaliation for calling police, six moved out of the neighborhood and the other four never called the police again.

Residents confirmed the gang's ability to damage the police's reputation. For example, the very evening that Anna reported a group of gang members on her block holding guns, the Latin Kings set her home on fire.

I sat with Anna in her living room as she recalled that day. After they threw the Molotov cocktail at her house, the gang members yelled, "This is the bitch who calls the cops! Next time, don't call them because we own them! They told us you called!"

"How are you certain that the police did that?" I asked.

"How else could it be?" Anna answered through tears. "I didn't tell anyone else about it! I know better than to go around complaining about the gangs to neighbors because you never know if they might tell the gang. So if I didn't tell anyone else, how could they [the gang] know?"

Similarly Martha, who called police after seeing weapons in the garage of a gang member, recalled her traumatic experience: "The very next day [after calling the police], my daughter picks up the phone and starts crying. It was one of the gangbangers. I got on the phone and he was yelling 'Bitch! You better watch your back for calling the cops on us!' I tried to say we didn't call the police, and he yelled back, 'We know it's you, the cops told us!' Then he hung up."

Like Anna, Martha could not imagine how the Latin Kings could have learned her identity other than by police collusion. "I've always instructed my kids that if they want to call 911, they should never give their name or phone number," she said. "But when I called 911, I made the mistake of giving them my address. I didn't think it would be a problem though, 'cause I didn't tell nobody else about it. But when that gangbanger called my house and said the cops ratted me out, I knew it was 'cause I gave 911 my address. The cops told [the gang]."

The gang's subversive actions paid off, as residents expressed deep cynicism toward police after experiencing retaliation. "The cops are on the side of the gangbangers," said Ernestina in the hallway of her apartment. "They [police] don't do anything. They don't care. You talk to anyone in this neighborhood and they'll tell you, 'Kings own cops.' Everyone says it and knows it. I don't even bother calling the cops because not only will they not do anything, they'll turn me in to the gang." During the entire data collection period between 2007 and 2012, I recorded residents using the phrase "Kings own cops" fifty times. That police revealed informants to the gang was accepted as fact and spread among friends, neighbors, and relatives in Little Village's east side.

My conversation with Vinny on Sal's porch confirmed that the Latin Kings were indeed responsible for retaliating against the residents I interviewed.

"Are there certain blocks where you've had a lot of problems with snitches?" I asked Vinny.

"Yeah," he replied, "we cocktailed a few places on Franklin 24, Roswell 28, Morgan 22, Cutler 27. We also had some where we didn't even have to use the scanner. Our boys just caught the bitches talking to police over on Woodcreek 28 and Timbuck 29." The identifiers Vinny used were shorthand for blocks; Franklin 24 meant the 2400 block of South Franklin Street, for instance. Vinny thus confirmed the stories I heard from residents whose homes had been firebombed.

In addition to calling 911, residents had the option of reporting gang activities at meetings of the Chicago Alternative Policing Strategy (CAPS). CAPS was the city's community policing initiative which brought together residents, police, and city agencies to identify and solve neighborhood crime problems. Yet, residents avoided CAPS meeting because they feared identifying themselves to the gang.

"I know the gangbangers send friends or family members to the beat meetings," said Beto. "They send someone so they know what the police are up to and where they're going to target. It's messed up." Wesley Skogan heard similar concerns from residents in his evaluation of CAPS.[24] I attended three CAPS meetings in beats within Latin Kings territory, and at each one I spotted a gang member from the basketball league in the audience. Beto's suspicion about the gang's presence at CAPS meetings was valid.

Despite the success of the gang's subversive acts, they did not always engage in retaliation to enforce the code of silence. Vinny explained as he opened another beer on Sal's porch: "One time, we caught this dude calling the cops with the scanner, so we lit up his house, and dude turned out to be the director of a program that runs my kids' basketball league at school. So when I saw this dude, I apologized to him and told our boys [younger gang members] to leave his house alone and make sure no one messes with it. Now I don't just tell boys to light up houses. When I find a snitch I check to see who it is. When it's somebody important, we talk. When it's some fucking new lady who doesn't want shit to do with us and calls [police] on us, we send a message and, you know, to scare the shit out of them."

The "dude" who operated the basketball league was Israel Palacios, a neighborhood activist and nonprofit organizer whom I met at a community meeting in Little Village. In addition to running the basketball league, Israel led a graffiti-removal effort with neighbors on his block, 7700 South Cutler, which also happened to be Vinny's block. Israel confirmed Vinny's account and described how the Latin Kings tried to undo the damage caused by their retaliation: "When we bought the house, it was wintertime and there weren't any gang members on the street, so we thought the block was safe. But then, when the weather got warmer, we saw that our block was a hot spot for King activity. This past June I saw a kid hiding a gun in a garden, and I knew I was risking it by calling police, but I couldn't help it because I knew I'd never forgive myself if that gun was used to kill a kid. So I called 911, and the Latin Kings ended up setting my house on fire and telling me how it was the police who ratted me out. A week later I was coaching my basketball team, and our league has quite a few active gang members in it, and one of the gang members on my team asked where I lived, and I gave him my block. And he was like, 'Oh, 77 and Cutler?' And I was like, 'Yeah,' and he was like, 'On which side?' I told him, 'The west side of the block near the corner,' and he was like, 'Oh no, not the big gray house?' And I was like, 'Yeah, the big gray house.' Then he said, 'Oh shit, I think my dad might've cocktailed your house!' The next day this short and tattooed guy [Vinny] rang my doorbell. He was a Latin King, and he apologized for what the gang did and gave me money to repair the damage. I invited him inside, and we talked for an hour about how to make the block safer, and he said he was willing to provide me with buckets of paint for my graffiti-removal program."

Vinny was true to his word: the Latin Kings decreased their activity around Israel's house and Vinny ordered every gang member not to lay a hand on Israel, his family, or his home. This finding supports other case studies showing relationship-building efforts by street gangs.[25] But even more important, it shows that gangs were strategic in their use of retaliation and misinformation to divide police and residents. Vinny's decision to build a relationship with Israel and apologize for the gang's retaliation suggested that gang members chose their strategies for securing resident cooperation based on the resources residents brought to the gang.

The Latin Kings also refrained from retaliating against organizers like Freddy at Youth Inc. Midway through the second basketball season, Freddy agreed to participate in a recorded interview at his office, where he described a tense incident: "We were on South Boulevard and we saw these guys going at it. I mean going at it! And we jumped out. I think my partner called 911, saying, 'We are on Forty-second and South Boulevard and there's a big fight going on.' So guess what? [The gangs] heard it on the police scanner! We get there and start breaking it up, and one of their boys on the sideline goes to us, 'Hey, did y'all call the cops?' The kid had the scanner in his hand. I was like, 'Nah, bro. We just got here.' And the boy tells us they heard the cops saying they got a call from a white van on Forty-second and South Boulevard. So I'm like... 'Aw, bro... we thought you were going to get shot, bro!' And the boy goes, 'Why'd you call the cops, man?' I kept repeating, 'We thought you were going to get shot!' So one gang [member] ran off, and the others got in our van and we got out of there. But that wasn't it. I got a call an hour later from another member of their gang, and he's like, 'Freddy! One of your guys called the cops on us, bro!'"

"How did you handle that?" I asked.

"That's when you tell the guys, you know, there were children, lots of children running around, old ladies, babies in strollers." He pauses. "See, a lot of people are understanding, and when you have a relationship you can tell them, 'This was the situation, man. We felt we had to call because we felt we were protecting some kids.' Without that relationship, you can have gangs boycotting organizations, so when shit like this breaks down, we tell the Latin Kings we're not showing up to court anyway."

Despite catching Freddy calling police, the Latin Kings chose to negotiate rather than violently retaliate because of the gang's long history with him. His fear was not that the Latin

Kings would retaliate with violence, but that they would stop Youth Inc. from effectively implementing their programs. "We know they ain't about to light up Youth Inc. for breaking the code," Freddy explained, "but instead, they'll boycott an organization. If an organization ain't got no kids in their programs, and no one shows up to their event, that organization dies. Because we have a relationship that goes back sixteen years, we know what we gotta do, and that's why we tell [the Latin Kings] we ain't showing up to court."

Tre, a twenty-two-year-old member of the Latin Kings, confirmed Freddy's story during a conversation at the halftime break of a basketball game. Tre and I were watching Freddy and some of the other violence prevention workers talking to an off-duty police officer when I asked Tre why he trusted Freddy. He responded, "He's been doing this shit since before I was born. I caught him calling the cops once when I had a scanner, but he only does that to protect us. He's never gone to court to testify against any of us for anything, and that man has probably seen more shady stuff go down than any of us." Like Israel, Freddy was a valuable and trusted resource to the gang, so they chose to negotiate rather than retaliate after learning that he called the police. Together these examples show that the Latin Kings refrained from retaliating against residents who had relationships with the gang and provided resources to the community.

The Latin Kings were careful with their decisions around retaliation because they knew from experience that a mistake could strengthen residents' relationship with police. One afternoon I was at a party Freddy organized to watch the Chicago Bulls play the Miami Heat. The halftime show was interrupted by a news report about a young girl who had just been killed by a gang in another part of Chicago. Vinny turned to Freddy and said, "Oh no. Not another Magda incident."

"Who was Magda?" I asked.

"A four-year-old who was killed when a Latin King shot at a Two Six," Freddy answered.

"Magda got killed when one of our boys lit up a Two Six," said Vinny, "and after that, all hell broke loose. The neighborhood turned against us and started working with the police. We made it through only because we gave our guy up to the cops."

"I remember it like it was yesterday," Freddy interjected. "It took these guys a year before they could even get out the house without a resident calling police on them."

Stylo walked over and looked directly at me: "You know, we got a code too. When an innocent kid gets hurt, we know there is a price to pay."

The tragedy of Magda Hernandez's death represented a clear lesson to the Latin Kings: the gang could not retaliate against residents indiscriminately without facing repercussions. As Martin Sánchez-Jankowski argues, when innocent children or well-respected community leaders are victimized by a gang, the gang loses its legitimacy, and relations between residents and police grow stronger.[26] The Latin Kings were able to restore their legitimacy in the neighborhood only by turning Magda's killer over to police. As Stylo said, the Latin Kings had "a code to follow."

PUBLICIZING POLICE MISTAKES

The gang also enforced the code of silence by simply taking advantage of police blunders. As Vinny explained, two of the gang's eleven recent retaliations happened by chance after gang members saw police talking to informants on the street.

The first of the two cases took place on the 2800 block of South Woodcreek, where the remodeled façade of one home stood out from the rest. Only a few doors away I met Raquel, a thirty-four-year-old mother of three, who invited me inside to administer a survey to her son. As we sat in the living room, I asked Raquel what she thought about the police in the neighborhood.

"They're terrible," she said, "absolutely terrible."

"What do you mean?" I asked.

She shared the following story about her neighbor Yolanda who had lived in the remodeled home a few doors down: "A woman [Yolanda] down the block reported a gang member with a gun, and the police knocked on her door to ask if she could identify who had the gun. The police had three guys in custody in front of her house! She pointed out the person, and the gang member got two years in prison, but in retaliation, the gangs set her house on fire. Her front façade had to be replaced. A year later my cousin who lives upstairs witnessed a shooting. A gang member ran [along] the side of the house and shot someone in front of our home. The detectives came to talk to her, and she said that she only saw a kid with a white T-shirt. She could have identified the culprit, but she wasn't going to risk it."

According to Raquel, the Latin Kings were able to easily identify Yolanda as the informant after the police's public lineup. Witnessing the retaliation against Yolanda led Raquel and her family to refrain from cooperating with police because they had no faith that the police would try to keep their identity safe.

While public discourse in Chicago suggests that residents adhere to the code of silence out of allegiance to criminals, the data from residents like Raquel show that the code stemmed from the turf war between gangs and police. A public relations campaign like Silence Kills would not convince the Little Village residents I interviewed to cooperate. Instead improving police communication and protocols for safeguarding informant identities might prove more effective at breaking the code. It is unreasonable to expect inner-city residents to risk their family's safety to cooperate with police when it is unclear whether the police are able to protect their anonymity.

After interviewing Raquel, I knocked on the door of Yolanda's home but received no answer. Glancing through their front window, I saw that the house was entirely empty. But interviews with other residents on the block confirmed Raquel's story and revealed that the Latin Kings publicized the incident to tarnish the police's reputation. Amada, a twenty-two-year-old college student who lived on the block, said, "We saw what happened to Yolanda, and what those stupid cops did, ... asking her to point out who had the gun. I don't know how they [police] could be so stupid. But after the Kings cocktailed her house, they let people know about it. A friend of mine who lives over on 7400 South Tremont told me she found out from a King on her block."

Amada's sixteen-year-old sister, Sonya, confirmed that the Latin Kings spread word of the police's disclosure of informants to students at her high school as well. In total, five residents on the block confirmed the retaliation had taken place. According to residents, Yolanda moved out of the neighborhood shortly after her house was set on fire, and the Latin Kings spread word of the incident throughout the neighborhood to further dis-credit the police. This strategy worked. All of the residents in-terviewed on 2800 South Woodcreek shared that they no longer reported crimes to the police after learning about Yolanda's experience.

Another informant was revealed on the 2900 block of South Timbuck, when two Latin Kings, sitting in custody in the back of a squad car, witnessed Florencia pointing out the location of a weapon to police at a crime scene Florencia's home had a "For Sale" sign in the front yard and moving boxes scattered around her backyard porch. A new teacher at a local elementary school, Florencia had just purchased the home but was already moving following her traumatic experience with the Latin Kings and police.

"I used to always call the cops on the Kings because twenty of them would just loiter out in front of my house," said Florencia.

"And I tried to be smart [to protect her identity] by never giving my name, address, or phone number to 911." But after she witnessed a drive-by shooting, she spotted one of the Latin Kings hiding a gun in a neighbor's mailbox. After seeing the police investigating the crime scene overlook the mailbox, she went outside to inform them of the gun's location. Just as she did, a police car pulled up in front of the house with two Latin Kings in the backseat. "At that moment," Florencia recalled, "I knew I was in trouble. From the back of the police car they were yelling and calling me a cop-calling rat." The police even told her to "lay low," and the next day the Latin Kings set fire to her home.

Two weeks after the gang set fire to Florencia's house, the police raided a gang member's house on the same block. Florencia and other neighbors on the block described the police raid as similar to a raid in a movie, with officers carrying machine guns and wearing bulletproof vests to enter the house. The raid uncovered some drugs, but gang members stayed away and no arrests were made. Later that evening, Florencia recalled, she was awoken by the sound of gunshots in the street. "I took cover behind my refrigerator," she said, "but then I heard voices from the street yelling, 'Whoever snitched! We're going to find out! We know the cops, they'll tell us who you are and you'll get yours! You saw what the cops did to this bitch that tried ratting us out! You know the police can't protect you!'"

The success of the gang's strategy to delegitimize police was apparent in interviews with six other residents on the block. "It's a shame what happened to Florencia. It just shows that you can't trust the cops," said Griselda, a fifty-four-year-old resident. "The Kings out here don't mess around," said Marco, a twenty-five-year-old construction worker, "They were pissed when the cops raided their house, and I'm sure they're gonna find out who tipped off the police."

The police's explanations for the inadvertent disclosure of informants revealed the role of resource scarcity in creating opportunities for the gang to subvert police. Randy, Mike, and Sean, three local beat officers, told me that police did not intentionally disclose informants, but the demands of an underresourced job pressured officers into making hard compromises. Mike, a four-year veteran of the police force, offered, "I didn't get into this job to be a beat officer my whole life. I want to make commander someday, or at least sergeant, but that's becoming harder because the department isn't replacing many of the guys retiring. They just don't have the money to do it." Resource constraints were a huge problem, according each of the police officers; I was astounded to learn that just five officers covered the patrols in a single beat in Latin Kings territory. Sean explained, "It [the small number of beat officers] sounds worse than it actually is because you gotta remember, we got detectives, special gang units, special drug units, et cetera, so we have a lot of officers, but the actual number of beat officers, the guys responding to everyday shit, there's just five of us. Five of us split up the three shifts, and whoever is lucky gets a partner, otherwise, on most days, we're out there on our own because the fifth guy stays at the district's headquarters as the designated 'rapid response car.' His job is to come flying in when we need backup. And that's it. It's worse when a guy takes his vacation or sick days because we got nobody to replace him, and the three or four of us left over are on our own. If we really get into trouble, we can always call a car from another beat or district, but when you do that, you're taking away another district's patrolmen. There's no way around it."

Studies have documented similar resource scarcity in police departments, but in Little Village resource scarcity was especially damaging because it limited the time police officers had to deal with informants.[27] Randy explained, "If you want to move up the ladder, the last thing you want [as a police officer] is to have the reputation of a 'milker,' the pieces of shit that take forever to finish a call and milk the clock for overtime. Not only is that bad for moving up, it also means that you get stuck with the shit jobs, like processing the mountains of paperwork for a homicide."

On most days Randy started his shift with dispatchers already backlogged by ten to twelve calls. "Supervisors pay attention to who is taking forever to get through two calls and who is going through eight or ten per shift," he said. "All it takes is one lazy asshole to make your shift hell," Mike added.

When career-oriented police officers like Randy, Mike, and Sean responded to residents, they were faced with conflicting goals of rationing time and protecting informant identities, which usually involved time-consuming precautions. In light of these resource constraints, Randy explained why a police officer might conduct a public lineup in front of a residents' home: "Inevitably guys are going to cut corners. . . . Let's say you witness a robbery in front of your house. You call 911 and give them a description of the suspect. On the way to the scene, the police pick up a guy matching the description of the robber and recover the stolen items on his person. Those officers probably came into their shift with a backlog of calls. They are not going to take all the time to process the suspect, arrange for someone to pick [the victim] up, bring them to the department, and grab another four guys to do the lineup. No, they are going to call you and bring the suspect to your house to identify them because they're just a few blocks away. Does that lead to informants being revealed? Yeah, sometimes." Though decisions like these prioritized the officer's time and reputation over protecting residents, these officers felt comfortable with their actions because, as Randy shared, "You can't protect everybody, you just can't. That's the reality."

In addition to simply trying to save time on a call, Randy revealed that police officers might disclose informants' identities as punishment for wasting officers' time: "The only other reason why cops would do a public lineup would be if the informant was making bullshit calls, giving the cops a hard time, or disrespecting an officer. Sometimes you get residents who call 911 a lot when a fight breaks out by their house and instead of arresting the guys, they want us to break it up. That's not our job. It's a waste of our time. And if you come across the same guy over and over again making these bullshit calls, then officers might do a public lineup to put their name out there as a snitch, so that street justice can teach them not to waste our time by making bullshit calls."

Officers' use of "street justice" highlights residents' difficult position: caught in the middle of a turf war between police and gangs. Gangs aimed to prevent residents from cooperating with police, and police aimed to prevent residents from taking time away from their efforts to suppress the gang. Incidents of violence in Little Village were not random acts, and they were not just the product of conflicts among gangs. Both the police and the gangs tried to use residents to their advantage in their efforts to resist or dominate one another. In the process, both sides used violence to discipline residents into cooperating.

* * *

In the aftermath of Derrion Albert's murder, Chief of Police Jody Weis angrily denounced the code of silence in poor Chicago communities: "The code of silence is killing our kids. How can someone witness such a brutal act and not come forward to talk to police?"[28] His question located responsibility for Albert's death with the residents of poor communities, treating the code of silence as a product of the culture of poor neighborhoods rather than complex interactions among residents, gangs, and police. The code of silence is much more complex than most scholars and policymakers think. In addition to a lack of resources constraining police, street gangs actively undermine police-resident relations by capitalizing on police mistakes and fostering mistrust among residents. Whereas public discourse on the code of silence typically asks how can we convince poor people to cooperate with police, the data from Little Village point to a different question: How can we prevent the turf wars between gangs and police from triggering violent gang retaliation against residents?

The findings from this chapter suggest that addressing the police's high caseloads and limited resources would help. Although criminologists argue that neighborhoods with high rates of poverty and violence produce cynical views of police among residents, these perceptions do not simply arise from exposure to a high-risk area.[29] Perceptions of police stem from the actions of people in relationships. By studying a field of actors in Little Village, we can see that both violence and negative perceptions of police were the product of police's and gangs' strategic actions. The Latin Kings capitalized on the police's constraints by engaging in covert surveillance, violent retaliation, and subversion. Resource scarcity and poverty certainly contributed to slow police response times and the conflicting goals of saving time while protecting informants, but it was the gang's strategic actions that reinforced the code of silence among residents. This suggests that the code of silence cannot be addressed simply by providing police with more resources.[30] An infusion of resources will not prevent gangs from monitoring police. The police also need to change their approach to gang control and safeguarding informants. When the police engage in unilateral gang suppression, they cannot assume that gangs go into hiding or disappear. Gangs can resist suppression in ways that exacerbate the effects of resource scarcity and police errors on the erosion of residents' willingness to cooperate with police.

In Little Village, the police gave minimal attention to the collateral damage of their unilateral strategy of suppression against the Latin Kings. This created a violent turf war between the gang and police, with residents caught in the middle. While the city may claim to be winning its war against gangs, the stories from Little Village reveal that its victories come at an enormous cost to residents. The following chapter sheds additional light on the negative consequences of this street turf war.

6

Locking Up Social Order

IN A COURTROOM FILLED WITH reporters present for the sentencing of Augustin Zambrano, convicted leader of the Latin Kings, U.S. Attorney Patrick Fitzgerald said, "This investigation has been held to hold the leaders of the Latin Kings like Zambrano responsible for their iron-fisted leadership of a criminal enterprise responsible for murders and attempted murder. As the CEO of this gang, Zambrano bears responsibility for its criminal acts."[1] The arrest and conviction of Zambrano and forty other leaders of the Latin Kings street gang in Little Village was seen as a major victory for law enforcement in its war against gangs.

"Correlation doesn't equal causation," the *Chicago Tribune* editorialized, "but we suspect the forces that consign [gang leaders] to the gray-bar hotel...also have helped lower Chicago's murder pace."[2] Eliminating gang leadership is widely viewed as an effective tactic in law enforcement's turf war with Chicago gangs.

Over the five-year period of this study, the FBI and Chicago Police Department arrested leaders of both the Latin Kings and 22 Boys in Little Village. Figures 6.1 and 6.2 show the monthly violent crime rates in these gangs' territories three years before and after the arrests.[3] Contrary to the *Tribune's* supposition, the violent crime rate in Latin Kings territory changed little, decreasing

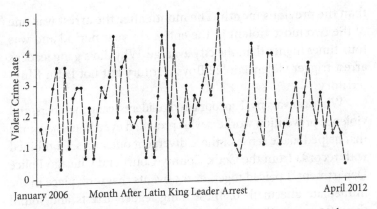

FIGURE 6.1 Monthly violent crime rates in Latin Kings territory in Little Village, 2006–2012.

Source: Chicago FBI Field Office Reports.

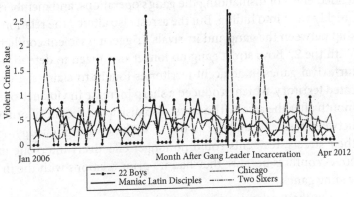

FIGURE 6.2 Monthly violent crime rates in 22 Boys territory.
Source: Chicago FBI Field Office Reports.

but then increasing the month after by less than 1 percent. Over the entire six-year period the violent crime rate remained within a consistent range in the territory. In Little Village's east side, however, the arrest of the 22 Boys gang leader resulted in a sharp increase in violent crime rate that was 2.5 times higher than the previous month. The month after the arrest was one of the two most violent in the entire six-year period and was four times higher than the city average. Why did a gang leader's arrest trigger violence in 22 Boys territory but not Latin Kings territory?

While canvassing, I encountered residents, gang members, and violence prevention workers who provided eyewitness accounts that helped make sense of these divergent outcomes. Combined with records from the Cook County Court and Chicago Police Department, I pieced together the events that took place in the immediate aftermath of these gang leader arrests and found they affect more than just the behavior of individual gang members in the neighborhood. It changes the relationship among multiple gangs in the neighborhood's field.

In the east side, the arrest of the 22 Boys' leader had the intended effect of dismantling the gang's operations, and members quickly went into hiding. But the arrest also altered the relationship between the gang and its rivals, triggering violent conflict. With the 22 Boys street gang no longer organized to defend its turf, rival gangs in adjacent territories fought to claim the vacated territory, which produced a sharp increase in violence one month after the arrest. The arrest also disrupted the social order between residents and the 22 Boys.[4] With new gangs occupying their streets, residents could no longer effectively intervene in street conflicts because they had no prior relations with the invading gangs.

On the west side, the arrest of the Latin Kings' leadership had no effect on violent crime. Though police apprehended the majority of the gang's leaders in the community, the gang still had operational leadership in prison and in other neighborhoods of Chicago. Residents and violence prevention workers reported that new leaders from other parts of the city came to Little Village to fill the positions made vacant by the police operation. The arrest of its leaders may have altered the gang's drug operations, but it did not change patterns of violence in the neighborhood as the gang quickly filled the leadership void.

Law enforcement agencies cannot fully understand the consequences of eliminating gang leadership without paying attention to the effects that these operations have on relationships between the gang, its competitors, and residents. While research on law enforcement tactics has resulted in multiple effective violent crime reduction strategies such as hot-spot policing, focused deterrence, and community policing, the science behind controlling organized criminal groups remains underdeveloped. By thinking of violence as the outcome of relationships among actors in a field it becomes possible to identify the conditions under which the arrests of gang leaders can unintentionally trigger violent conflict among gangs. The lessons from this Little Village case study have the potential to help law enforcement address the street gang problem with fewer unintended consequences.

THE ADVERSE EFFECTS OF THE POLICE'S WAR ON GANGS

Social scientific research demonstrates two adverse effects of gang interventions.[5] The most commonly studied is spatial displacement, or the shift of gang crime from the original target area to another area as the gang finds new places to operate.[6] The second is souring police-community relations. For example, in Los Angeles, police implemented massive gang sweeps in Operation Hammer, using one thousand officers to arrest hundreds of suspected gang members.[7] Yet, only about half of all Operation Hammer arrestees were gang members, and fewer than 2 percent were convicted of a crime.[8] This created intense community resentment toward police.

While the research on these adverse effects has contributed to important policy changes, much less is known about the adverse effects of police crackdowns on gang leaders.[9] To date only two studies have examined the arrest of a gang's leader, and each focused on the Gangster Disciples street gang in Chicago during the 1990s. Both George Knox and Andrew Papachristos interviewed fifteen members of the Gangster Disciples and found that the arrest of Larry Hoover (the highest ranking leader) and thirty-seven midlevel leaders had a debilitating effect on the gang's organizational structure.[10] Given the dearth of knowledge on this type intervention and its effectiveness, how could law enforcement agencies rely on such a gang control strategy?

Part of the answer lies in the strategy's political expediency. Arresting leaders of criminal groups like gangs and the mafia has been a goal of U.S. law enforcement throughout the nation's history.[11] From Billy the Kid in the old West to the crackdowns on mafia families during Prohibition, public officials and law enforcement agents can reap tremendous political rewards from apprehending high-profile leaders of criminal organizations. Chicago in particular has a long history of federal and local law enforcement agents pursuing leaders of organized crime. Figures like J. Edgar Hoover and Eliot Ness made their names chasing down infamous gangsters like John Dillinger and Al Capone.[12]

Contemporary operations against gang leaders serve a similar role. In 2001, Patrick Fitzgerald was appointed U.S. attorney for the northern district of Illinois and spearheaded numerous raids on gang leadership throughout Chicago. As a result, he was lauded by media outlets as one of Chicago's most upstanding public officials.[13] After sting operations against gangs, Fitzgerald often shared the stage with local law enforcement agencies at press conferences to announce gang leader arrests and assert that arresting high-profile gang leaders reduces violence by deterring inner-city youth from the gang life. For example, after the arrest of the Latin Kings gang leader Fernando "Ace" King, Joseph Ruzevich, an agent with the Bureau of Alcohol, Tobacco,

Date	Gang	Arrests
February 23rd 2011	Maniac Latin Disciples	17
October 1st 2011	Latin Kings	4
November 17th 2010	Travelling Vice Lords	70
September 30th 2010	Cobras and Gangster Disciples	55
September 16th 2010	Jokers	24
July 21st 2010	Insane Latin Deuces	25
June 16th 2010	Gangster Disciples	8
February 10th 2010	Four Corner Hustlers	8
November 5th 2009	Black P Stones Nation	4
September 24th 2009	Latin Kings	18
October 1st 2008	Spanish Cobras	30
December 1st 2007	Conservative Vice Lords	13

FIGURE 6.3 Gang leader arrests in Chicago, 2007–2011.
Source: Chicago FBI Field Office Reports.

and Firearms, said, "It's going to be the choice of the next Latin King: Does he want to take a chance of being infiltrated in the future and possibly arrested and spending the rest of his time in jail? That's the chance that that person has to take. [Sting operations] show to the gangbangers that it's not worth taking a leadership position because they know that we will eventually bring them to justice."[14]

Law enforcement's belief that arresting gang leaders reduces violence was common among Chicago's leadership despite little evidence.[15] Figure 6.3 shows the frequency of operations to apprehend gang leaders in Chicago between December 2007 and September 2011. In that time period 293 gang leaders were arrested across just six Chicago neighborhoods.

When police arrest gang leaders, they destabilize not just one gang but also the broader array of relationships among gangs in the area.[16] With gangs engaged in wars over street territory and status, the removal of a gang from a local drug market can create a void that leads to violent competition among other gangs for a bigger share of the market.[17] Conflict triggered by the police intervention can set off a chain of retaliations as gangs fight for the territory made vacant by the crippled street gang.[18] The events that unfolded after the arrest of the leader of the 22 Boys showed how this process can play out.

THE ARREST OF THE 22 BOYS' LEADER

"Why are you wearing so much black on this hot day?" I asked Ruben Martinez, a sixteen-year-old sitting on his front porch.

"So that the gangs around here don't think I'm one of them," Ruben explained. "There's so many with all these different colors, and black is a neutral color. It's the only way I can skateboard around here." Ruben lived in the territory of the 22 Boys street gang, a small gang with a three-block territory sandwiched between two larger gangs, the Latin Kings to the west and the Satan Disciples to the east. Ruben's block had what scholars call an "alternative form of social organization," where residents followed a code of conduct to protect themselves from gang violence.[19]

"What do you think about the violence on your block?" I asked Ruben.

"It's gotten really bad," he answered, "especially after they arrested the gang leader here."

"What do you mean?"

"The head of the 22 Boys. Basically, ever since he's been gone, the gangs from the two other sides have been coming to try and take over this block." Ruben stood up and pointed down the street. "It's so bad that the 22 Boys out here have checkpoints some days where they stop cars driving by [pointing at a stop sign]. They tell people to get out and take off their shirts."

"Why?"

"So they can see if they have any tattoos of rival gangs on them. They stopped me once, and when they saw I had nothing they let me go. But a few months ago it was really bad, there were a lot of shootings. Now there's just gangbangers everywhere on the lookout." According to Ruben, the gang leader's arrest severely disrupted the social order in 22 Boys territory.

The leadership style of twenty-nine-year-old 22 Boys' gang leader Rudy Cantu can best be described as charismatic. With an estimated membership of at most one hundred, the gang had no set of written rules, no formal midlevel managers, and no prison leadership like some of Chicago's more corporatized street gangs.[20] Instead, the gang's organizational structure consisted of Cantu and a group of his close friends who operated the drug- and weapon-selling activities in their small territory. Most residents and gang members in those three blocks simply referred to Cantu as "the Chief."

"The Chief knew everybody on the block," said Miranda, a resident living in 22 Boys territory. "He lived across the alley from me and would invite my husband to play basketball on the rim on his garage. They would be playing till late at night sometimes."

George, another of Cantu's neighbors, described the gang leader as accessible: "He always told us to come to him if we ever had any problems. Once, I saw a 22 Boy walking on the street carelessly holding a gun, and I gave the Chief a call, telling him one of his boys is out there being stupid. And he went out there and grabbed the kid off the street."

Residents and gang members remembered Cantu most for his strong desire to protect residents and gang members. Wearing a bright blue Charlotte Hornets basketball jersey, Spikey, an eighteen-year-old member of the 22 Boys, told me stories about Cantu as he played fetch with his pit bull in his backyard. "I once heard the Chief broke a dude's jaw for fucking with an old man on the block. He didn't fuck around when one of us was messing with anyone on our blocks. He really cared about this block."

"Have you ever met him?"

"Yeah, he would run our meetings. I didn't get to talk with him much, but he was really cool." Another 22 Boy, Angel, recalled the story of Cantu going to a grocery store on their corner and being confronted by members of the Satan Disciples: "He was pissed that they came on our turf, so he came home and got into his van, pulled up next to the [Satan Disciples], and blasted them." Cantu had a mythic reputation. 22 Boys gang members perceived him as a strong protector of their territory.

With no nonprofits or responsive alderman to turn to for help, residents of the three-block territory felt they could count on Cantu to look after them. Karen, a twenty-year-old college student who grew up next to Cantu's residence, described the positive influence he and the gang had on her life. Karen and I met when I canvassed her block, though she preferred to be interviewed at her college campus instead of outside in the view of everyone on the block. Sitting across from me in the student center, she explained, "I grew up with these guys. I got straight A's in grade school, and when my school put me in the gifted classes I still hung out and played with them." Karen won a scholarship to attend a local university and regularly commuted from the same Little Village home where she grew up. "Even now, when I get home from college, they'll tell me, 'Keep doing well at school' or 'Don't get a boyfriend and get pregnant.' They really look after us."

"Really?" I pressed.

"Yeah, and it's not just with me," Karen insisted. "They also helped my father. He worked as a day laborer working odd jobs here and there, then he really hurt his back bad, and we were in trouble because we didn't make much money."

"Did the gang help out?"

"Yeah, they came and knocked on our door to see if we needed money. My dad refused their help, but every week one of them would come by and sweep our front porch and cut our grass. They knew my dad was hurt so they tried to make things easier for us."

Cantu and the 22 Boys built a social order in their small territory within Little Village, but on January 14, 2010, that order collapsed when Chicago Police raided a house where Cantu stored drugs and weapons; after tracking the gang's drug business for months, they arrested Cantu.[21] Because the 22 Boys were smaller and less organized than their adjacent rivals, the loss of their leader had a profound effect on the gang's organization, relations with residents, and competition with rival gangs.[22]

Residents living in 22 Boys territory observed a drastic difference in the gang's activities before and after Cantu's arrest. Juliana said that when the gang leader was still around, she was able to get gang members to stay away from her front steps: "A 22 Boy was sitting on my front steps, and as he got up to talk to his friend, I came out and asked if he was looking for someone. He said no, so I told him... 'I don't mean any disrespect, but I don't like it when you sit on my front porch. I have two daughters, and if you get shot, the bullets coming through my house put my kids in danger.' He apologized, and no one ever sat on my front porch again." After Cantu's arrest, however, Juliana could no longer appeal to 22 Boys' interest in preserving the neighborhood because the gang members on the block were from other neighborhoods: "In February I saw a group of them [Satan Disciples gang members] with bats and bottles, looking as if they were headed to a fight. I got out and told them not to fight because everyone on this block is innocent, the gang leader isn't living here anymore, he got locked up. And this kid tells me to not worry, that they are here to protect me and my kids now. When the 22 Boys on the block disappeared, the block became the worst I have ever seen in the twelve years I've lived here."

When the Satan Disciple told Juliana not to worry, he was telling her that the gang was now taking over 22 Boys territory. This news was not welcomed by Juliana, who believed this would only result in more violence when the 22 Boys or Latin Kings returned. Cantu's arrest disrupted the social cohesion and shared expectations that residents like Juliana had built with the 22 Boys on her block. According to her, the gang virtually disappeared, and members of rival gangs came to her block to claim the territory. Prior to the raid, residents said the block was safe because the gang leader knew their faces, but after his arrest, 22 Boys gang members stopped protecting the neighborhood.

Residents Ben, Alonzo, and Alicia all said that their block became more dangerous after Cantu's arrest. Ben hardly ever went outside anymore because the Satan Disciples and Latin Kings were fighting over the territory. Alonzo shared a harrowing experience: "I was driving down the block and an SD [Satan Disciple] got in front of my car and told me to get out. They asked [which gang] I was with, and I said, 'Nobody.' They patted me down and told me to take my shirt off to see if I had any gang tattoos. When I showed them, they told me I could go."

The 22 Boys went into hiding after the arrest of their leader out of fear of violent aggression from rivals. I spoke with one 22 Boy, Deron, in his backyard just four months after Cantu's arrest. Wearing a bright blue football jersey, Deron recalled the gang's troubles: "We was in trouble a few months ago, when our boy [Rudy Cantu] got locked up. A lot of us didn't leave our houses for months because we knew Latin Kings and SDs [Satan Disciples] would be coming in from both sides [of the block] shooting each other up for this block. They've been eyeing our territory for years, and when word got around that Rudy got locked up, shit broke out like the Wild Wild West. Thankfully we got some help from our older guys in the burbs, who came in and helped us hold this shit down, but it's still dangerous to be out here. I still don't go out on the street much."

While Deron attributed the aggressiveness of rival gangs to "word getting around" that Cantu had been arrested, interviews with Latin Kings at Youth Inc. revealed that the absence of 22 Boys on street corners was the factor that spurred violent competition over the turf. After their leader was arrested, members of the 22 Boys fearfully refrained from patrolling their blocks and street corners in anticipation of aggression from rival gangs.

Eusebio, a Latin King, described how the disappearance of 22 Boys gang members created the perception of vulnerability: "Soldiers be always going back and forth over blocks and territories. A 22 Boy will spray 'Latin King Killer' on one of our blocks, and we'll go back and spray '22 Boy Killer' to let them know we ain't gonna take their bullshit. But after a while, if you don't protect your turf, then dudes will see that and think you weak. First, we spray graffiti on your territory, and if you don't do anything, we take your corner. If you don't protect your corner, we take your block. So when those 22 Boys weren't holding down their [corners and blocks], some of our boys tried to take them over."

After the gang leader's arrest, I drove through 22 Boys territory in the early morning to avoid confrontation with the warring gangs and saw Latin Kings graffiti sprayed on sidewalks and garage doors, which signified to gangs in the area that the Latin Kings were claiming the block. A few of the graffiti images were vandalized not by the 22 Boys but by the Satan Disciples, who were also attempting to take over the territory.

As the Latin Kings encroached upon 22 Boys territory from the west, they came into contact with the Satan Disciples encroaching from the east. According to police records and the Cook County Criminal Records Division, blocks within 22 Boys territory experienced a sharp increase in shootings during the month after the gang leader's arrest: three shootings occurred, and figure 6.4 illustrates where each incident took place in relation to the gang territories in the area.

The first shooting took place on February 3, 2010. According to court documents, Christian Correa, a member of the Satan Disciples, was walking in 22 Boys territory when a car pulled up and the assailant, Jesus Rios, a member of the Latin Kings, fired multiple shots.[23] The victim was struck in the shoulder and ear and was rushed to the hospital, where he survived. The shooter was charged with attempted first-degree murder. The Chicago

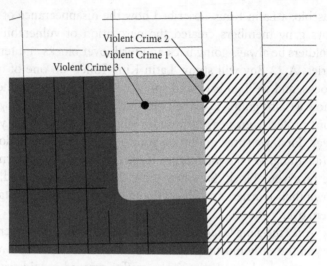

FIGURE 6.4 Location of shootings after gang leader's arrest.
Source: Chicago FBI Field Office Reports.

Crime Commission described the area near the shooting as the primary site of violent conflict between the 22 Boys and their rivals, but in this case the Latin Kings had advanced into 22 Boys territory and were fighting with the Satan Disciples. Juliana, who lived on the corner where the shooting occurred, believed the shooting was related to Cantu's arrest: "After they arrested the Chief, Latin Kings started coming from the other side to fight these guys [the Satan Disciples]. Thankfully, when the shooting took place here on the corner, my house didn't get hit, but now I don't let my kids out the house anymore."

The second shooting occurred three days later. Fernando Correa, a member of the Satan Disciples and a cousin of Christian Correa, saw members of the Latin Kings standing on the corner of Cermak and California, a corner typically occupied by the 22 Boys. According to police records, Correa retrieved a gun and with the help of a fellow gang member fired toward the group of Latin Kings.[24] No Latin Kings were injured, but two innocent bystanders waiting by a bus stop were struck multiple times and rushed to the hospital; they survived. The street corner where the shooting took place was home to a restaurant. The restaurant's owner, Juan, vividly remembered the shooting: "I remember the shooting happened in February because it was cold, and there were all these Kings in their black and gold standing outside my restaurant. Then all of a sudden I heard these pops and the gang members all ran away and two ladies were on the ground screaming for help."

The third shooting took place two weeks later, on February 23. Carlos Villagomez, a member of the 22 Boys, spotted Jose Fuentes, a member of the Satan Disciples, walking near 2877 West 22nd Place, a block occupied by the 22 Boys. Villagomez retrieved a gun and fired multiple times at Fuentes, hitting his leg and torso. Fuentes survived and Villagomez was charged with attempted first-degree murder and unlawful use of a weapon. According to court documents, Villagomez's residential address was in the western suburbs of Chicago, but police suspected that he came to the 22 Boys territory in Little Village to help the gang hold on to their territory.[25] The Chicago Crime Commission described Villagomez as an enforcer for the 22 Boys who provided muscle for the gang.[26] His street nickname was "Assassin," and his action defending the gang's territory ended the spree of shootings.

According to residents, unreported violent crimes also occurred between the gangs in the month after Cantu's arrest, though they did not involve guns or result in serious bodily harm. Javier, who lived next door to the final reported shooting, recalled how it restored some order to the block: "For a little while, there was nobody from the 22 Boys out representing the block. But then one of them came out of the house next door and started blasting away at the SDs [Satan Disciples], who tried to take over." Javier and other residents said that when 22 Boys gang members returned to the sidewalks and street corners, they displayed their weapons and fired shots into the air to make sure everyone knew they were armed. They believed that when Villagomez returned to reclaim the territory from the encroaching rival gangs, he also brought a supply of guns for lower-ranking gang members to defend themselves.

When put to the test of a rigorous statistical analysis, the stories shared by residents and gang members held up. Using violent crime data from 2006–12 and controlling for alternative explanations, results showed a significant increase in violent crime after the arrest. In addition, I used police records to determine the gang affiliations of the victims and perpetrators involved in shootings in 22 Boys territory one year before and after the arrest.[27] During this time period the majority of shootings involved a 22 Boy and a Latin King or a 22 Boy and a Satan Disciple. The month after the gang leader's arrest, however, marked the only time when a Satan Disciple and Latin King got into a violent conflict in 22 Boys territory. This provided stronger evidence that the gang leader's arrest sparked an unprecedented and violent competition between the Satan Disciples and Latin Kings over 22 Boys territory.

The gang leader's arrest also increased residents' cynicism toward law enforcement. "Things are out of control here," said Mario, a forty-seven-year-old resident in 22 Boys territory. "Before, the gangs had respect, they went to church, they mentored the new generation of gangbangers, but now they don't do that anymore." Speaking from behind his window screen, Mario continued, "The guys in charge of these gangs know they are targets and that they can be liable for a lot because of the RICO Act. And so they do things to separate themselves from the lower-ranking gangbangers." The Racketeer Influenced and Corrupt Organizations (RICO) Act allows the leader of an organized crime group to be held liable for the crimes of the organization.[28] "This separation has allowed a lot of these new and younger gang members to go unsupervised," said Mario, "and they're the ones doing a lot of these stupid shootings."

Rodolfo, a thirty-nine-year-old community organizer for CARE, an organization near 22 Boys territory, similarly lamented, "There used to be a code of the streets. You wouldn't mess with people when they were with their mother or kids. There was a respect, as crazy as it sounds. That's just out the window at this point. The arrests that have been made in the past year has played a role in that. They took a lot of the leadership from the gangs. So now you have a lot of younger guys in those positions, trying to make a name for themselves. Trying to be the ruthless leader. That plays a tremendous role in the violence we've seen lately."

According to Rodolfo, the absence of leaders allowed small internal conflicts to spiral into episodes of violent crime. He explained this process during a training session for newly hired youth group coordinators. On a chalkboard he diagrammed the gang's bureaucratic structure. A woman in the audience asked, "How does the gang settle internal disputes?" Rodolfo answered, "Conflicts usually start with the soldiers, and it's typically over a girl. The gang leader is supposed to take care of it by beating the crap out of all parties involved. That's how it's supposed to work because those kind of things hurt business. [Pointing to his illustration on the chalkboard] Whenever connections in the hierarchy of the gang dissolve, things get out of hand, with kids shooting dudes in their own gang." Residents like Rodolfo and Mario saw crackdowns on gang leaders as not simply ineffective but also disruptive of the social cohesion between gangs and the neighborhoods where they operate.

Some advocates of gang suppression might argue that the disruption of social cohesion was the desired outcome of the arrests. But for blocks like those in 22 Boys territory, which had little cohesion with the formal political system as a result of the political turf wars described in previous chapters, the loss of the gang leader meant the loss of a key community protector. The absence of nonprofits and responsive aldermen left residents dependent on the gang for protection. When the police operation was over, there was no law enforcement presence to protect residents from the ensuing violence between rivals competing for their blocks. Consequently residents saw little upside to the gang leader's arrest.

THE ARREST OF LATIN KINGS LEADERS

The Latin Kings' leader Augustin Zambrano, age fifty-one, oversaw the operations of the gang's activities and midlevel leaders. The Latin Kings had a large presence in federal prisons, and Zambrano answered to Gino Colon, the gang's national leader, who was in a maximum security federal prison. Colon maintained oversight of the gang through his wife, who served as his eyes and ears for monitoring the gang's activities.[29] As the highest-ranking leader outside of prison, Zambrano oversaw the Latin Kings' four-square-mile territory in Little Village. The territory was organized into twenty-four block sections, each with a designated block leader to supervise lower-ranking soldiers.

Zambrano's leadership activities could best be described as what Martin Sánchez-Jankowski calls "structured leadership," making key decisions but relying on trusted lieutenants to put those decisions into effect.[30] According to the FBI's indictment, "Zambrano did not carry out any violence by himself. He was insulated. He was behind the scenes. He entrusted others to do it. The result was an organization with its own rules, its own laws, and a savage code of violence."[31] My fieldwork supported the FBI's description of Zambrano's behind-the-scenes leadership style. Neither the residents nor the gang members I interviewed knew Zambrano's identity. Each of the Latin Kings I interviewed stated that the gang had a president, or what they called "Inca," but no one had seen the Inca or even knew his name. Residents knew only the names of midlevel leaders, or "block chiefs," who supervised the soldiers on their blocks.

On September 24, 2008, the FBI served arrest warrants on the home of Augustin Zambrano and seventeen Latin King block leaders in Little Village. The names and addresses of the gang leaders were published in the indictment released by the U.S. attorney's office.[32] Zambrano was denied bail because of the severity of the charges against him, which included murder, identity theft, and intent to distribute fake identification.

On the streets, the arrest of the leadership appeared to have little effect on the gang's use of space. The gang's prison leadership quickly appointed replacements for Zambrano as well as for the seventeen block leaders.

"What changed after Zambrano's arrest?" I asked Freddy, a Youth Inc. violence prevention worker.

"It got quiet for a week." Freddy laughed. "That's about it. No one was causing any trouble on the streets or anything, but things got back to normal quick. It actually made us [violence prevention workers] more busy because we had to figure out who was calling the shots now. After a couple days, we figured out who replaced the old guys."

"How did you find out who was in charge?"

"After riding around the neighborhood asking soldiers who was calling the shots now, I was given an address and I went and visited the new guy."

"How do you know he was the new leader?"

"Everyone in the house was calling him *jefe* [boss], and he was fresh out of prison, which is where the new guys usually come from. He still had a GPS tag on his ankle. He said he was put in charge by the *jefes* in prison."

Accounts from residents living in Latin Kings territory during the spring and summer of 2010 supported the conclusion that the Latin Kings had quickly replaced their leaders. Residents overwhelmingly agreed that the gang's activities on their blocks changed little after the police intervention. For example, asked whether he had heard of the police raids on the gang, Maurice, who had lived in Latin Kings territory for fifteen years, recalled the 2008 raid: "There were tons of unmarked police cars everywhere and SWAT teams with machine guns. They went into one of the homes on our block and got some of the Kings living there."

"Do you think these raids work?" I asked.

"I've seen these raids happen before and it's all the same," Maurice responded. "They come in, arrest the guys, it gets quiet for a day or two, and then it goes back to normal. They have their meetings where they collect dues, and their peewees [youngest gang members] are still out patrolling the streets on their bikes."

Tony, a violence prevention worker at the PCG, had a similar reaction to the FBI raid: "The Kings are the last supergang left in Chicago. The police have been able to dismantle the Disciples, Black P Stones, and Vice Lords, but they [the Latin Kings] have constantly been able to adapt to whatever the law throws at them."

"What makes the Kings different?" I asked.

"Loyalty. They do a really good job of ingraining loyalty to their members. It's a pseudo-religion to these guys. The young guys might not get it, but the older guys have been indoctrinated. It's like a cult."

* * *

Arresting gang leaders may have consequences that reverberate throughout the community, altering the relationships among actors in the neighborhood's field. As this chapter has shown, residents in neighborhoods like Little Village can establish a social order with gangs built on trust and shared expectations. But when law enforcement agencies aim to foster distrust and conflict within a gang by arresting its leader, they also foster distrust and conflict among residents and nearby gangs.[33]

Social scientists argue that reducing gang violence requires a balance of law enforcement suppression and provision of social services, but the arrests of the two gang leaders in Little Village show city government strategies were contradictory in Chicago.[34] On the one hand, police worked to suppress gang activity by arresting gang leaders to damage gangs' organizational cohesion. On the other hand, residents and state-funded violence prevention organizations tried to prevent violence by building relationships with gangs. The conflicting approaches of the police's gang suppression and nonprofits' violence prevention programming reinforce the violent turf wars in Little Village.

Though the outcomes of the gang leaders' arrests were far different from what law enforcement expected, this analysis should not be taken as a defense of gang leaders. Rather, the case of Little Village highlights the need for a more nuanced approach to gang control that begins with recognizing the importance of relationships to violent crime. In neighborhoods with multiple gangs, it is difficult to envision how dismantling a single gang would reduce overall levels of violence in the area. Even if law enforcement were able to dismantle each gang one by one, these tactics might result in the splintering of organized crime groups into smaller cells or factions. In Chicago, the dismantling of other supergangs like the Gangster Disciples and the Vice Lords created an archipelago of gang factions in poor neighborhoods where, in the absence of leadership, small gangs rose to represent blocks instead of entire neighborhoods.[35] Suppression may have dismantled large organized gangs, but it did not end the relational conflicts triggering violence. When law enforcement disrupts the social order among gangs and residents, history shows that it is eventually replaced by a new social order.

Gang control policies need to reassemble, not dismantle, the social order in which gangs operate. With the use of data and with collaboration with social service agencies, law enforcement crackdowns on gang leaders can be done in smarter ways. In addition to planning how to detain the gang leaders, policymakers need to devise a plan on how to fill the void created by the removal of the gang from the neighborhood. Where will lower-level gang members go? How can the community defend its blocks and sidewalks from the aggression of outside gangs coming to take over the turf? Gangs survive, in part, through the relationships they forge within the communities where they operate. Thus, failing to mend or replace the gang's role in the neighborhood will only create an opportunity for a new gang or rival to take its place.

It is important to note that not all gang leader arrests result in null effects or increases in violence. Some conditions in Little Village made the east side more likely to experience an outburst of violence after a gang leader's arrest. The 22 Boys were a small gang with territory adjacent to two larger and more organized gangs. Proximity to the larger Latin Kings and Satan Disciples made the 22 Boys especially vulnerable to aggression in the aftermath of their leader's arrest.[36] By contrast, when the Latin Kings leaders were arrested, it would have been highly unlikely for the 22 Boys to have the resources and level of organization necessary to encroach on their territory. More case studies are needed to better understand the conditions shaping the outcomes of gang leader arrests, but the case of Little Village highlights the importance of paying close attention to the dismantling of small gangs with territories adjacent to larger and more organized gangs.

Other interventions such as gang sweeps and targeted deterrence may also have consequences extending beyond the targeted gang.[37] By highlighting the consequences of law enforcement's turf war with gangs, the case of Little Village instructs policymakers and scholars to be more cautious when attempting to dismantle gangs. Even further, the east side of Little Village demonstrates how political and street turf wars can concentrate violence on particular blocks of a neighborhood.

7

Conclusion

Toward a Relational Understanding
of Urban Violence

THE VIOLENCE CONCENTRATED IN PARTICULAR areas
within Chicago neighborhoods cannot be understood without
accounting for the political and street turf wars fought over
blocks. Areas like Little Village's east side exist throughout the
city. The *Chicago Tribune* has described them as "a no-man's
land" for both police and politicians.[1] While cities and police
departments deploy a variety of policing tactics to combat
violent hot spots, these efforts are limited by the fact that they
are not designed to intervene in the political processes rendering areas hot spots to begin with. As this study showed, violent hot spots are not created by social disorder or broken windows. Rather, the actions of actors inside and outside the
neighborhood shape blocks' capacity to prevent violence and
can trigger violent conflict among gangs or residents. In Little
Village's east side, relationships between gangs and residents
were routinely disrupted in ways that ignited violent conflict
and undermined violence prevention, whereas the west side
had a nonprofit infrastructure in place to help prevent conflicts
from erupting into violence. Researchers and policymakers
need to identify the small clusters of blocks within neighborhoods that account for the majority of violent crimes and work
to integrate the people living in those areas with city government and nonprofit agencies working to prevent violence.

Governments and foundations can easily map the underserved and politically underrepresented areas within cities and devise ways to build partnerships with residents in those areas. In contrast to popular perceptions of residents in poor communities being incapable of collective action, residents of Little Village's most violent blocks in the east side worked hard to address the violence. Eastside residents would be eager to receive similar resources and collaborative efforts from nonprofits or city violence prevention agencies.

Addressing urban violence requires taking urban politics seriously. As Little Village's political history showed, it was no coincidence the east side lacked meaningful ties to city resources. Little Village was once, and in many ways still is, the base of a growing independent political movement that challenged the city's mainstream Democratic Party. To heal the wounds of street violence in Chicago, the city's political actors must also heal the wounds of the city's racial and political history. Chicago's political turf wars continue to this day. The historic 2015 Chicago mayoral election reignited the battle between the Democratic machine and independents. Jesus "Chuy" Garcia was a former close ally of Mayor Harold Washington, an independent, while Mayor Emanuel was a close ally of former mayor Richard M. Daley, a Democrat.

It may be unreasonable to expect political rivals to put aside their differences and collaborate, but it is still possible for urban violence to become a nonpartisan issue. No politician wants neighborhood violence to continue injuring young people and taking lives. By allocating violence prevention resources to the places where it is most needed, such as Little Village's east side, mayors may not only help reduce violence but may also build a new political base for reelection. As Clarence Stone argues, politics do not always have to lead to control over a particular group of people; politics can be productive.[2] For example, in Boston leaders of the African American community worked alongside the predominantly white police department to reduce youth homicides.[3]

At a national level, Democrats and Republicans worked across the aisle to pass important laws such as the Americans with Disabilities Act and the Children's Health Insurance Program. In Chicago, violence is an issue that can and should be addressed through cooperation between Democratic and independent political groups.

This book attempts to bring groups with a history of conflict together by moving the political conversation about violence away from broad policy prescriptions and toward a discussion of the specific places and relationships triggering or preventing violence. Little Village's past and present reveal a neighborhood where violence persists not because the community lacks values, but because political and street turf wars have wounded relationships in small spaces within the neighborhood. These findings have several implications for social science and policy approaches to violence prevention.

INTEGRATING SPACE AND NETWORKS FOR A RELATIONAL CRIMINOLOGY

Scholars tend to conceptualize neighborhoods as either geographically bounded places or fields of relationships among actors. This study illuminated a few useful ways these two conceptualizations can be integrated. In Little Village, space affected relationships among actors and relationships among actors affected neighborhood spaces. The west side had public and nonprofit resources to broker an informal social order with the gangs, while the social order in the east side was routinely disrupted by turf wars among politicians, gangs, and police that transformed blocks into hot spots for shootings and arson. The boundaries delineating spaces in Little Village, such as ward boundaries, gang boundaries, and neighborhood boundaries, were the outcome of strategic actions among various actors engaged in competitive relations for different forms of power, such as control of the Chicago city council, drug territory, or residents.

These spaces also influenced relationships. Violence on the east side caused residents to fear police and to avoid spending time outside. When the 22 Boys' gang leader was arrested, the geographic proximity of rival gangs contributed to a sudden spike in shootings. The turf wars over streets and political power can be thought of as having the ability to amplify or weaken a neighborhood effect. For example, Little Village shows how the relationship between collective efficacy and neighborhood violence might be stronger after taking into account the political wards in which neighborhood spaces are embedded. Neighborhood spaces that have been gerrymandered by the dominant local political party might have lower levels of collective efficacy than structurally similar spaces. Neighborhoods are not just places where exposure to an environment can influence individual behavior. They are also places constructed by the strategic actions (such as arresting a gang leader or changing a ward boundary) of actors in competitive relations. Changes in the relationships among residents, gangs, police, neighborhood leaders, and city officials can result in changes in neighborhood conditions that, in turn, can affect residents' behavior.[4]

BRIDGING THE FIELDS OF URBAN POLITICS AND NEIGHBORHOOD INEQUALITY

Scholars of neighborhood inequality and urban political economy have long been in dialogue with one another, building and critiquing each other's perspectives but ultimately falling short of establishing a bridging theoretical framework. Neighborhood researchers have focused on everyday interpersonal interaction, negotiation, and conflict to understand the dynamics of neighborhood social organization, but they have largely overlooked the influence of political economy.[5] The theory of collective efficacy is the most recent formulation of this perspective, arguing that neighborhood violence stems from the absence of trust and social cohesion among residents.[6] Yet despite volumes of research on collective efficacy and neighborhood social organization in Chicago, only a handful of studies incorporate an analysis of Chicago city government or Chicago's history of racial politics and exclusion.[7] This omission is problematic considering that Chicago is the site of many key studies on urban social processes. While concepts like collective efficacy and legal cynicism help explain neighborhood homicide rates, they are measures of individual attitudes or collective action among residents and do not capture the political structures that can facilitate or impede residents' collective efficacy. If, as Robert Sampson argues, urban sociology should be primarily concerned with explaining neighborhood capacity for collective action, then political turf wars must be included in any analysis of neighborhood inequality.[8]

In Little Village, the political turf wars between the neighborhood's politically independent leadership and the Chicago Democratic Party helped explain different blocks' ability to socially control gang members. Areas like the burbs in Little Village's west side benefited from the political victories of the 22nd ward's leaders, who funneled resources (surveillance cameras and violence prevention programs) to blocks in the area. In the east side, poverty and residential instability were not the only barriers to collective efficacy; residents also had no political support or nonprofit infrastructure due to gerrymandering.

Scholars of neighborhood inequality could better incorporate urban politics by focusing on neighborhoods' political ecology, such as ward boundaries, congressional districts, police districts, zoning ordinances, tax increment financing districts, and empowerment zones.[9] Besides the ecological environment, urban neighborhoods are also embedded in bounded political spaces.

Collaborations and turf wars among political actors produce the political and ecological spaces within neighborhoods and shape the allocation of resources across a city. Urban sociologists should examine the overlap between neighborhood and political boundaries to develop what I call "political ecometrics," or measures of political spaces within neighborhoods that indicate who is governing the neighborhood and how.[10] The case of Little Village highlights the salience of gerrymandering, which is one mechanism of political ecology shaping neighborhood space. Researchers could also explore the political affiliations of neighborhood representatives, relationships between city and ward officials, and other factors to identify additional political sources of neighborhood inequality.[11] Testing measures of a neighborhood's political ecology would give urban sociology the much-needed connection between extralocal political processes and neighborhood social organization that critics have been arguing has been missing from urban sociology for decades.[12]

Incorporating urban politics could also help disentangle the relationship between race and neighborhood violent crime. In an effort to move beyond "culture of poverty" and "relative deprivation" explanations, Robert Sampson and William Julius Wilson argue that African Americans and whites reside in very different ecological contexts that spur differences in neighborhood violent crime rates.[13] The findings from this study indicate that these racial differences might also stem from variation in the outcomes of political turf wars among white, African American, and Latino political groups. In Chicago, the gerrymandering of African American and Latino neighborhoods could have consequences for the broader geographic concentration of violence throughout the city. Examining differences in the ways mayors, city managers, and city councils govern African American, white, and Latino neighborhoods may help explain the race effect on neighborhood violent crime. Studies by Maria Velez and others find that cities with greater political representation and incorporation of racial minorities have lower violent crime rates.[14] Such studies are a great start at incorporating the urban political economy into the study of urban racial inequality.[15]

A RELATIONAL UNDERSTANDING OF THE STATE

The political turf wars over Little Village demonstrate how conflict among state actors can shape the social organization of poor neighborhoods. To date, many scholars of urban political economy have understood urban conditions as derivative of capitalism or neoliberalism.[16] For example, John Logan and Harvey Molotch argue that governing coalitions of the rich and politically powerful, which they call "growth machines," determine land use in urban areas. Loïc Wacquant argues that the U.S. government's coordinated neoliberal agenda produced mass imprisonment and welfare retrenchment, which have turned poor neighborhoods into ghettos void of resources and overflowing with law enforcement agents.[17] These perspectives have been criticized for being too deterministic and failing to account for resistance to or fragmentation among political and economic elites.[18]

Battles between government officials at the city and neighborhood level heavily shaped Little Village's social organization, contributing to the creation of violent hot spots in some areas and low violent crime rates in others. These findings reflect the workings of a fragmented state with multiple levels of power and multiple geographic jurisdictions. By studying neighborhoods as fields, scholars can identify the conflicts and collaborations among multiple state actors that result in the unequal distribution of resources as well as unequal social and physical conditions across urban space. The deals brokered, grants applied for, and relationships built among state actors on different blocks within a neighborhood have consequences for residents' ability to address problems like violence. Though welfare reform, the war on drugs, and other large-scale government policies certainly shape neighborhood conditions, low-income neighborhood conditions still vary considerably, and variation in the relationships among state actors may help explain why certain policies have had devastating effects on some poor neighborhoods but not others.

Studying political turf wars—or, more broadly, how relationships among state actors affect urban inequality—is critical because city governments vary tremendously in their powers, structures, and modes of governance. Urban sociologists often use blanket terms such as *the state* and *the ghetto* to describe the government's contribution to the formation of poor neighborhoods as a coordinated process involving the absence of institutions and a heavy-handed criminal justice system.[19] But this case study of Little Village showed that even neighborhoods with high levels of violent crime have multiple political structures governing them. Rather than conceptualizing the role of government broadly, scholars should specify the particular relationships that produce urban poverty, violence, and other social problems.

Scholars can start by studying a neighborhood's relationship to political actors such as legislators, political parties, mayoral administrations, state representatives, or even U.S. congressional representatives. Like Little Village, other neighborhoods with a history of opposing the local dominant political party might have less access to government resources. Neighborhoods subject to gerrymandering might also have a more difficult time lobbying for funds or programs to address local problems. The consequences of these relationships may vary from place to place even within a single neighborhood, leading to very different configurations of problems with unique solutions. Advancing such a research agenda would provide a more accurate description of how the diverse political structures comprising US government shape urban inequality within cities.

TOWARD SMARTER POLICING

In the current historical context the rate of violent crime is dropping in urban areas, but it is also becoming more concentrated in clusters of blocks within cities. Yet many city governments are still increasing spending on policing and surveillance.[20] To make matters worse, city police departments across the country share little data with the public on how police resources are spent or distributed across districts. Recent cases of police brutality and the subsequent unrest in places like Baltimore, Maryland, and Ferguson, Missouri, reveal the difficulty of creating accountability in urban policing. But the stories from Little Village suggest a few ways that police might work to create safer neighborhoods and break the code of silence.

First, the U.S. criminal justice system needs to understand that preventing violence should involve not just destroying relationships among criminals but also building relationships in communities. Studies have shown that when an arrest is made, not just the individual but also family members and neighbors feel the effects.[21] The case of Little Village showed that arresting gang leaders left a gap in community relationships that were simply filled by the next generation of gangs or organized crime groups. Criminal enterprises do not just introduce violence into communities; they also create forms of social cohesion. They can create order among criminal groups competing over drug markets or informal social control through relations with residents. Interventions aimed at dismantling the gang's criminal activities must also consider how to replace the social cohesion provided by the gang.

The street watchers around Farragut High School did just that by relationship building that preserved peace and social order among gang members, residents, and police on the streets. The work of preserving order was a joint venture brokered by Youth Inc. and PCG violence prevention workers, police, street watchers, and even members of the gang. Violence decreased not because gang members feared police but because they felt a sense of social obligation toward these other community actors. Violence prevention workers like Tony, Freddy, and Santino engaged in important relationship-building work that should be incorporated into a smarter set of strategies for urban violent crime fighting. Police play an important role in preserving law and order, but they are only part of the solution. As the policing of violent crime begins to focus on small pockets within neighborhoods, the role of police in preserving order will need to be supplemented by relationship brokers who can serve as key mediators between a poor neighborhood's formal and informal economies.

The stories of Little Village residents demonstrated that adherence to the code of silence can also be concentrated within particular areas of a neighborhood, and that efforts to curb the code of silence could be enhanced by focusing on those areas. Contrary to public perceptions, the majority of Little Village residents did not adhere to the code of silence. Rather, pockets of the east side were dominated by the Latin Kings, who seized upon police mistakes to reinforce the code. A more critical and focused intervention, centered on where the code of silence is most prevalent within neighborhoods, would help cities more efficiently address the issue through efforts targeting specific areas and relationships. This would be better than a broad public relations campaign. Another potential fix would be to update the police's outdated use of radio communication. With the rise of social media and cell phone usage, investment in better internal communication technologies could help prevent small mistakes from revealing informant identities to gangs, and inadvertently supporting residents' reluctance to report crime to the police.

THE FUTURE OF LITTLE VILLAGE

Much has changed in Little Village since my data collection ended in 2012, but the political turf wars have continued. After Karen Lewis, the head of the Chicago Teacher's Union, dropped out of the 2015 mayoral race because of health problems, Jesus Garcia ran for mayor in her place and forced the first runoff election in the history of Chicago. The election was heated, and for a moment it appeared as though history was repeating itself. Little Village was on the verge of capturing a close relationship to city hall. But Mayor Emanuel defeated Garcia by 11 percentage points.

In contrast to 1983, when African Americans and Latinos were united in opposition to the machine, Emanuel received the majority of black votes (58 percent). Garcia won decisively in Little Village's 22nd ward, but with just 4,509 votes cast in his favor.[22] Voters had a difficult time discerning Garcia's plan for improving Chicago's budget problems, relieving its pension obligations, and decreasing violent crime. Many questioned whether he could fund his promise to put one thousand more police officers on the street, and some voters in African American communities voiced concern that additional police officers would lead to more police harassment. Political analysts viewed the election as a referendum on Mayor Emanuel's failure to curb violence and his unpopular policies: closing fifty Chicago public schools in mostly minority neighborhoods, installing red-light cameras, and taking on the teacher's union.[23]

The election reignited political turf wars in Little Village when Kimberly Wasserman, a neighborhood environmental justice advocate, was featured in a television advertisement supporting Emanuel's reelection. The advertisement credited the mayor with helping to close a coal plant that had been polluting the air quality in Little Village for decades. Wasserman's endorsement infuriated Garcia's supporters and was seen by some as a betrayal. This conflict was the most recent manifestation of the political turf wars described in this book, as Emanuel and the city's mainstream Democratic Party continue to divide activists in the neighborhood. In the time since my fieldwork ended, Alderman Ricardo Muñoz has opened his doors to more resident input by hosting participatory budget hearings throughout the ward. These budget meetings have been widely attended, which suggests that more residents have a venue to request violence prevention resources in the west side.

The new ward boundaries in effect in 2015 have once again carved up Little Village's east side into the 24th, 28th, and 12th wards; however, the 12th ward has been redrawn to incorporate the majority of east Little Village (see figure 7.1).

This has created a new opportunity for renewal of the east side as the 12th ward Alderman, George Cardenas, has increased his investment of time and resources into that section of Little Village. In 2014, the city opened a new park in the 12th ward, a green space for youth who have for decades felt unsafe venturing outside the east side because of the various surrounding

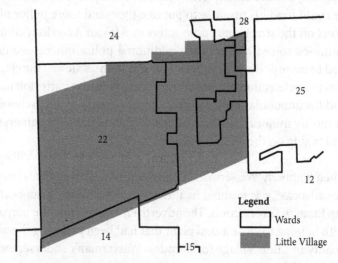

FIGURE 7.1 Ward boundaries in Little Village, 2015.
Source: City of Chicago 2015.

gang territories. Leadership in the 12th ward has been especially active in rebranding Little Village's east side as a new neighborhood called "Marshall Square." In fact, community organizers in adjacent neighborhoods formed a new organization, the Marshall Square Resource Network, aimed at building strong organizational capacity to address the area's needs. It's unclear whether these efforts at renewal will be successful, but things are certainly headed in the right direction within the 12th ward. Unfortunately the same is not true for the sections of Little Village's east side in the 24th and 28th wards. The 24th ward in particular now slithers through a much larger section of Little Village, while the 28th ward has been reduced to just one small precinct. The struggle for neighborhood improvement continues in the east side.

IMPLICATIONS FOR VIOLENCE PREVENTION

The case of Little Village demonstrates that violence prevention advocates have to fight both political and street turf wars to be successful. The PCG in Little Village's 22nd ward provides a good example of success on both of these fronts. After decades of struggle for political representation, a hunger strike, and applying for and implementing a variety of nonprofit social services, the west side's leadership developed the capacity to implement innovative violence prevention programs.

Outside Little Village, organizers and concerned residents could learn a great deal from the PCG's work. This begins with training violence prevention workers and organizers to develop a better understanding of city and neighborhood politics alongside their understanding of the criminal underworld. An analysis of political turf wars would be a useful addition to the public health model for violence prevention, which conceptualizes gang violence as a disease infecting communities one individual at a time.[24] This model has informed the design of several interventions, such as Ceasefire, which employs former gang members to prevent retaliations. "For every shooting," Freddy would say, "there's at least six or seven retaliations. So if you stop the retaliations you can stop the violence." As effective as these interventions might be, there is nothing in the public health model that instructs residents or organizers on how to prevent a governor or mayor from slashing a program's funding. Over the course of its existence Ceasefire has had its funding cut by the governor several times, and Chicago police have refused to cooperate with Ceasefire workers and vice versa. Violence prevention models need to work toward repairing not just the physical wounds caused by violence but also the institutional wounds inflicted by acts of political violence on low-income neighborhoods through budget cuts, public school closings, gerrymandering, and police brutality.

The political socialization of violence prevention workers could be supplemented by educating and empowering residents in violence-plagued areas about civic action and Chicago's political structure. Residents and organizers must learn how to identify the power structures impeding their efforts and devise strategies to neutralize them or call upon alternative sources of power to acquire resources. Civic participation and collective action is not just about voting. It also involves understanding the political systems and institutions that structure everyday urban life, gerrymander neighborhoods out of key resources, and impede the pursuit of collective goals.

One example of this type of consciousness-raising took place on December 19, 2013, when Reverend Al Sharpton and the National Action Network held a town hall meeting to discuss solutions to the problem of violence in Chicago. To the surprise of many, the residents in attendance did not discuss changing gun laws or getting guns off the streets. Instead, the meeting turned into a rally against Chicago machine politics, the mayor, and the city council. Attendees offered solutions to the gang violence problem that involved political action.

"If you're not a part of the patronage army, you can't get a job, you can't get a grant, your community suffers," said Wendy Pearson, a Chicago activist. "The manner in which we have been voting needs to change."

"Stop blaming just anybody for the violence in the city of Chicago," said Paul McKinley, an ex-convict and activist. "Blame the right people. Not white people. Blame the right people. Because it ain't white folks, it's on the fifth floor [of city hall, i.e., the mayor's office]. The fifth floor took your schools [referring to the closing of fifty public schools]. The fifth floor took all your jobs."

The sentiments expressed by these activists highlight the kind of political consciousness that can trigger collective action to address the political turf wars sustaining violence in pockets of Chicago. When policymakers seek to reduce violence, they usually do so with the goal of better managing the problem, *not* altering the political power structures impeding its eradication. Criminologists have provided little insight into political turf wars and efforts to properly apply the knowledge put forth from criminological research. For example, while social network analysis can tell policymakers who among the population is most likely to be victimized by violence, this knowledge has not been used in constructive ways. In particular, Chicago police have used this knowledge to implement "two degrees of separation," a strategy that identifies gang members deemed "likely" to fall victim to gang violence, arrests them, and holds them in custody over a weekend to make sure they do not get shot.[25] This strategy does nothing to change the political turf wars undermining violence prevention or street turf wars triggering violent conflicts.

Urban politics presents a challenge for criminologists. It complicates efforts to make knowledge productive for facilitating collective action among residents in violent neighborhoods and the political leaders governing them. When addressing violence, social scientists should not ignore political issues but, instead, address them head on by incorporating them into research questions and theoretical frameworks. The social scientific knowledge on reducing violence can suggest ways to rehabilitate violence-plagued communities, but it must also help heal the wounds from decades of political turf wars between city hall, neighborhood leaders, and residents in American cities.

Appendix A

Ethnographic Uncoupling and the Challenges of Relational Ethnography

HISTORIAN AND SOCIAL ACTIVIST Howard Zinn often said "You can't be neutral on a moving train" to describe the impossibility of being objective on important political issues. This was a lesson I quickly learned when conducting my relational ethnography of violence in Little Village. Matt Desmond describes relational ethnography as studying "at least two types of actors or agencies occupying different positions within the social space and bound together in a relationship of mutual dependence or struggle."[1] In contrast to ethnographic studies of groups or places, such as gangs and street corners, relational ethnography focuses on chains, threads, connections, and mutual influence among actors.[2] For this project, I followed relations among five types of actors (local politicians, nonprofit organizations, police, gangs, and residents) across a variety of settings (street corners, homes, schools, recreational basketball leagues, and offices). While the study focused on two types of turf wars, arriving at this argument involved a long and strenuous process of data collection and analysis that required entering into conflict with research subjects.

In an ideal situation, the relational ethnographer enters the field humble and impartial, and navigates both sides of a contentious relationship to get at the truth. This was not how data collection unfolded for this project. At the start, I had no intention of conducting relational ethnography. I was intrigued by certain questions as they emerged from the field: Were police colluding with gangs? Were nonprofits and politicians intentionally ignoring residents' requests for help with preventing violence? These questions demanded data collection from multiple actors who were hesitant to talk to me and who despised one another. In the process of developing close relationships with residents and gang members (the first groups I studied), I found myself not only understanding but also adopting my research subjects' point of view in ways that profoundly altered how I framed and theorized early drafts of this book.

Arriving at my final thesis required engaging in multiple rounds of what I call, ethnographic uncoupling, a process of distancing and disconnecting from both the relationships with informants and physical spaces in an ethnographer's field site. Diane Vaughan originally coined the term *uncoupling* to refer to the process of how married couples transition out of intimate relationships.[3] After conducting the fieldwork for this book, it struck me that relational ethnographers must go through a similar process. After immersing myself in the lives of individuals on one side of a turf war (such as the gangs), I had to pull myself out, cleanse my analytical mind-set, then immerse myself in the lives of their rivals (the police), and then repeat the process to study the other turf wars. This involved immersion with residents and gangs at the outset, then immersion with nonprofits and the police. After completing data collection, I once again had to uncouple myself from the relationships I built with people involved in these turf wars. I had to clear my thoughts by giving talks at universities, circulating chapters to colleagues, losing contact with research subjects, and staying away from my field site.

This methodological appendix describes my process of ethnographic uncoupling for conducting this relational ethnography and arriving at my major conclusions. When advising graduate students, many professors oversimplify the process whereby an ethnographic project becomes a published book: the ethnographer collects the data, takes time off after completing the dissertation, spends a year revising, maybe collecting more data, and then writing a book. While sufficient for some, these instructions do not provide much help to the relational ethnographer who is attempting to draw conclusions from the vantage point of multiple rival actors. The challenges of conducting relational ethnography lie not only in fieldwork tasks such as gaining access to research subjects and navigating boundaries but also in the post-fieldwork task of ethnographic uncoupling such as unlearning one's profound dislike of a research subject or deciphering whether one has fairly portrayed both sides of an issue.

For this project, my process was not perfect or pretty, but neither is ethnography or social science more generally. The notion of the humble, dispassionate, and objective ethnographer is not only a myth; it's also not a useful way to think about doing relational ethnography.[4] Rather than striving for an unattainable ideal, I describe my own struggle for objectivity, fairness, and balance in the hope that ethnographers can pay greater attention to the important yet rarely discussed post-fieldwork task of ethnographic uncoupling. My experiences might serve as a useful guide for scholars aspiring to conduct their own relational ethnographies, especially of actors engaged in highly contentious and antagonistic relations.

STEPPING INTO A TURF WAR

Before starting my graduate studies at Northwestern in 2007, I knew that once I started working toward my PhD, the majority of my time was going to be spent in class or conducting research. To maintain a connection to the real world, I wanted to spend my last free summer volunteering for a nonprofit organization working on social justice–related issues in Chicago. My undergraduate advisor recommended I volunteer at the Little Village Environmental Justice Organization (LVEJO), a nonprofit addressing a number of environmental issues afflicting the neighborhood. After meeting with the LVEJO director, I was assigned to volunteer for the clean power campaign, an effort to lobby city and state governments to close a nearby coal factory that has polluted the neighborhood's air quality for decades.

My experience as a volunteer gave me my first wind of the neighborhood's political turf wars. Organizers on the clean power campaign spoke disapprovingly of 22nd ward's alderman Ricardo Muñoz and the Puebla Community Group (PCG) for their lack of support with closing the coal plant. "We don't like the PCG or alderman because they take money from the coal plant company," said one organizer.

Initially I did not think much of this conflict. Most of my time was spent canvassing or conducting research on the links between air quality and asthma in Little Village.

As my time as a volunteer came to an end, I decided to stay and conduct an ethnography of the youth group at LVEJO. Every Friday, a group of neighborhood youth met to discuss neighborhood social issues, eat food, and do some volunteer work for the organization. As my scholarly interests at the time lay primarily in the educational achievement of Mexican American youth, the group seemed like a useful field site to begin an ethnographic project. From the fall of 2007 to the end of summer 2008, I spent close to 180 days in Little Village shadowing and interviewing youth in three friendship groups. I would hang out with them after school, at the youth group, on the streets, and at LVEJO events. In the process, I heard both organizers and youth speak negatively about the PCG and alderman. It was clear that some of the neighborhood nonprofits were not fond of one another.

My motivation to study violence arose from one particular night at the youth group. The meeting was wrapping up when a young male entered the room and announced, "Hey yo, on your way home tonight, avoid South Boulevard. The Latin Kings are doing an initiation tonight and they may be looking to stir up some trouble with the Two Six." Immediately, the teenagers in attendance asked around for a ride home. That night my car was packed with teens I took to their homes. When I arrived at my apartment later that evening, I looked through my field notes and found so many instances of neighborhood violence constraining young peoples' everyday decisions. Youth chose to spend time with certain people, in certain places, and at certain times based on their knowledge of the neighborhood's violent hot spots. I went to sleep that night feeling that, to understand young people and their educational outcomes, I needed to first understand the neighborhood's geography of violence.

After completing the ethnography of the youth group, I spent 2009 analyzing violent crime statistics and police intelligence maps of the neighborhood's gang territories. To build upon my qualitative findings on neighborhood youth, I designed a survey with 120 questions to administer to young people between fourteen and nineteen years old in a random sample of households in Little Village. In addition, I designed three open-ended questions to interview parents as their child was completing the survey (mainly to distract them from checking on their child's answers). Specifically I asked parents: What do you think about the violence on your block? What do you think of police in the neighborhood? What do you think of the local alderman? For a more technical description of the survey, see appendix B.

The project's focus drastically changed as the canvassing produced puzzling research questions related to neighborhood politics, gangs, police, and nonprofits that were impossible for me to refrain from investigating ethnographically. These included stories of residents feeling excluded by the alderman and the PCG, as well as stories of police officers disclosing informant identities to the gang. At first I thought these stories were idiosyncratic, but the longer I canvassed blocks, the more I heard resident stories of being disappointed by community organizations, politicians, and the police on some blocks and stories of being satisfied on others.

It was at this stage that my closeness to my research subjects and previous involvement in turf wars among nonprofits began to interfere with my objective ethnographic sensibilities. While I did not believe residents' stories about corrupt police officers intentionally disclosing informant identities to the gang, I did believe that the PCG and alderman were failing them. After spending years with youth and organizers who spoke derisively about the PCG and alderman, and after empathizing with residents' frustration with the lack of violence prevention on their block, I adopted my research subjects' views of these actors. My biases were even being reinforced during my time away from the field.

"Where are you doing your research?" a stranger asked me at an alumni event in a Southside Chicago neighborhood bar.

"Little Village," I answered.

"Oh, then you must know about the big bad organization, the PCG. They're shady." It seemed that no matter where I went, I could not escape people reinforcing my negative perceptions of these actors in my field site.

To begin unraveling all the negativity surrounding the PCG, I interviewed Arianna, a former PCG staff member at the time, in September 2010. "What have relationships been like between the PCG, other nonprofits, and the police?" I asked.

"I have an issue with the question, actually," she replied, "because you are framing it within the context of what LVEJO have thrown out there. Why is the question specific to the PCG?"

"I'm not sure what you're asking me," I answered. "I'm not trying to go after the PCG. I apologize, I don't mean for it to sound that way at all. That's not my intention. I ask because regardless of what I've heard from organizations, there have been a lot of complaints about police and how they protect informant identities. So I'm wondering how community organizations handle resident complaints about policing."

"Okay, that makes more sense than the way you phrased it before." Arianna continued, "I tell you that because you need to interview other people, especially more neutral people, you know, like people who work at the PCG. It's just, like, knowing where you're coming from [LVEJO] is already telling me that you already have perceptions of the way things are."

By entering the neighborhood through the LVEJO, I unknowingly took sides in turf wars among the neighborhood's nonprofits. In addition, some LVEJO organizers had become close friends of mine, and my immersion in their world impeded my attempt at relational ethnography. The interview with Arianna left me feeling like I was the PCG's enemy. In my mind the PCG were questioning me because they had something to hide. I had never had my integrity questioned in such a direct manner. I was being forced to take a side in the neighborhood's turf wars and, rather than stay neutral, I picked a side. I was against the PCG. I was against the alderman. I internalized so much of my research subjects' opinions that I began to believe them myself.

With the PCG being uncooperative, I interviewed other nonprofits and learned about the Anti-Violence Network (AVN) from organizers at Youth Inc., a violence prevention organization that also had issues with the PCG. More important, Youth Inc. quickly provided me access to interview and observe their staff. The network met once a month to discuss neighborhood violence prevention efforts, and the PCG was part of the group. After a couple of weeks, I signed up to give a fifteen-minute presentation of my survey findings to the AVN and recruit more organizations for one-on-one interviews. The title of my PowerPoint presentation was "The Causes and Consequences of Violence in Little Village." I described some statistics from the survey and offered to share it with organizations at the AVN for their own work or grant proposals. At the end of the presentation, I asked if organizations would be willing to participate in one-one-interviews. My final PowerPoint slide remained on the screen as a Q&A session began. It listed three questions that I was trying to answer through the interviews. I read them aloud to the group: How are violence prevention resources allocated? How do you navigate Chicago politics to acquire them? And what are the challenges of collaborating to prevent violence? By asking these questions so openly and directly, I was unknowingly casting a spotlight on an enormous elephant in the room: the tension between the PCG and other neighborhood nonprofits. I was not prepared for what unfolded during the Q&A session.

"How will you be held accountable?" Arianna asked. "What follow-up will you do? How will the community be portrayed?" When Arianna spoke of "community," I believed she was really talking about the PCG. Maria, another PCG staff member, added, "We know what is going on with the violence, we just don't know which policy is really hurting the neighborhood."

"I just want to conduct interviews with organizers to make sense of what I heard from residents on the streets," I responded.

"Why don't you explain to everyone who you worked for in the neighborhood? And why you are studying Little Village," Arianna asked. I felt she was trying to expose me as an ally of the LVEJO and that I was out to make all of them look bad. I answered Arianna honestly. I explained that I was originally interested in the educational achievement of Mexican American youth and had volunteered at LVEJO because my undergraduate advisor suggested that the youth group would be an ideal field site. After fifteen minutes of back and forth with PCG staff, other organizers spoke up. "Why don't we give him our contact info?" suggested

Anthony, a staff member from a local health clinic. "And whoever wants to sign up for an interview can sign up. Whoever doesn't, doesn't. I don't know what's going on here, but my organization has had good collaborations in the past with researchers from DePaul." Arianna interrupted: "Yeah, but he's not from DePaul, he's from Northwestern."

Besides my affiliation with LVEJO, my affiliation with an elite private academic institution also impeded my relational ethnography. As a young and naïve graduate student with no real experience as a community organizer, I had a very difficult time coming to grips with the fact that my affiliation with Northwestern University was a source of distrust and resentment. I did not come from an elite background. My parents were working-class Mexican immigrants. I was the first in my family to go to college and one of the first undergraduates from DePaul to gain admission to the sociology graduate program at Northwestern. The experience was so troubling to me that I considered dropping out of graduate school.[5] A large reason why I pursued a PhD was to conduct research that would produce knowledge useful for improving the conditions of low-income communities of color, but I wasn't prepared nor mature enough at the time to understand the broader social context constraining relations between elite universities and low-income communities. The experience further entrenched me in one side of the neighborhood's turf wars.

While I was conducting interviews with several organizations in the AVN, organizers told me to watch my back because the PCG organizers were speaking poorly of me, referring to me as "the biased researcher." At public meetings, PCG staff would make disparaging comments to me about my research, saying that it would not amount to anything useful. From that point forward it was really difficult for me to objectively study the PCG. During the next year I conducted the bulk of my ethnography through Youth Inc., which was assisting with the implementation of

Culture of Calm and providing services to the Latin Kings street gang. Early drafts of the manuscript argued that violence was the result of rogue nonprofit organizations and local politicians.

Despite the rich and varied data I collected in the field, my lens for interpreting the data was still tinted from my involvement in the neighborhood's turf wars. I was taking sides, and my dissertation committee members were the first to help me step away.

"You need to interview the PCG," said Mary Pattillo, one of my advisors.

I wasn't sure how to proceed. The PCG did not trust me, they bruised my ego, and I was still convinced they were the antagonists in the neighborhood's story. After some thinking I reached out to Gabriel Cortez, a professor at Northeastern Illinois University who had studied the PCG in the past. He told me, "You need to humble yourself and get to know some of them personally, see them as people and help them."

The one saving grace I had while immersed in the neighborhood turf wars was the breadth and depth of my data. I wrote down everything I saw on the streets, in board rooms, or in hallways. Constantly going back to the data served as the basis for my ethnographic uncoupling.

STEPPING OUT OF THE TURF WAR

Reengaging with the PCG changed the book's focus. After being immersed in the neighborhood's nonprofit turf war and being indoctrinated into one side, I was pulled out by the wise words of my advisors. In the summer of 2012, I sent an email to PCG staff members inviting them to lunch, and two agreed. Following Gabriel's advice, I got to know them as people first, and then followed up to conduct a one-on-one in-depth interview. Getting to know Steve Beltran and Howard Ramirez at the PCG on a personal level helped me understand that the nonprofit turf

wars I learned about through LVEJO were really part of larger
political turf wars between neighborhood leaders and the mainstream Democratic Party in Chicago.

The interviews informed me of the history of the PCG and
the 22nd ward, and their struggles with bringing resources to
the east side transformed the project into a story about political
turf wars. Instead of violence stemming from neighborhood
politicians and nonprofits, the varying levels of violence within
the neighborhood were the product of various relationships between blocks and their nonprofit or ward structures. Digging
deeper into the neighborhood's political history helped me
understand that the variation in blocks' political relations were
the result of ward boundaries and the history of the neighborhood's political turf wars with the Chicago Democratic Party.
At the end of my interview with Steve, he shook my hand and
said, "You know, your questions were the most fair and balanced questions I've ever been asked about the neighborhood's
politics."

Stepping out of the turf war and revising the book to reflect
this relational argument took quite some time. I revised the
manuscript and circulated it to several violence prevention
workers who caught some inaccuracies in my depiction of relations among nonprofits. I organized a book conference while at
Harvard with three leading sociologists who read the entire
manuscript and provided in-depth comments. I presented chapters of the book to several university audiences, and some pieces
still didn't fit together. Several colleagues and my copy editor
read the entire manuscript and continued to find pieces that
were too one-sided. Every inch of the manuscript needed to be
rewritten, and I needed to consistently revisit my field notes and
interview transcripts to rid the book of as much bias as possible.

The experience taught me that writing a relational ethnography requires a particular type of reflexivity, in which the
ethnographer needs to be especially attuned to taking on the

attitudes and beliefs of his or her research subjects. Earlier drafts of the manuscript relied on data interpreted from the vantage point of one side in the neighborhood's turf wars (the residents). Later drafts interpreted data from the vantage point of some nonprofits. The final draft emerged three years after I left the neighborhood's turf wars behind, and it relied more heavily on a relational analysis than any actor's point of view. The process of revision was a process of uncoupling myself from the relationships that colored my view of the data.

My experience collecting data for this project holds several lessons that I hope can prove useful for future efforts at relational ethnography. First, when conducting relational ethnography with several actors enmeshed in serious conflict, it is important to take time and have an ethnographic support group across all stages of the project. As ethnography involves immersing oneself in the lives of one's research subjects, getting to know their points of view, and understanding their lived experiences, it takes time to step out of one group's life and restart the process of immersion with a new group, let alone a rival group. Being embedded in a support group or writing group of ethnographers, both during and after fieldwork, was critical for recognizing when I was steering too far in one group's perspective versus another's. It helped me become more objective, step out of the turf wars, and see the bigger picture of what was really happening at my field site.

Conducting relational ethnography with antagonistic groups or actors also requires great humility. As a young and naïve graduate student who had entered a PhD program straight after finishing my BA, humility was something I needed to learn. It took some time, but I came around to understanding that nonprofits were justified in their suspicion of me and academics in general.

"Professors come to us all the time," Arianna told me. "They offer to collaborate, they come, collect their data, leave, and never come back. Then they keep all the data to themselves to get grant money or publish, and we can't even access these publications because they cost thousands of dollars!"

I had no answer for Arianna. She was right. After all the knowledge produced by neighborhood studies in urban sociology, how many researchers have gone back to their field sites and shared the spoils of data collection with their research subjects? Ethnographers like Mitch Duneier and Annette Lareau have done so, but these revisits have been the exception, not the rule.[6]

The benefits to neighborhoods from urban ethnographies pale in comparison to the grants, tenure promotions, book sales, and prestige received by academic authors. Initially, I felt the PCG's scrutiny was unfair, and even found myself believing other organizers' negative perceptions. But after reflecting on my position as a privileged academic affiliated with a prestigious elite university, I realized that I too was a political actor. Ethnographers' hustle to collect data, publish, and compete for academic jobs is not all that different from the political or street turf wars I observed in Little Village. One only needs to visit some of the anonymous message boards where academics spit fire at one another over the ever shrinking pool of academic jobs.

Researchers' power, politics, and motivations cannot be pushed to the side in relational ethnography; they must be confronted and navigated to fully understand the facts. In retrospect, knowing this would have made data collection for this project faster, a bit easier, and certainly less emotionally taxing. I am grateful that both my research subjects and ethnographic colleagues made me aware of when I was taking sides. Not all ethnographers may benefit from such active or passionate research subjects. It is my hope that the lessons from this project prove useful in future ethnographic efforts to immerse oneself in one side of a conflict, switch sides to get the other side of the story, and then step away completely to arrive at relational ethnography.

Finally, I hope my experience helps dispel the myth that research is easier for ethnographers of the same race or ethnicity as the communities they study. As a Mexican American studying a predominantly Mexican American community, I might be dismissed as doing "me-search," but my experience collecting data could not have been any different. Just as Mary Pattillo argues that there is no such thing as a unified black political agenda, I learned that there is no unified Latino political agenda in Chicago, let alone within Latino neighborhoods.[7] Scholars cannot assume that navigating insider versus outsider status is easy or requires less work for researchers of color.

Appendix B

Methods

IN THIS APPENDIX I DESCRIBE the logic informing my use of a case study approach involving mixed methods of ethnography, quantitative data analysis, and historical description.

THE CASE STUDY LOGIC

My study of the Chicago neighborhood of Little Village followed a case study approach to identify important processes in the relationship between politics and gang violence that may also manifest in other settings. Though the ideal approach to studying an urban social problem would involve gathering in-depth qualitative data from a representative sample of neighborhoods and cities, most studies on gangs, policing, and nonprofit community organizing use case studies to build a theoretical framework.[1] The topic of politics and gang violence is understudied, and small case studies are a good approach to develop a theoretical foundation that later scholarship can refine through larger samples and additional case studies in other settings. This book does not claim to have uncovered processes that are common to the political structures of all poor neighborhoods; rather the book illuminates the importance of a topic that few have evaluated (the relationship between politics and gang violence) and shows how scholars can test ideas and hypotheses emerging from the case study.[2]

DATA SOURCES

Survey Canvassing and Fieldwork with Residents

Originally I designed a survey with the goal of assessing the consequences of youth exposure to violence for a variety of outcomes, including community organization participation, health, and grades. However, my street observations and conversations with youth and parents took the study in a different direction, and the survey became a source of data to contextualize both questions and findings emerging from the field.

To obtain a sample of the residential population with variation in exposure to violence, I used a cluster sampling design. I randomly selected twenty blocks from three regions in the neighborhood: the east side, the west side, and four blocks along the Latin Kings and Two Six gang border, resulting in a total random sample of sixty blocks. I then randomly sampled one third of the households on each block. Households without youth were not included in the sample. Along with five research assistants, all of whom were fluent Spanish speakers, I canvassed blocks in Little Village for a six-month period at the rate of three days per week, five to seven hours a day. Each research assistant carried a clipboard to log nonresponses. Respondents were compensated $20 for their participation. While the youth respondent completed the survey in another part of the home, the research assistants or I interviewed his or her parent in the backyard or on the front steps of the home. Parents ranged from thirty to fifty years old; 78 percent were female, and 22 percent were male. The survey response rate was 40 percent (355 out of 904 households).

Parents' stories were recorded as field notes written by me and the research assistants, and I always confirmed research assistants' observations by visiting each residence myself. Research assistants were used only while canvassing blocks to administer the survey; I conducted all other fieldwork alone. Unfortunately, interviews were not audio-recorded because most residents either refused or said very little after agreeing to be recorded. To best record residents, I took exhaustive field notes in a small notebook I always carried or repeated what they said into an audio recorder upon completion of an interview.

The survey data collection included several precautions to ensure the researchers' safety. The most potent danger while canvassing was being caught in a drive-by shooting. A year after the survey data collection ended, a six-year-old was killed in broad daylight in a drive-by shooting on one of the blocks I had surveyed. Drive-bys were a real and persistent danger in Little Village. Though it was impossible to mitigate this danger entirely, a few basic safety guidelines helped keep me and my research assistants safe. First, while conversing with residents and implementing the survey, I asked residents if we could move to their backyard so that we were not standing in front of their house for a long period of time. Early in the survey data collection process, I made the mistake of not asking to move to the backyard while surveying a home where a few Latin Kings gang members lived. As one research assistant and I stood on the front sidewalk waiting for the teens to finish the survey, two research assistants (who had been knocking on doors on the other side of the street) quickly walked up to me. They informed me that residents were not answering their doors because a drive-by shooting had occurred on the block the night before, and they were expecting the rival gang to retaliate with another drive-by shooting on the block at any time. Hearing this, I wrapped up the surveys as quickly as possible and left the area.

This experience taught us to pay careful attention to blocks with little street activity. In contrast to stereotypical beliefs about the danger of intimidating men standing on street corners or graffiti sprayed on walls, the most dangerous blocks in Little Village were often the most quiet and empty. This did not mean that blocks with gang members were safe; rather it meant that even on blocks that appeared well-kept, peaceful, and quiet, we could not let our guard down. In the event that we had to stand in front of a house for an extended period of time, we sat or stood behind a large barrier such as a tree or car or underneath the front steps of a home to avoid a direct line of sight to cars passing by. Such precautions may seem commonsensical, but knocking on doors can become monotonous after months of the same routine, and all it took was one mistake for something to go wrong.

Second, for the most part, the research assistants and I canvassed in pairs. When randomly knocking on doors, we encountered some uncomfortable situations. For example, we once knocked on a door at the same time as a man was negotiating a price with a prostitute near his doorstep. Navigating such awkward situations was easier when canvassing in pairs than alone. Dressing in business casual attire with name tags and clipboards helped us blend in as part of the neighborhood alongside mail delivery workers, census workers, and Jehovah's Witnesses, and we were never mistaken for police or rival gang members. We knew the colors of the local gangs and wore black and white on most days to avoid being mistaken for a rival.

Third, all the research assistants I hired were college students (or recent college graduates), Spanish speakers, and, most important, grew up in Little Village or a neighborhood like it. By relying on contacts within Little Village's community-based organizations, I easily found Spanish-speaking research assistants who felt comfortable talking with gang members and walking on streets with violent reputations.

Statistical Analysis of Violent Crime

Data for all the analyses of violent crime in Little Village come from the City of Chicago Urban Data Portal, a publicly available data set of all individual crimes in Chicago from 2001 to the present. All the violent crime incidents were assigned a block address. Using geographic information systems, I mapped each violent crime incident and grouped them into blocks and census tracts to analyze violence in various areas of Little Village. I divided these crime rates by census tract population (using figures taken from the 2010 U.S. census) to produce violent crime rates. The statistical analyses relied on only three types of violent crime (as coded by the City of Chicago): aggravated arson, aggravated battery with a firearm, and homicide.

Besides the urban data portal, I also used data from the Chicago Homicide Database compiled by Richard and Rebecca Block, which codes all homicides in Chicago from 1965 to 1995. In this data set I used the lowest level of aggregation (census tract) to analyze trends in homicides within various areas of Little Village. I merged the results from this analysis with homicide data from the Chicago data portal to create trajectories of homicide by census tract within Little Village. I relied on the census tract as the unit of analysis for all mapping of violent crime hot spots to maintain the anonymity of the individual blocks surveyed.

Fieldwork with Gangs and Police

I began fieldwork with the Latin Kings by volunteering at Youth Inc., where gang members met weekly to hang out and shoot pool. In my first week at Youth Inc. a violence prevention worker asked if I played basketball because they needed a few more players for their team in a local league. Having played basketball most of my life, I eagerly volunteered. I arrived at the first game only to discover that the league was composed entirely of teams representing block sections of the Latin Kings street gang. In the process of playing basketball, I developed relationships with gang members, violence prevention workers, and police officers working security at the league. Unlike ethnographies of gangs in which the researcher is integrated into the everyday operations of the gang, I did not have access to the inner workings of the Latin Kings, their bookkeeping, or monthly meetings.[3] Rather, I used informal interviews and conversations with gang members before, during, and after basketball games to make sense of the puzzles emerging from my fieldwork with residents.

My basketball team consisted of violence prevention workers, most of whom were much older and less athletic than the gang members in the league. We typically lost by about twenty points. Nevertheless, thanks to my experience as a basketball player, the gang members respected my ability to score, which led to conversations about basketball strategy or Derrick Rose and the Chicago Bulls. The gang members were aware of my status as an academic; violence prevention workers introduced me as a PhD student writing a book on gang violence in the neighborhood.

In the first basketball season I did not ask questions about the retaliations. Instead, I focused on establishing rapport with gang members. The games were held once a week at a local elementary school gym from 7:00 p.m. until midnight; each game lasted one hour, giving participants plenty of time to converse. I explained to gang members that I was doing a school project on how violence affects kids. I established rapport by saying that most researchers do not talk directly to gang members like themselves. They responded positively to my intentions, and with violence prevention workers vouching for my integrity, the gang members did not suspect that I was an informant.

At the basketball league, I developed good relationships with twelve Latin Kings gang members in particular and one Latin Kings block leader, who coached one of the teams. These particular gang members lived on or near blocks where residents alleged that corrupt police disclosed informants' identity to the gang. After six months of participating in the league and spending time at Youth Inc., I felt I had established enough trust to ask gang members about the retaliations during the second basketball season. These informal interviews took place between games as we sat in the stands. Gang members refused to be audio-recorded but were willing to answer my questions. When the basketball season ended in September 2011, I maintained contact with the gang members and block chief by visiting their homes and the Youth Inc. office.

The basketball league also allowed me to ask police officers questions. The principal of the elementary school gym hosting the league wanted a police presence at the games, so through their relationship with the local police commander, organizers at Youth Inc. hired three local beat officers to work as security guards while off duty. I recruited police officers through the basketball league after failed recruitment attempts at the local district headquarters, where the designated public relations officer repeatedly failed to return my phone calls and emails. Only one officer at a time was present at the basketball league because they rotated shifts each week. They wore bright yellow security jackets, with their firearm tucked in a holster underneath. Gang members tolerated their presence because it was the only way that Youth Inc. was allowed to rent gym space for the league.

To converse with the police officers without raising gang members' suspicions, I accompanied violence prevention workers when they spoke to officers about league scheduling conflicts. This gave me the opportunity to introduce myself as a researcher and ask officers for their phone numbers, so I could recruit them for interviews. Police officers were hesitant to participate at first, but after sharing that I grew up in Chicago and had several friends and extended family members in the police force, they were willing to answer questions. Though three police officers may seem like a small number to interview, only five officers in total worked the beat within Latin Kings gang territory. The public relations officer at police headquarters confirmed this; budget cuts had forced police to decrease the number of beat officers. The two other beat officers refused to participate in the study, but I spoke with the majority of police officers working in the beat where retaliations took place.

Because I did not observe violent incidents firsthand, I relied on an analytical strategy of triangulation to separate fact from fiction. Specifically, I made sure that each data point was confirmed by multiple sources (police, residents, gang members, violence prevention workers, and police reports). Data that were not confirmed by multiple sources were omitted from the analysis. For example, residents actually reported fifteen separate incidents of gang retaliation, but I included only ten in this study because they were the only incidents I could confirm with gang members, residents, and violence prevention workers. The gang's use of police scanners was confirmed by multiple sources and my firsthand observations. I confirmed instances of police inadvertently disclosing informant identities by speaking with the informants, multiple neighbors who witnessed the incidents, and the police. Though police officers refused to name officers who disclosed informants, their general confirmation of this practice, coupled with confirmation from the victim and multiple eyewitnesses, gave me confidence that the incidents indeed took place.

Triangulation is a common method used in ethnographic studies of phenomena that are difficult to observe firsthand.

Diane Vaughan used triangulation in a process she called "historical ethnography" to understand the decision-making process that led to the *Challenger* disaster because she did not witness the launch preparations firsthand.[4] Triangulation is also used by other ethnographers of gang violence. For example, Sudhir Venkatesh documented a spree of shootings between the Black Kings street gang and a group of car thieves by interviewing gang members and police to confirm the events.[5] Ruth Horowitz maintained close relationships with gang members but never accompanied them when they left their territory to fight other gangs, instead relying on interviews from multiple actors at the fights.[6] Though some ethnographers witnessed gang violence during their fieldwork, firsthand accounts constitute just a small fraction of their data.[7] Instead, as Papachristos explains, ethnographers must rely on building relationships with multiple sources to get ethnographers "as close as possible to gang violence or, at least, close to the actual facts of the violent events."[8] Through triangulation based on close relationships with residents, police, violence prevention workers, and the gang in Little Village, I presented the most accurate possible reconstruction of retaliations.

Fieldwork with Nonprofits

In the fall of 2010, I attended a public hearing in Little Village on neighborhood violence, hosted by representatives of Illinois governor Pat Quinn. There I met Freddy and Santino from Youth Inc. and Tony from the Puebla Community Group (PCG). After introducing myself as a researcher, I offered to volunteer for Youth Inc. The violence prevention workers were skeptical at first, but after I attended several of their events and became a familiar face at the organization, we developed trusting relationships. During the basketball league seasons, I spent three days a week shadowing Freddy and Santino in their daily work activities. In this shadowing stage, I observed the implementation of the Street Watchers program and began to build a relationship with the PCG through Tony, who was Freddy and Santino's close friend and collaborator. By regularly going out to lunch with them and shadowing them in and around the school grounds, I formed a close relationship with Tony, who was eager to share his wisdom about the neighborhood's gangs. Tony also regularly attended the basketball league, and our friendship facilitated my access to both the street watchers and the gang members he supervised. In addition to shadowing the violence prevention workers, I spent two days a week observing street watchers on the job on street corners from the inside of my car a block away. After observing their interactions and conflicts, I approached the street watchers to ask about what took place. Because I attended their training sessions, all of the street watchers were aware of my status a researcher and were happy to talk to me.

After establishing a working relationship with the violence prevention workers at Youth Inc., I recruited additional nonprofit organizers for in-depth interviews by attending a meeting of the Anti-Violence Network, which was led by the PCG. The AVN was a small group of neighborhood organizations engaged in violence prevention work. To begin recruiting organizations for this study, I presented an overview of my research project to the AVN and gathered the contact information of all organizers interested in an interview. In total, I interviewed the directors of fifteen neighborhood organizations for this study. Each of the interviews was recorded and transcribed, and each took place at the organization's offices. The length of the interviews ranged from forty minutes to two hours, and the same interview questions were asked of all the organizations. When puzzles or inconsistencies emerged during data analysis, I scheduled meetings with organizers and communicated with them over the phone to make sure that I had correctly interpreted certain situations or quotes.

Historical Analysis

Data on the history of the neighborhood came from a variety of sources. I started by interviewing community organizers, former gang members, and residents who had lived and worked in the neighborhood all their lives. After my participation in the basketball league ended, I interviewed five ex-gang members whose ages ranged from forty-two to sixty-five to understand the history of the neighborhood's street gangs. The stories from the interview data were triangulated with additional data sources. Using newspaper archives from 1965 to the present, I did keyword searchers for articles containing the words *Little Village, 22nd ward, Alderman Stemberk, Latin Kings,* and South Lawndale. These searches yielded over twenty-five articles on gang violence in Little Village from 1965 to the present that describe the gangs in the area, residents' efforts to prevent violence, and local politicians' action (or inaction) on the issue. The newspaper archives also confirmed the details of the gang war of 1981 that sparked conflict between the Two Sixers and the Latin Kings.

In addition, I used the Chicago Historical Society's collection of neighborhood oral histories to validate the dates and details of stories emerging from other sources. The Cook County Crime Commission also published reports (in irregular years only, due to budget constraints) that describe organized criminal groups in Little Village. The reports from 1971 and 1981 included maps of the neighborhood's gang territories in the 1970s. Records from the Cook County Courts at 26th Street and Pulaski confirmed the dates and details of violent crime incidents I learned about through interviews with residents and gang members. For example, when residents and gang members discussed a shooting they witnessed, I asked for the date of the occurrence and the name and approximate age of the perpetrator, and I cross-checked these details with the records at Cook County. I regularly accessed these records on the third floor of the Cook County Court building, where they were stored electronically on pass-word-protected desktop computers. The computers were old and dusty and used an MS-DOS operating system, where key-board commands, instead of a mouse, were the only way to nav-igate the electronic system. By entering the name and date of birth of the perpetrator, I was able to confirm whether the acts of violence were reported to police.

In addition to these primary sources, secondary sources such as Irving Spergel's Little Village Gang Violence Reduction Project and Frank Magallon's *Chicago's Little Village* provided great insight into the neighborhood's history.[9] Biographies of Harold Washington, Richard M. Daley, and Richard J. Daley also provided historical context to Little Village's relationship with city hall since the 1960s.

Finally, I downloaded the shapefiles required to reproduce maps of the neighborhood's ward boundaries from 1970 to the present from the University of Chicago GIS lab. Overall the qual-itative and historical data used in the book were confirmed by multiple sources.

MIXED METHODS

I used mixed methods for several chapters in the book with the goal of providing an accurate description of events and compel-ling evidence to support my arguments. But I did not design a mixed-method project from the outset. Instead, after immers-ing myself ethnographically in the field and employing induc-tive analysis, I chose my methods by reflecting on the types of data that would best answer the emerging questions. For ex-ample, the first chapter I drafted was on the arrest of the gang leaders. After hearing residents say that violence increased after arrest of the 22 Boys gang leader, I reflected on the type of data

I would need to test this hypothesis. I went to the Cook County records office to learn the precise dates of the gang leader's arrest and concluded that a time-series analysis of violent crime trends before and after the arrest would provide the best test of this hypothesis. Similarly, after hearing from residents and gang members that the Latin Kings were enforcing the code of silence by monitoring police communication, I decided to test the location of arsons in the neighborhood. I also returned to my survey data to examine the percentage of residents who adhered to the code of silence by census tract (based on the survey data). I followed the same procedure when assessing the effects of the Street Watchers program on violence around Farragut High School. After hearing stories and observing incidents where violence was diffused near the school, I decided to test whether this was a trend using a statistical analysis of violent crime in the area. These additional analyses ultimately produced a mixed-methods study, but it emerged through a series of stages that involved inductive fieldwork, triangulation, hypothesis testing with statistical data, and reentering the field to make sense of the quantitative findings.

My use of mixed methods was possible only through the proliferation of open-access data sources for crime analysis and mapping, as well as easier survey implementation tools. It would have been much more difficult for me to write this kind of book twenty years ago, when data on ward boundaries and the locations of violent crimes would have taken much more time to organize and analyze. Social media, handheld touch computers, big data, and open-access data on city municipal services can and should be incorporated into the toolkit of urban ethnographers to better understand the complex dynamics of neighborhoods and cities.

NOTES

Chapter 1

1. Sampson et al. 1997; Sampson and Raudenbush 1999.
2. Eck et al. 2000; Weisburd et al. 2012.
3. Blumstein and Wallman 2006; Lafree 1999.
4. For a similar ethnographic study of violent hot spots within a neighborhood, see Peter St. Jean's (2007) *Pockets of Crime*. Although St. Jean's focus is on robbery, drug dealing, and assault instead of gang-related shootings and arsons, his findings suggest the importance of studying relationships as he found that certain families (as opposed to places) were hot spots for assaults because of frequent interpersonal conflicts. His work questions the utility of "broken windows" theory because the robbers and drug dealers he observed did not interpret physical disorder (like trash, graffiti, and abandoned properties) as markers of ideal places to commit crimes.
5. Anderson 1999; Spergel 2007; St. Jean 2007; Venkatesh and Levitt 2000.
6. Papachristos 2009.
7. Papachristos et al. 2013.
8. Cure Violence 2015.

9. Aside from gang disputes over turf, social scientists know remarkably little about relationship dynamics that trigger violence or inhibit its prevention on neighborhood blocks. We know that violence is more common on blocks near the boundaries of rival gangs (Curry and Decker 1996; Kennedy 2011; Spergel 2007; Tita and Papachristos 2010). We know that gangs follow an honor code and that violations of the code can incite a violent reaction (Anderson 1999; Horowitz 1983; Papachristos 2009). Yet we know little about the broader social and political relations that may concentrate and perpetuate violence on certain blocks in a neighborhood.

10. By violence, I mean specifically homicide or physical attacks occurring in public spaces like sidewalks, streets, or alleys. The findings from this study shed little light on the workings of domestic violence.

11. Alexander 2012; Clear 2007; Pattillo et al. 2004; Rios 2011; Western 2006.

12. Curry and Decker 1996; Kennedy 2011; Spergel 2007; Tita and Papachristos 2010.

13. Childress 2013.

14. City of Chicago 2015.

15. City of Chicago 2015.

16. Data are not publicly available for shootings prior to 2006.

17. Ford 2015.

18. Kirk and Papachristos 2011; Krivo and Peterson 1996; Lauritsen and White 2001; Morenoff and Sampson 1997; Morenoff et al. 2001; Peterson et al. 2000; Sampson et al. 1997; Sampson and Raudenbush 1999; Taylor and Covington 1993; Warner and Rountree 1997.

19. See Heller et al. (2013) for a notable exception.

20. The concept of field has a long history in sociological theory (Bourdieu and Wacquant 1992; DiMaggio and Powell 1983; Fligstein and McAdam 2012; Levi-Martin 2003). In this book, I use Fligstein and McAdam's (2012, 9) definition of field as a "meso-level social order in which actors are attuned to and interact with one another on the basis of shared understanding (which is not to say consensual) about the purpose of the field, relationships to others in the field, and the rules governing

legitimate action in the field." A handful of scholars have shown the usefulness of studying urban settings as fields. In their description of the systemic model of social organization, Bursik and Grasmick (1993) emphasize the importance of collaboration among residents, neighborhood leaders, and city-level public officials for creating neighborhood social control (also see Carr 2005). Nicole Marwell (2007) demonstrates that political and economic fields were critical for understanding how nonprofit community-based organizations delivered housing and employment resources to neighborhoods in Brooklyn. For a good overview of ethnographic studies employing a field analysis, see Desmond 2014.

21. To clarify, in this study I use the notion of field as a heuristic to develop greater insight into the dynamics triggering and preventing violence. While a full treatise on field theory is beyond the scope of this project, I raise a number of questions that future urban studies incorporating field theory should address, such as Where do fields begin and end? and How do fields overlap to produce outcomes? In Little Village, multiple fields overlapped to concentrate violence in the neighborhood's east side. The political turf wars constituted one field that shaped blocks' capacity to prevent violence. Street turf wars between gangs and police constituted another field that triggered violence on some blocks but not others.

22. Lublin 1999; Shotts 2002; Overby and Cosgrove 1996.

23. Building on the work of Hunter (1985) and Bursik (1999), Patrick Carr (2005) introduces the concept of "new parochialism" to describe how neighborhoods build informal social control through relationships among actors in the private, parochial, and public spheres in a neighborhood. This book advances this line of research by showing how these relationships can vary across blocks, even within the same neighborhood. In Chicago, the public sphere is not monolithic. City government is composed of political parties that compete for power and resources. By emphasizing the importance of political turf wars, this book advances the systemic social organization framework by showing how horizontal as well as vertical relationships among public and parochial actors affect blocks' capacity to prevent violence.

24. In criminology, collective efficacy is considered a significant predictor of neighborhood violent crime rates (Browning and Cagney 2002; Duncan et al. 2003; Sampson et al. 1997; Sampson and Raudenbush 1999; Silver and Miller 2004). Defined as social cohesion and shared expectations for social control (Sampson 2012, 152), the concept recently expanded beyond social ties among residents (Warner and Rountree 1997) to include their connections to institutions. Concentrated poverty and residential instability are forces shown to undermine the formation of collective efficacy in neighborhoods, and these forces were indeed present in Little Village. However, my empirical data show that political turf wars were key determinants of collective efficacy on Little Village's most violent blocks.

25. For the Chicago school ecological perspective see Park 1915; Park and Burgess 1921; Shaw and Mckay 1969; Thomas and Znaniecki 1918; Wirth 1938. For critiques of the Chicago school see Castells 1977; Dear 2002; Harvey 1972; Logan and Molotch 1987; McQuarrie and Marwell 2009; Wacquant 2009.

26. Loïc Wacquant's (2009) research has been at the forefront of theories on the role of the state in the marginalization of the poor. He argues that the political entrepreneurship of elected officials led to policies creating what he terms the "hyper-ghetto," a neighborhood characterized by high levels of racial and class segregation, few job opportunities, a retrenched welfare safety net, and an intrusive and omnipresent police. While welfare retrenchment and mass incarceration indeed have devastating effects on poor neighborhoods, one major limitation in this framework is that not all poor neighborhoods are hyper-ghettos. Poor neighborhoods vary significantly both within and across cities. Using a national sample of cities, Small and McDermott (2006) found that as a neighborhood's poverty rate increased, the number of establishments also increased. Similarly, in Chicago the number of poor black neighborhoods with no nonprofit organizations was very small (six), and the presence of organizations in poor neighborhoods varied tremendously (Small 2008).

It is also inaccurate to claim that poor neighborhoods have been abandoned by the state. Regardless of the level of poverty or marginalization in a given neighborhood, most poor neighborhoods have some form of political representation at the city, county, state, or federal level. As Small (2008) argued, "If governments truly matter, the logical conclusion is that differences among local governments in their level of institutional involvement (or detachment) should produce remarkably different ghettoes from city to city." This book advances Wacquant's work by showing how turf wars among political actors can produce variation in neighborhood conditions.

Studying interactions between government actors at various levels is becoming increasingly important for understanding the relationship between the state and the urban poor. Scholars like Joe Soss et al. (2011) and David Garland (2001) show that federal and state governments expand and restructure programs for the poor through privatization and the adoption of market principles. The welfare state has been transformed by an unprecedented rise in collaboration between state agencies and nonprofit organizations (Salamon 1995). This makes it very difficult for urban scholars to ignore local nonprofit organizations when studying the relationship between state action and neighborhood conditions. For example, Marwell's (2007) research shows that public and nonprofit collaborations can help explain variation in the physical and social conditions of poor neighborhoods. In contrast to the notion that the state has abandoned urban, poor, and minority communities, Marwell finds that some poor neighborhoods have strong political actors who can successfully acquire job and housing resources. To understand the state's role in shaping neighborhood conditions, scholars must study the various public, private, and nonprofit actors involved in governing poor neighborhoods. Studying turf wars among state actors allows for a more accurate reflection of the workings of the state as a fragmented and diffuse entity.

27. Todd Clear (2007) finds correlations between neighborhood incarceration rates and crime rates, showing that arrests can undermine neighborhood collective efficacy; however, much of the research on the consequences of arrests for violent crime does not identify the mechanisms triggering criminal acts.

28. Sánchez-Jankowski (1991) and Venkatesh (2002, 2006) describe gang members' rationale for refraining from violence against

police. This is not the case in Brazil, for instance, where police are routinely involved in shootouts with drug gangs (Arias and Rodrigues 2006; Goldstein 2013).

29. Legewie 2016.
30. Jacobs and Wright 2006; Jacques and Wright 2015; Sánchez-Jankowski 1991; Skarbek 2014; Venkatesh 2006; Venkatesh and Levitt 2000.
31. Anderson 1999; Decker and Van Winkle 1996; Hagedorn 1988; Harding 2010; Horowitz 1983; Papachristos 2009; Papachristos et al. 2013; Suttles 1968; Vigil 1988.
32. Small 2008.
33. Small 2009.
34. Ragin and Becker 1992; Small 2009.
35. Sampson 2012; Wilson 1987.
36. Berrien and Winship 1999; Braga et al. 2007; McRoberts 2004.
37. Kennedy 2011.
38. Sánchez-Jankowski 1991; Venkatesh 2006.

Chapter 2

1. Simpson 2001.
2. Kallina 1985.
3. Simpson 2001.
4. Rhodes 2013.
5. Tritsch 2010.
6. Simpson 2001.
7. Moser 2015.
8. Simpson 2001.
9. Simpson 2001.
10. Jaffe 2015.
11. Rivlin 1993, 349.
12. U.S. Bureau of the Census 1970, 1980, 1990, 2010.
13. Rivlin 1993.
14. Rosen 1989.
15. Fremon 1988.
16. Healy 1980.
17. Coakley 1979.
18. Papachristos 2001; Venkatesh and Levitt 2000.

19. Knox 2000.
20. Circuit Court of Cook County 1986.
21. Galvan 1981.
22. Rosen 1989.
23. Rosen 1989.
24. Rosen 1989.
25. Rivlin 1993, 196.
26. Rivlin 1993.
27. Strong 1985.
28. Galvan 1981.
29. Brown 2011; Davis and Strong 1985.
30. Rosen 1989.
31. Fremon 1988.
32. Cordova 1998.
33. Rivlin 1993.
34. Rivlin 1993.
35. Fremon 1988.
36. Fremon 1988; Rivlin 1993.
37. Koeneman 2013, 137.
38. Koeneman 2013.
39. Rivlin 1993; Pattillo 2007.
40. Kass 1995.
41. Dawson 2015.
42. Spergel 2007, 59.
43. Puente 1998.
44. Lutton 1998.
45. Poe 1998.
46. Cortez 2008, 144.
47. Cortez 2008, 65.
48. Cortez 2008, 30.
49. Cortez 2008, 107.
50. The Illinois Violence Prevention Authority (IVPA), the Chicago Violence Prevention Authority (CVPA), and the Chicago Project for Violence Prevention were the agencies that allocated state funded contracts for violence prevention work in Little Village. The IVPA operated as an office of the IL Governor, whereas the CVPA operated as an office of the Chicago Mayor. These agencies awarded contracts to nonprofit organizations for implementing small

violence prevention programs that involved mentoring, after school crossing guard patrols, and neighborhood watch. The largest state-funded violence prevention program was Ceasefire, a program that attempted to reduce gang violence by hiring ex-gang members to work as interrupters, or social workers mediating conflicts among gang members. Ceasefire identified neighborhoods that could benefit from the program and selected a community-based organization to administer and house the program locally. As Skogan et al. (2008) described, politics played a role in the selection of neighborhoods and host organizations. "Politically influential places had some advantages: they often had strong community-based organizations, vocal political representatives, and activists who were able to bring Ceasefire to the community through political clout... Size also mattered. Larger and longer-established host organizations typically had a solid financial base and regarded Ceasefire as an add-on." Having established itself as the "lead organization" in Little Village with close ties to local elected officials, the PCG were successful at securing the contracts for implementing all six of the state funded violence prevention programs.

51. Bursik 1999.
52. Fremon 1988.
53. Casuso and Joravsky 1987.
54. Lutton 2003.
55. Lutton 2003.

Chapter 3

1. Rueff et al. 2012.
2. "Mom of Girl Killed on Front Porch" 2012.
3. I focus on these blocks because these were areas where, in my street observations, I saw residents attempting to control the behavior of gang members on their blocks. Street gangs did not have a physical presence on all blocks on the neighborhood, and not all blocks wanted to get rid of their street gangs. Thus, this chapter compares only the blocks that tried to reduce the threat of drive-by shootings to explain differences in outcomes.
4. In total, I canvassed four blocks in the eastside borderlands region, eight in the burbs, and fifteen in the westside borderlands

(the regions are shown in figure 3.1). I focused on seven blocks in this chapter because they were most representative of the patterns I uncovered in each region. Most blocks in the burbs and westside borderlands had very few instances of gun violence. The only violent hot spots in the westside borderlands at the time of the study were 2800 Shedd Street and 2700 May Street, and neighborhood efforts to reduce violence on these blocks provided a compelling contrast to the other regions. The east side was a much smaller area, and the blocks I chose for this chapter were the most violent in the region.

5. Sampson 2012; Sampson et al. 1997.
6. St. Jean 2007.
7. I do not disclose precise details of the block's location to keep residents' identities anonymous.
8. La Vigne et al. 2011.
9. Greenhouse 1999.
10. Criminologists call this collective efficacy (Sampson 2012; Sampson et al. 1997).
11. Bursik 1999; Carr 2005.
12. Gutierrez 2010.
13. Two years after data collection, the Chicago Park District opened a new park on Little Village's east side.
14. Anderson 1999; Horowitz 1983.
15. Hagedorn 1988; Horowitz 1983; Pattillo-McCoy 1999; Sánchez-Jankowski 1991; Tita et al. 2003; Venkatesh 2006.
16. Scholars have referred to these factors as collective efficacy (Sampson 2012) and ecological disadvantage (St. Jean 2007).

Chapter 4

1. Billups 2009.
2. Saulny 2009.
3. Vevea 2011.
4. Spohn and Holleran 2000.
5. Levenstein et al. 2011.
6. Spergel 2007.
7. Studies have shown the importance of clergy (Venkatesh 2006; Winship et al. 2000), nonprofit organizations (Kennedy 2011;

Sánchez-Jankowski 1991), and parent groups (Pattillo-McCoy 1999) in mediating disputes among gangs or other actors in a neighborhood's informal economy.

8. Bursik 1999; Kasarda and Janowitz 1974.

Chapter 5

1. Daley 2010.
2. Pattillo-McCoy 1999; Sánchez-Jankowski 1991; Venkatesh 2006.
3. Finn and Healey 1996.
4. Clearmap Chicago 2015.
5. For a more complete breakdown of the number of survey respondents in each tract, see appendix B.
6. Chicago Crime Commission 2012.
7. There is an extensive debate over the definition of *gang*, but I follow Sánchez-Jankowski's (1991, 28–29) definition: "an organized system that is both quasi-private (not fully open to the public) and quasi-secretive (much of the information concerning its business remains confined with the group) ... and governed by a leadership structure that has defined roles and pursues goals whether the action is legal or not." My fieldwork with the Latin Kings suggested that they were more than what Klein (1995) or Spergel (1995) would call a territorial and loosely associated group of people engaged in criminal acts. They were highly organized with a hierarchical leadership structure, codes of conduct, and a dues structure. Thus it is important to emphasize that these findings may apply to more structured and hierarchical street gangs like those studied by Sánchez-Jankowski (1991), Venkatesh (2006), and Pattillo-McCoy (1999) but not to gangs defined as "street corner groups" or "crews."
8. U.S. Department of Justice 2009a.
9. Spergel 2007.
10. Coen and Bush 2006.
11. Coen 2008.
12. Sweeney 2012.
13. Since this fieldwork, Mayor Rahm Emanuel has taken slightly different approaches toward controlling gangs than Mayor Daley used. The results of these alternative approaches are yet to be determined.

14. Main 2010.
15. Main 2010.
16. Kennedy 2011.
17. Thomas 2010.
18. Garcia 2010.
19. "Governor Quinn Signs Legislation to Fight Street Gang Crime" 2012.
20. Byrne and Ford 2010; Janssen 2011.
21. Sánchez-Jankowski 1991; Venkatesh 2002.
22. To transcribe police communication, I played the audio of the police radio on a speaker and recorded it using a handheld device with the microphone pointed at the speaker.
23. Sánchez-Jankowski 1991; Venkatesh 2002, 2008.
24. Skogan and Hartnett 1997.
25. Pattillo-McCoy 1999; Sánchez-Jankowski 1991; Venkatesh 1997, 2002.
26. Sánchez-Jankowski 1991.
27. Klinger 1997; Manning 2003; Skolnick 1966.
28. Lutz 2009.
29. Kirk and Papachristos 2011; Klinger 1997; Sampson and Bartusch 1998.
30. Anderson 1999; Carr et al. 2007; Kane 2005; Klinger 1997.

Chapter 6

1. Seper 2012.
2. "What's Squeezing the Latin Kings" 2014.
3. By violent crime, I mean homicide and aggravated battery with the use of a firearm. Ideally one would study trends in gang violence using relations between gangs as the unit of analysis, for example, by assessing changes in the rate of violence between the Latin Kings and 22 Boys before and after the gang leader's arrest. This would allow for analysis of whether the gang leader's arrest sparked violence beyond any particular geographic space. Although I acquired police reports on all gang-related shootings from the Chicago Police Department's Research and Development Division, the majority had missing data on the gang affiliation of either the perpetrator or the victim. As an alternative, I chose to

compare violent crime rates across gang territories that were and were not subject to the police intervention.

4. Scholars of urban sociology debate whether gangs provide social order in poor communities. Klein (1995) argues that the benefits gangs provide are minimal, while Sánchez-Jankowski (1991) argues that gangs are major players in the social order of poor neighborhoods. Sampson 2012 offers a middle position, describing the relationships gangs strike up with residents as alternative or unconventional forms of social order.

5. McCord 2003. Many investigators fail to assess whether an intervention had adverse effects, and many studies fail to report such effects in their results (Sherman et al. 1997).

6. Reppetto 1976.

7. Klein 1995.

8. Klein and Maxson 2006. Similar interventions, such as "stop and frisk" (Gelman et al. 2007; Reitzel et al. 2004; Rice et al. 2005) and "zero tolerance" policies for gun and drug possession (Fagan et al. 1997; Greene 1999) have also been shown to decrease police legitimacy in high-crime communities.

9. The absence of research on the effects of arresting a gang's leader on gang violence stems in part from some scholars' contention that gangs are not capable of engaging in organized violence (Decker and Curry 2002; Fleisher 1998; Klein 1995). Though scholars recognize patterns in gang violence, such as the consistent use of firearms (Bjerregaard and Lizotte 1995; Decker and Pennell 1995), its spatial concentration (Block and Block 1993; Kennedy et al. 1996; Maxson 1999), and its retaliatory nature (Decker 1996; Maxson et al. 1985), some have concluded that most gangs lack the cohesion and structure to generate compliance among members and engage in organized violence (Decker 1996; Decker and Van Winkle 1996; Klein 1995; Klein and Maxson 2006). However, the introduction of social network analysis to the study of gang violence now suggests that gang violence in cities such as Boston, Chicago, and Los Angeles can be structured as a series of retaliations between gangs that erupt in short episodes over time (Kennedy et al. 1996; McGloin 2005; Papachristos 2009; Tita et al. 2003). Papachristos et al. (2013) found that gangs with adjacent turf and a history of conflict were more likely to engage in patterns of retaliatory violence. These network studies suggest

that in cities where gang violence is structured and organized, the arrest of a particular gang's leader may significantly alter the behavior of not only the targeted gang but also its rivals. Yet most studies on police crackdowns focus on massive sweeps of drug markets or prostitution rings, which involve the arrest of several low-level gang members but not leadership (Fritsch et al. 1999; Kent and Smith 2001; Langworthy 1989).

10. Knox 2001; Papachristos 2001. While these studies found that intragang violence may be an adverse effect of arresting a gang's leader, they relied on interviews with gang members and journalist accounts of violent incidents. They provided little insight into the magnitude of violence after the gang leader's arrest.
11. Beckett 1999; Garland 2001; Western 2006.
12. Gentry 2001.
13. Kass 2012.
14. Maguire 2011.
15. Beckett 1999; Western 2006.
16. Criminologists have used the notion of the embeddedness of social relations to explain other forms of violent crime. For example, to explain individual criminal behavior, Hagan (1993) introduced "criminal embeddedness," referring to an individual's ties to criminal others, involvement in criminal acts, and isolation from pro-social networks. Criminal embeddedness was thought to limit individuals' employment prospects and present opportunities for engaging in criminal acts. Pyrooz et al. (2013, 5) have similarly employed the concept of gang embeddedness to explain gang membership, finding that "the varying degrees of involvement, identification, and status among gang members" influenced involvement among youth.
17. Decker 1996; Sánchez-Jankowski 1991; Venkatesh 1997.
18. Papachristos 2009.
19. Pattillo-McCoy 1999; Sánchez-Jankowski 1991; Venkatesh 1997.
20. Chicago Crime Commission 2012.
21. *County of Cook v. Rudy Cantu* 2010.
22. Chicago Crime Commission 2012.
23. *County of Cook v. Jesus Rios* 2010.
24. City of Chicago Police Records 2012.
25. *County of Cook v. Carlos Villagomez* 2010.
26. Chicago Crime Commission 2012.

27. I only use data from 2009 to 2011 because the reports of gang-related shootings in this time period and in this geographic location had no missing data. Seventy percent of police reports of shootings in 22 Boys territory prior to 2009 had missing data on either the victim or offender and thus could not be used in this analysis.
28. U.S. Department of Justice 2009b.
29. U.S. Department of Justice 2009a.
30. Sánchez-Jankowski 1991.
31. U.S. Department of Justice 2009c.
32. U.S. Department of Justice 2009c.
33. Sánchez-Jankowski 1991; Venkatesh 1997.
34. For a good discussion of gang violence reduction strategies and public policy, see the special issue of *Criminology and Public Policy* 10 (4), 2011.
35. Gorner 2012.
36. This finding supports previous research showing that gangs with adjacent territories are more likely to engage in retaliatory violence with one another (Tita et al. 2005; Venkatesh 1997). In his network analysis of gang homicide in Chicago, Papachristos (2009) found that size differences between gangs were highly predictive of reciprocal murders between gangs: larger and more organized gangs were more aggressive and likely to be involved in turf disputes with smaller gangs. In other words, previous research suggests that larger and more organized gangs are more likely to be aggressive toward smaller gangs weakened by the loss of their leader.
37. Braga et al. 2001; Klein 1995; Maxson et al. 2005; Meares and Kahan 1998.

Chapter 7

1. Sweeney and Byrne 2013.
2. Stone (1989) distinguishes between two functions of politics: power over (social control) and power to (social production).
3. Tyler 2007.
4. Studies by Sharkey (2010) and Legewie (2016) demonstrate the usefulness of a focus on relationships and events for neighborhood effects research.

5. Browning and Cagney 2002; Morenoff et al. 2001; Park 1915, 1936; Sabol et al. 2004; Sampson 1988, 1991; Sampson et al. 1997, 1999; Sampson and Wilson 1995; Silver and Miller 2004; Thomas and Znaniecki 1918; Wirth 1938.
6. Sampson 2012, 127.
7. See Carr 2005; Pattillo 2007.
8. Sampson 2012.
9. Robbins 2011.
10. My concept of political ecometrics draws on what Raudenbush and Sampson (1999) call "ecometrics."
11. Studies of political ecology have centered on issues of environmental justice in the United States (Heynen et al. 2006) and abroad (Grossman 1998; Kull 2004).
12. Logan and Molotch 1987; Marwell 2007.
13. Sampson and Wilson 1995.
14. Vélez et al. 2015.
15. Velez 2009; Lyons et al. 2013.
16. Castells 1977; Harvey 2012.
17. Wacquant 2009.
18. For example, religious leaders in Boston helped reduce violence through the ten-point coalition (Winship and Berrien 1999), black and Latino leaders helped Harold Washington defeat the Chicago political machine during the 1980s (Ferman 1996), and activists in Philadelphia elected its first black mayor in 1983 (Hunter 2013).
19. Goffman 2014; Wacquant 2009.
20. Kent and Carmichael 2014; Kent and Jacobs 2005.
21. Clear 2007; Haskins 2014; Massoglia 2008.
22. "2015 Election Results" 2015.
23. Bosman 2015; Kass 2015; Nair 2015.
24. McGloin 2005; Papachristos 2009; Papachristos et al. 2013; Ritter 2009; Winett 1998.
25. Chicago Police Department 2014.

Appendix A

1. Desmond 2014.
2. Becker 1996; Marcus 1998.
3. Vaughan 1986.

4. See Fine (1993) for a great discussion of myths in ethnographic work.
5. Thanks to a conversation with Hector Carrillo, I did not.
6. Duneier 1999; Lareau 2011.
7. Pattillo 2007.

Appendix B

1. Fritsch et al. 1999; Kent and Smith 2001; Marwell 2007; Moore and Hagedorn 1996; Padilla 1992; Sánchez-Jankowski 1991; Taylor 1990; Venkatesh 1997, 2006; Vogel and Torres 1998; Weisel and Painter 1997.
2. Building a theoretical base with small, in-depth empirical case studies is a common approach to advance knowledge of processes that are difficult to access, measure, and sample in large quantities. See Ragin and Becker 1992; Small 2009.
3. Sánchez-Jankowski 1991; Venkatesh 2006.
4. Vaughan 1996.
5. Venkatesh 2006, 310–11.
6. Horowitz 1983.
7. Anderson 1999; Sánchez-Jankowski 1991; Venkatesh 2006, 2008.
8. Papachristos 2009, 87.
9. Magallon 2010; Spergel 2007.

REFERENCES

Alexander, Michelle. 2012. *The New Jim Crow: Mass Incarceration in the Age of Colorblindness.* New York: New Press.

Anderson, Elijah. 1999. *Code of the Street: Decency, Violence, and the Moral Life of the Inner City.* New York: Norton.

Arias, Enrique Desmond, and Corinne Davis Rodrigues. 2006. "The Myth of Personal Security: Criminal Gangs, Dispute Resolution, and Identity in Rio De Janeiro's Favelas." *Latin American Politics and Society* 48(4): 53–81.

Becker, Howard S. 1996. "The Epistemology of Qualitative Research." Pp. 53–71 in *Ethnography and Human Development: Context and Meaning in Social Inquiry,* edited by Richard Jessor and Richard A. Shweder. Chicago: University of Chicago Press.

Beckett, Katherine. 1999. *Making Crime Pay: Law and Order in Contemporary American Politics.* New York: Oxford University Press.

Berrien, Jenny, and Christopher Winship. 2003. "Should We Have Faith in the Churches? Ten-Point Coalition's Effect on Boston's Youth Violence." In *Guns, Crime, and Punishment in America,* edited by B. Harcourt. New York: New York University Press.

Billups, Andrea. 2009. "36 Chicago Area Students Killed Sets Record." *Washington Times,* May 13. Retrieved May 21, 2009. http://www .washingtontimes.com/news/2009/may/13/record-36-students-killed-this-school-year-across-/?page=all.

Bjerregaard, Beth, and Alan J. Lizotte. 1995. "Gun Ownership and Gang Membership." *Journal of Criminal Law and Criminology* 86(1): 37–58.

Block, Carolyn R., and Richard Block. 1993. *Street Gang Crime in Chicago*. Washington, DC: U.S. Department of Justice, Office of Justice Programs, National Institute of Justice.

Blumstein, Alfred, and Joel Wallman. 2006. *The Crime Drop in America*. Cambridge, UK: Cambridge University Press.

Bosman, Julie. 2015. "Candidates for Chicago Mayor Struggle to Unite Latinos and Blacks." *New York Times*, April 4. Retrieved April 10, 2015. http://www.nytimes.com/2015/04/04/us/candidate-for-chicago-mayor-struggles-to-unite-latinos-and-blacks.html.

Bourdieu, Pierre, and Loïc J. D. Wacquant. 1992. *An Invitation to Reflexive Sociology*. Chicago: University of Chicago Press.

Braga, Anthony A., David Hureau, and Christopher Winship. 2007. "Losing Faith: Police, Black Churches, and the Resurgence of Youth Violence in Boston." *Ohio State Journal Criminal Law* 6: 141–172.

Braga, Anthony A., David M. Kennedy, Elin J. Waring, and Anne M. Piehl. 2001. "Problem-Oriented Policing, Deterrence, and Youth Violence: An Evaluation of Boston's Operation Ceasefire." *Journal of Research in Crime and Delinquency* 38(3): 195–225.

Brown, Mark. 2011. "In Illinois Politics, You Live Where You Say You Live." *Chicago Sun-Times*, January 25. Retrieved January 30, 2011. http://www.suntimes.com/news/brown/3490571-452/ward-chicago-address.html.

Browning, Christopher R., and Kathleen A Cagney. 2002. "Neighborhood Structural Disadvantage, Collective Efficacy, and Self-Rated Physical Health in an Urban Setting." *Journal of Health and Social Behavior* 43(4): 383–99.

Bursik, Robert J., Jr. 1999. "The Informal Control of Crime through Neighborhood Networks." *Sociological Focus* 32(1): 85–97.

Bursik, Robert, and Harold G. Grasmick. 1993. *Neighborhoods and Crime*. New York: Lexington Books.

Byrne, John, and Liam Ford. 2010. "Cops, Feds Meet with Gang Leaders." *Chicago Tribune*, August 28. Retrieved September 1 2010. http://articles.chicagotribune.com/2010-08-28/news/ct-met-gangs-0829-20100828_1_gang-leaders-gang-members-gang-violence.

Carr, Patrick J. 2005. *Clean Streets: Controlling Crime, Maintaining Order, and Building Community Activism*. New York: New York University Press.

Carr, Patrick J., Laura Napolitano, and Jessica Keating. 2007. "We Never Call the Cops and Here Is Why: A Qualitative Examination of Legal Cynicism in Three Philadelphia Neighborhoods." *Criminology* 45(2): 445–80.

Castells, Manuel. 1977. *The Urban Question: A Marxist Approach*. Cambridge, MA: MIT Press.

Casuso, Jorge, and Ben Joravsky. 1987. "Party of Juan." *Chicago Reader*, April 23. Retrieved July 10, 2015. http://www.chicagoreader.com/chicago/party-of-juan/Content?oid=870567.

Chicago Democracy Project.

Chicago Homicide Database.

Chicago Crime Commission. 2012. *The Chicago Crime Commission Gang Book*. Chicago: Chicago Crime Commission.

Chicago Police Department. 2014. "Gang Violence Reduction Strategy." *Directives*. Retrieved August 24, 2014. http://directives.chicagopolice.org/lt2015/data/a7a57bf0-136d1d31-16513-6d1d-382b311ddf65fd3a.html.

Childress, Sarah. 2013. "Chicago Drops Ceasefire from Anti-Violence Strategy." *PBS.org*, October 17. Retrieved October 21, 2013. http://www.pbs.org/wgbh/pages/frontline/social-issues/interrupters/chicago-drops-ceasefire-from-anti-violence-strategy/.

Choolijan, Lauren. 2015. "Where Do the Mayoral Candidates Stand on Chicago's Big Issues." *Chicago Sun-Times*, February 17. Retrieved February 20, 2015. http://www.wbez.org/news/where-do-mayoral-candidates-stand-chicagos-big-issues-111583.

City of Chicago. 2015. "Urban Data Portal: Crimes 2001–Present." Retrieved February 26, 2013. https://data.cityofchicago.org/.

City of Chicago Police Records. 2012. "Fernando Correa: Arrest #17813640." Cook County, Chicago, Criminal Records Division. Retrieved June 15, 2012.

Clear, Todd R. 2007. *Imprisoning Communities: How Mass Incarceration Makes Disadvantaged Neighborhoods Worse*. New York: Oxford University Press.

Clearmap Chicago. 2015. "Crime Type Categories: Definition and Description." Retrieved July 20, 2015. http://gis.chicagopolice.org/CLEARMap/startPage.htm.

Coakley, Michael. 1979. "Latino Progress Slow in Chicago." *Chicago Tribune*. May 25.

Coen, Jeff. 2008. "40 Charged in Major Sweep in Little Village." *Chicago Tribune*, September 9. Retrieved September 12, 2008. http://articles.chicagotribune.com/2008-09-25/news/0809242068_1_latin-kings-gang-informant:.

Coen, Jeff, and Rudolph Bush. 2006. "Top-Level Member of Gang Collared: 17 Other Latin Kings Taken into Custody." *Chicago Tribune*, June 12. Retrieved September 12, 2008. http://articles.chicagotribune.com/2006-12-06/news/0612060027_1_gang-member-violent-street-gang-drug-and-gun-violations:.

Cordova, Teresa. 1998. "Harold Washington and the Rise of Latino Electoral Politics in Chicago: 1982–87." Pp. 31–57 in *Chicano Politics and Society in the Late Twentieth Century*, edited by David Montejano. Austin: University of Texas Press.

Cortez, Gabriel. 2008. "Education, Politics, and a Hunger Strike: A Popular Movement's Struggle for Education in Chicago's Little Village Community." PhD diss., University of Illinois at Urbana-Champaign.

County of Cook v. Carlos Villagomez. 2010. Cook County, Chicago, Criminal Records Division. Case Number 10CR0556701.

County of Cook v. Jesus Rios. 2010. Cook County, Chicago, Criminal Records Division. Case Number 10CR0424501. Retrieved June 1, 2012.

County of Cook v. Rudy Cantu. 2010. Cook County, Chicago, Criminal Records Division. Case Number 09CR1710901. Retrieved June 1, 2012.

Cure Violence. 2015. "The Cure Violence Health Model." Retrieved July 27, 2015. http://cureviolence.org/the-model/.

Curry, G. David, and Scott H. Decker. 1996. "Understanding and Responding to Gangs in an Emerging Gang Problem Context." *Vanderbilt Law Review* 31: 523–59.

Daley, Richard M. 2010. "Mayor Daley Announces Public Service Campaign against Code of Silence." *YouTube*, February 9. Retrieved December 5, 2012. http://www.youtube.com/watch?v=7aPz5sDSOyw.

Davis, Robert, and James Strong. 1985. "Alderman's Residency Investigated." *Chicago Tribune*, May 10. Retrieved June 10, 2012. http://articles.chicagotribune.com/1985-05-10/news/8501290181_1_chicago-alderman-riverside-richard-daley.

Dawson, Michael C. 2015. "Welcome to the Chicago Democracy Project." Chicago Democracy Project. Retrieved June 12, 2015. http://chicagodemocracy.org/.

Dear, Michael. 2002. "Los Angeles and the Chicago School: Invitation to a Debate." *City & Community* 1(1): 5–32.

Decker, Scott H. 1996. "Collective and Normative Features of Gang Violence." *Justice Quarterly* 13(2): 243–64.

Decker, Scott H., and G. David Curry. 2002. "Gangs, Gang Homicides, and Gang Loyalty: Organized Crimes or Disorganized Criminals." *Journal of Criminal Justice* 30(4): 343–52.

Decker, Scott H., and Susan Pennell. 1995. *Arrestees and Guns: Monitoring the Illegal Firearms Market.* Washington, DC: National Institute of Justice.

Decker, Scott H., and Barrik Van Winkle. 1996. *Life in the Gang: Family, Friends, and Violence.* Cambridge, UK: Cambridge University Press.

Desmond, Matthew. 2014. "Relational Ethnography." *Theory and Society* 43(5): 547–79.

DiMaggio, Paul J., and Walter W. Powell. 1983. "The Iron Cage Revisited: Institutional Isomorphism and Collective Rationality in Organizational Fields." *American Sociological Review* 48(2): 147–60.

Duncan, Terry E., Susan C. Duncan, Hayrettin Okut, Lisa A. Strycker, and Hollie Hix-Small. 2003. "A Multilevel Contextual Model of Neighborhood Collective Efficacy." *American Journal of Community Psychology* 32(3–4): 245–52.

Duneier, Mitchell. 1999. *Sidewalk.* New York: Farrar, Straus and Giroux.

Eck, John E., Jeffrey S. Gersh, and Charlene Taylor. 2000. "Finding Crime Hot Spots through Repeat Address Mapping." Pp. 49–64 in *Analyzing Crime Patterns: Frontiers of Practice*, edited by Victor Goldsmith, John Mollenkopf, and Timothy Ross. New York: Sage.

Fagan, Jeffrey, Franklin E. Zimring, and June Kim. 1997. "Declining Homicide in New York City: A Tale of Two Trends." *Journal of Criminal Law & Criminology* 88: 1277–324.

Ferman, Barbara. 1996. *Challenging the Growth Machine.* Lawrence: University of Kansas Press.

Fine, Gary A. 1993. "Ten Lies of Ethnography: Moral Dilemmas of Field Research." *Journal of Contemporary Ethnography* 22(3): 267–94.

Finn, Peter, and Kerry Murphy Healey. 1996. *Preventing Gang- and Drug-Related Witness Intimidation*. New York: DIANE.

Fleisher, Mark S. 1998. *Dead End Kids: Gang Girls and the Boys They Know*. Madison: University of Wisconsin Press.

Fligstein, Neil, and Doug McAdam. 2012. *A Theory of Fields*. New York: Oxford University Press.

Ford, Matt. 2015. "America's Largest Mental Hospital Is a Jail." *theAtlantic.com*, June 8. Retrieved June 20, 2015. http://www.theatlantic.com/politics/archive/2015/06/americas-largest-mental-hospital-is-a-jail/395012/.

Fremon, David K. 1988. *Chicago Politics, Ward by Ward*. Bloomington: Indiana University Press.

Fritsch, Eric J., Tory J. Caeti, and Robert W. Taylor. 1999. "Gang Suppression through Saturation Patrol, Aggressive Curfew, and Truancy Enforcement: A Quasi-Experimental Test of the Dallas Anti-Gang Initiative." *Crime & Delinquency* 45(1): 122–39.

Galvan, Manuel. 1981. "Little Village Cries 'Enough' after Gangs Kill 2 Innocents." *Chicago Tribune*, August 23.

Garcia, John. 2010. "Gang Leaders Going Public after Police Warning." *ABC.go.com*, September 2. Retrieved September 10, 2010. http://abclocal.go.com/wls/story?section=news/local&id=7645350:.

Garland, David. 2001. *The Culture of Control: Crime and Social Order in Contemporary Society*. Chicago: University of Chicago Press.

Gelman, Andrew, Jeffrey Fagan, and Alex Kiss. 2007. "An Analysis of the New York City Police Department's 'Stop-and-Frisk' Policy in the Context of Claims of Racial Bias." *Journal of the American Statistical Association* 102(479): 813–23.

Gentry, Curt. 2001. *J. Edgar Hoover: The Man and the Secrets*. New York: Norton.

Goffman, Alice. 2014. *On the Run: Fugitive Life in an American City*. Chicago: University of Chicago Press.

Goldstein, Donna. 2013. *Laughter out of Place: Race, Class, Violence, and Sexuality in a Rio Shantytown*. Berkeley: University of California Press.

"Governor Quinn Signs Legislation to Fight Street Gang Crime." 2012. Illinois Government News Network, June 11. Retrieved July 2, 2012. http://www3.illinois.gov/PressReleases/ShowPressRelease.cfm?SubjectID=3&RecNum=10299.

Greene, Judith A. 1999. "Zero Tolerance: A Case Study of Police Policies and Practices in New York City." *Crime & Delinquency* 45(2): 171–87.

Greenhouse, Linda. 1999. "Loitering Law Aimed at Gangs Is Struck Down by High Court." *New York Times*, June 11. Retrieved June 1, 2013. http://www.nytimes.com/1999/06/11/us/loitering-law-aimed-at-gangs-is-struck-down-by-high-court.html.

Grossman, Lawrence S. 1998. *The Political Ecology of Bananas: Contract Farming, Peasants, and Agrarian Change in the Eastern Caribbean.* Chapel Hill: University of North Carolina Press.

Gutierrez, Theresa. 2010. "Call for More Police Cams in Little Village." *ABC.go.com*, February 16. Retrieved February 20, 2010. http://abclocal.go.com/story?section=news/local&id=7278822.

Hagan, John. 1993. "The Social Embeddedness of Crime and Unemployment." *Criminology* 31: 465–91.

Hagedorn, John M. 1988. *People and Folks: Gangs, Crime and the Underclass in a Rustbelt City.* Chicago: Lake View Press.

Harding, David J. 2010. *Living the Drama: Community, Conflict, and Culture among Inner-City Boys.* Chicago: University of Chicago Press.

Harvey, David. 1972. "Revolutionary and Counter Revolutionary Theory in Geography and the Problem of Ghetto Formation." *Antipode* 4(2):1–13.

———. 2012. *Rebel Cities: From the Right to the City to the Urban Revolution.* New York: Verso Books.

Haskins, Anna R. 2014. "Unintended Consequences: Effects of Paternal Incarceration on Child School Readiness and Later Special Education Placement." *Sociological Science* 1(1): 141–58.

Healy, Patrick. 1980. *The Chicago Crime Commission Annual Report.* Chicago: Chicago Crime Commission.

Heller, Sara, Harold A. Pollack, Roseanna Ander, and Jens Ludwig. 2013. "Preventing Youth Violence and Dropout: A Randomized Field Experiment." NBER Working Paper No. 19014 (May). Cambridge, MA: National Bureau of Economic Research.

Heynen, Nik, Harold A. Perkins, and Parama Roy. 2006. "The Political Ecology of Uneven Urban Green Space: The Impact of Political Economy on Race and Ethnicity in Producing Environmental Inequality in Milwaukee." *Urban Affairs Review* 42(1): 3–25.

Horowitz, Ruth. 1983. *Honor and the American Dream: Culture and Identity in a Chicano Community*. New Brunswick, NJ: Rutgers University Press.

Hunter, Albert. 1985. "Private, Parochial, and Public Social Orders: The Problem of Crime and Incivility in Urban Communities." Pp. 230–42 in *The Challenge of Social Control: Essays in Honor of Morris Janowitz*, edited by Gerald Suttles and Maurice N. Zald. Norwood, NJ: Ablex.

Hunter, Marcus A. 2013. *Black Citymakers: How the Philadelphia Negro Changed Urban America*. New York: Oxford University Press.

Jacobs, Bruce A., and Richard Wright. 2006. *Street Justice: Retaliation in the Criminal Underworld*. Cambridge, UK: Cambridge University Press.

Jacques, Scott, and Richard Wright. 2015. *Code of the Suburb: Inside the World of Young Middle-Class Drug Dealers*. Chicago: University of Chicago Press.

Jaffe, Alexandra. 2015. "Rahm Emanuel Wins Second Term as Chicago Mayor." *CNN.com*, April 8. Retrieved April 9, 2015. http://www.cnn.com/2015/04/07/politics/chicago-mayoral-runoff-results-rahm-emanuel-chuy-garcia/.

Janssen, Kim. 2011. "Police Supt. Weis: Secret Gang Meeting Reduced Murder." *Chicago Sun-Times*, February 13. Accessed February 20, 2011. http://www.policeone.com/gangs/articles/3328192-Chicago-PD-credits-secret-gang-meeting-for-drop-in-crime/.

Kallina, Edmund F. 1985. "Was the 1960 Presidential Election Stolen? The Case of Illinois." *Presidential Studies Quarterly* 15: 113–18.

Kane, Robert J. 2005. "Compromised Police Legitimacy as a Predictor of Violent Crime in Structurally Disadvantaged Communities." *Criminology* 43: 469–98.

Kasarda, John D., and Morris Janowitz. 1974. "Community Attachment in Mass Society." *American Sociological Review* 39: 328–39.

Kass, John. 1995. "Latinos Slam Gang Politics." *Chicago Tribune*, February 27. Retrieved July 1, 2015. http://articles.chicagotribune.com/1995-02-27/news/9502270154_1_gangster-disciples-street-gang-gang-behavior.

———. 2012. "Ex-Senator Tells How He Picked an Untouchable, Patrick Fitzgerald, to Be U.S. Attorney in Chicago." *Chicago Tribune*, May 24. Retrieved May 25, 2012. http://articles.chicagotribune.com/

2012-05-24/news/ct-met-kass-0524-20120524_1_pat-fitzgerald-illinois-politicians-patrick-fitzgerald.

———. 2015. "Are Political Winds of Change Blowing in Chicago." *Chicago Tribune*, March 29. Retrieved March 29, 2015. http://www.chicagotribune.com/news/columnists/kass/ct-kass-chicago-mayor-36th-ward-met-0329-20150329-column.html.

Kennedy, David M. 2011. *Don't Shoot: One Man, a Street Fellowship, and the End of Violence in Inner-City America*. New York: Bloomsbury.

Kennedy, David M., Anne M. Piehl, and Anthony A. Braga. 1996. "Youth Violence in Boston: Gun Markets, Serious Youth Offenders, and a Use-Reduction Strategy." *Law and Contemporary Problems* 59: 147–96.

Kent, Douglas R., and Peggy Smith. 2001. "The Tri-Agency Resource Gang Enforcement Team: A Selective Approach to Reduce Gang Crime." Pp. 292–96 in *The Modern Gang Reader*, edited by Cheryl Maxson, Malcolm W. Klein, and Jody Miller. Los Angeles: Roxbury.

Kent, Stephanie L., and Jason T. Carmichael. 2014. "Racial Residential Segregation and Social Control: A Panel Study of the Variation in Police Strength across U.S. Cities, 1980–2010." *American Journal of Criminal Justice* 39(2): 228–49.

Kent, Stephanie L., and David Jacobs. 2005. "Minority Threat and Police Strength from 1980 to 2000: A Fixed-Effects Analysis of Nonlinear and Interactive Effects in Large U.S. Cities." *Criminology* 43: 731–60.

Kirk, David S., and Andrew V. Papachristos. 2011. "Cultural Mechanisms and the Persistence of Neighborhood Violence." *American Journal of Sociology* 116(4): 1190–233.

Klein, Malcolm W. 1995. *The American Street Gang: Its Nature, Prevalence, and Control*. Oxford: Oxford University Press.

Klein, Malcolm W., and Cheryl L. Maxson. 2006. *Street Gang Patterns and Policies*. New York: Oxford University Press.

Klinger, David A. 1997. "Negotiating Order in Patrol Work: An Ecological Theory of Police Response to Deviance." *Criminology* 35: 277–306.

Knox, George. 2001. "The Impact of the Federal Prosecution of the Gangster Disciples." *Journal of Gang Research* 7(2): 1–64.

Koeneman, Keith. 2013. *First Son: The Biography of Richard M. Daley*. Chicago: University of Chicago Press.

Krivo, Lauren J., and Ruth D. Peterson. 1996. "Extremely Disadvantaged Neighborhoods and Urban Crime." *Social Forces* 75(2): 619–48.

Kull, Christian A. 2004. *Isle of Fire: The Political Ecology of Landscape Burning in Madagascar*. Chicago: University of Chicago Press.

LaFree, Gary. 1999. "Declining Violent Crime Rates in the 1990s: Predicting Crime Booms and Busts." *Annual Review of Sociology* 25(1): 145–68.

Langworthy, Robert H. 1989. "Do Stings Control Crime? An Evaluation of a Police Fencing Operation." *Justice Quarterly* 6(1): 27–45.

Lareau, Annette. 2011. *Unequal Childhoods: Class, Race, and Family Life*. Berkeley: University of California Press.

Lauritsen, Janet L., and Norman A. White. 2001. "Putting Violence in Its Place: The Influence of Race, Ethnicity, Gender, and Place on the Risk for Violence." *Criminology and Public Policy* 1(1): 37–60.

La Vigne, Nancy G., Samantha S. Lowry, Joshua Markman, and Allison Dwyer. 2011. "Evaluating the Use of Public Surveillance Cameras for Crime Control and Prevention." Washington DC: Urban Institute. Retrieved November 21, 2011. http://www.urban.org/research/publication/evaluating-use-public-surveillance-cameras-crime-control-and-prevention.

Legewie, Joscha. 2016. "Racial Profiling and Use of Force in Police Stops: How Local Events Trigger Periods of Increased Discrimination." Working Paper, New York University.

Levenstein, Rachel, Sue Sporte, and Elaine Allensworth. 2011. "Findings from an Investigation into the Culture of Calm Initiative." Chicago: Consortium on Chicago School Research. Retrieved May 30, 2015. https://ccsr.uchicago.edu/sites/default/files/publications/Culture%20of%20Calm%20Findings.pdf.

Levi-Martin, John. 2003. "What Is Field Theory?" *American Journal of Sociology* 109(1): 1–49.

Logan, John, and Harvey Molotch. 1987. *Urban Fortunes: The Political Economy of Place*. Berkeley: University of California Press.

Lublin, David. 1999. *The Paradox of Representation: Racial Gerrymandering and Minority Interests in Congress*: Princeton, NJ: Princeton University Press.

Lutton, Linda. 1998. "War on Independents: Was Jesus Garcia Beaten by a New Machine? How Many Other Progressives Are Being Targeted for Removal?" *Chicago Reader*, September 3. Retrieved

February 21, 2012. http://www.chicagoreader.com/chicago/war-on-independents/Content?oid=897166:.

———. 2003. "Dumped for Another Man." *Chicago Reader*, February 6. http://www.chicagoreader.com/chicago/dumped-for-another-man/Content?oid=911136.

Lutz, B. J. 2009. "Three More People Sought in Derrion Albert's Death." *NBCChicago.com*, September 29. Retrieved September 30, 2009. http://www.nbcchicago.com/news/local/derrion-albert-fenger-high-beating-death-092909-62660787.html:.

Lyons, Christopher J., María B. Vélez, and Wayne A. Santoro. 2013. "Neighborhood Immigration, Violence, and City-Level Immigrant Political Opportunities." *American Sociological Review* 78: 604–32.

Magallon, Frank S. 2010. *Chicago's Little Village: Lawndale-Crawford*. Chicago: Arcadia.

Maguire, Rachel, director. 2011. "Divide and Conquer," episode of *Gangland*. DVD. New York: A&E Home Video.

Main, Frank. 2010. "Chicago Cops to Gangs: Stop the Killing—Or Else." *Chicago Sun-Times*, August 28. Retrieved August 30, 2010. http://www.policeone.com/gangs/articles/2556625-Chicago-cops-to-gangs-Stop-the-killing-or-else/.

Manning, Peter K. 2003. *Policing Contingencies*. Chicago: University of Chicago Press.

Marcus, George E. 1998. *Ethnography through Thick and Thin*. Princeton, NJ: Princeton University Press.

Marwell, Nicole P. 2007. *Bargaining for Brooklyn: Community Organizations in the Entrepreneurial City*. Chicago: University of Chicago Press.

Massoglia, Michael. 2008. "Incarceration as Exposure: The Prison, Infectious Disease, and Other Stress-Related Illnesses." *Journal of Health and Social Behavior* 49(1): 56–71.

Maxson, Cheryl L. 1999. "Gang Homicide: A Review and Extension of the Literature." Pp. 239–54 in *Homicide: A Sourcebook of Social Research*, edited by M. D. Smith and M. A. Zahn. Newbury Park, CA: Sage.

Maxson, Cheryl L., Margaret A. Gordon, and Malcolm W. Klein. 1985. "Differences between Gang and Nongang Homicide." *Criminology* 23(2): 209–22.

Maxson, Cheryl L., Karen M. Hennigan, and David C. Sloane. 2005. "It's Getting Crazy Out There: Can a Civil Gang Injunction Change a Community." *Criminology & Public Policy* 4(3): 577–606.

McCord, Joan. 2003. "Cures That Harm: Unanticipated Outcomes of Crime Prevention Programs." *Annals of the American Academy of Political and Social Science* 587(1): 16–30.

McGloin, J. M. 2005. "Policy and Intervention Considerations of a Network Analysis of Street Gangs." *Criminology & Public Policy* 4(3): 607.

McQuarrie, Michael, and Nicole P. Marwell. 2009. "The Missing Organizational Dimension in Urban Sociology." *City & Community* 8(3): 247–68.

McRoberts, Omar. 2004. *Streets of Glory: Church and Community in a Black Urban Neighborhood*. Chicago: University of Chicago Press.

Meares, Tracey L., and Dan M. Kahan. 1998. "Law and (Norms of) Order in the Inner City." *Law and Society Review* 32: 805–38.

"Mom of Girl Killed on Front Porch: 'They're Not People, They're Animals.'" 2012. *CBSChicago*, March 19. Retrieved May 19 2012. http://chicago.cbslocal.com/2012/03/19/prosecutors-slain-6-year-old-was-victim-of-gang-violence/.

Moore, Joan W. and John M. Hagedorn. 1996. "What Happens to Girls in the Gang?" Pp 205–218 In *Gangs in America*. Edited by C. Ronald Huff. Thousand Oaks: Sage.

Morenoff, Jeffrey D., and Robert J. Sampson. 1997. "Violent Crime and the Spatial Dynamics of Neighborhood Transition: Chicago, 1970–1990." *Social Forces* 76(1): 31–64.

Morenoff, Jeffrey D., Robert J. Sampson, and Stephen W. Raudenbush. 2001. "Neighborhood Inequality, Collective Efficacy, and the Spatial Dynamics of Urban Violence." *Criminology* 39(3): 517–58.

Moser, Whet. 2015. "What Martin Luther King Jr. Wanted for Chicago in 1966." *Chicago*, January 19. Retrieved May 30, 2015. http://www.chicagomag.com/city-life/January-2015/Martin-Luther-King-Jrs-Policy-Ideas-for-Chicago-Circa-1966/.

Nair, Yasmin. 2015. "Rahm, Chuy, and the Real Problem with Chicago Politics." *Yasmin Nair: Writer, Academic, Activist, Commentator*. Retrieved April 10, 2015. http://www.yasminnair.net/content/rahm-chuy-and-real-problem-chicago-politics.

Overby, L. Marvin, and Kenneth M. Cosgrove. 1996. "Unintended Consequences? Racial Redistricting and the Representation of Minority Interests." *Journal of Politics* 58(2): 540–50.

Padilla, Felix M. 1992. *The Gang as an American Enterprise*. New Brunswick, NJ: Rutgers University Press.

Papachristos, Andrew V. 2001. *A.D., After the Disciples: The Neighborhood Impact of Federal Gang Prosecution*. Peotone, IL: National Gang Crime Research Center.

———. 2009. "Murder by Structure: Dominance Relations and the Social Structure of Gang Homicide." *American Journal of Sociology* 115(1): 74–128.

———. 2011. "Too Big to Fail." *Criminology & Public Policy* 10(4): 1053–61.

Papachristos, Andrew V., David M. Hureau, and Anthony A. Braga. 2013. "The Corner and the Crew: The Influence of Geography and Social Networks on Gang Violence." *American Sociological Review* 78(3): 417–47.

Park, Robert E. 1915. "The City: Suggestions for the Investigation of Human Behavior in the City Environment." *American Journal of Sociology* 20(5): 577–612.

———. 1936. "Succession, an Ecological Concept." *American Sociological Review* 1(2): 171–79.

Park, Robert Ezra, and Ernest Watson Burgess. 1921. *Introduction to the Science of Sociology*. Chicago: University of Chicago Press.

Pattillo, Mary. 2007. *Black on the Block: The Politics of Race and Class in the City*. Chicago: University of Chicago Press.

Pattillo, Mary, Bruce Western, and David Weiman. 2004. *Imprisoning America: The Social Effects of Mass Incarceration*. New York: Russell Sage Foundation.

Pattillo-McCoy, Mary. 1999. *Black Picket Fences: Privilege and Peril in the Black Middle Class Neighborhood*. Chicago: University of Chicago Press.

The People of the State of Illinois v. Clayton Rockman. 1986. May 27. Illinois Appellate Court. Retrieved September 30 2010. http://il.findacase.com/research/wfrmDocViewer.aspx/xq/fac.19860527_0000689.IL.htm/qx.

Peterson, Ruth D., Lauren J. Krivo, and Mark A. Harris. 2000. "Disadvantage and Neighborhood Violent Crime: Do Local Institutions Matter?" *Journal of Research in Crime and Delinquency* 37(1): 31–63.

Poe, Juanita. 1998. "School Board Finalizes $24 Million Spending Plan: Officials Still Beaming over Kudos from President." *Chicago Tribune*, January 29. Retrieved March 21, 2012. http://articles.

chicagotribune.com/1998-01-29/news/9801290353_1_school-funding-schools-ceo-paul-vallas-education-reform.

Puente, Teresa. 1998. "Pilsen Area Jolted by Legislative Upset." *Chicago Tribune*, March 23. Retrieved March 21, 2012. http://articles.chicagotribune.com/1998-03-23/news/9803230128_1_voter-senate-race-longtime-latino-residents.

Pyrooz, David C., Gary Sweeten, and Alex R. Piquero. 2013. "Continuity and Change in Gang Membership and Gang Embeddedness." *Journal of Research in Crime and Delinquency* 50(2): 239–71.

Ragin, Charles C., and Howard S. Becker. 1992. *What Is a Case? Exploring the Foundations of Social Inquiry.* Cambridge, UK: Cambridge University Press.

Raudenbush, Stephen W., and Robert J. Sampson. 1999. "Ecometrics: Toward a Science of Assessing Ecological Settings, with Application to the Systematic Social Observation of Neighborhoods." *Sociological Methodology* 29: 1–41.

Reitzel, John D., Stephen K. Rice, and Alex R. Piquero. 2004. "Lines and Shadows: Perceptions of Racial Profiling and the Hispanic Experience." *Journal of Criminal Justice* 32(6): 607–16.

Reppetto, Thomas A. 1976. "Crime Prevention and the Displacement Phenomenon." *Crime & Delinquency* 22(2): 166–77.

Rhodes, Steve. 2013. "Why Chicago's Spineless City Council Just Can't Say No." *Chicago*, March 19. Retrieved April 21, 2015. http://www.chicagomag.com/Chicago-Magazine/April-2013/The-Yes-Men/.

Rice, Stephen K., John D. Reitzel, and Alex R. Piquero. 2005. "Shades of Brown: Perceptions of Racial Profiling and the Intra-Ethnic Differential." *Journal of Ethnicity in Criminal Justice* 3: 47–70.

Rios, Victor. 2011. *Punished: Policing the Lives of Black and Latino Boys.* New York: New York University Press.

Ritter, Nancy. 2009. "Ceasefire: A Public Health Approach to Reduce Shootings and Killings." *National Institute of Justice Journal* 264: 20–25.

Rivlin, Gary. 1993. "Fire on the Prairie: Chicago's Harold Washington and the Politics of Race." New York: Henry Holt and Co.

Robbins, Paul. 2011. *Political Ecology: A Critical Introduction.* New York: John Wiley & Sons.

Rosen, Dale. 1989. "Interview with Garcia Jesus." *Eyes on the Prize II Interview.* April 15. Retrieved January 31, 2012. http://digital.wustl.

edu/e/eii/eiiweb/gar5427.0524.055marc_record_interviewee_
process.html.

Rueff, Ashley, Jeremy Gorner, and Jason Meisner. 2012. "Shooting Death
of 6-Year Old Girl Punctuates Lethal Chicago Weekend." *Chicago
Tribune*, March 20. Retrieved March 21, 2012. http://articles.
chicagotribune.com/2012-03-20/news/ct-met-weekend-mayhem-
0320-20120320_1_aliyah-shell-shooting-death-chicago-police.

Sabol, William J., Claudia J. Coulton, and Jill E. Korbin. 2004.
"Building Community Capacity for Violence Prevention." *Journal
of Interpersonal Violence* 19(3): 322–40.

Salamon, Lester M. 1995. *Partners in Public Service: Government-
Nonprofit Relations in the Modern Welfare State*. Baltimore: Johns
Hopkins University Press.

Sampson, Robert J. 1988. "Local Friendship Ties and Community
Attachment in Mass Society: A Multi-Level Systemic Model."
American Sociological Review 53: 766–79.

———. 1991. "Linking the Micro and Macrolevel Dimensions of
Community Social Organization." *Social Forces* 70: 43–64.

———. 2012. *Great American City: Chicago and the Enduring
Neighborhood Effect*. Chicago: University of Chicago Press.

Sampson, Robert J., and Dawn Jeglum Bartusch. 1998. "Legal Cynicism
and (Subcultural) Tolerance of Deviance: The Neighborhood
Context of Racial Difference." *Law & Society Review* 32: 777–804.

Sampson, Robert J., Jeffrey D. Morenoff, and Felton Earls. 1999.
"Beyond Social Capital: Spatial Dynamics of Collective Efficacy
for Children." *American Sociological Review* 64: 633–60.

Sampson, Robert J., and Stephen W. Raudenbush. 1999. "Systematic Social
Observation of Public Spaces: A New Look at Disorder in Urban
Neighborhoods." *American Journal of Sociology* 105(3): 603–51.

Sampson, Robert J., Stephen W. Raudenbush, and Felton Earls. 1997.
"Neighborhoods and Violent Crime: A Multilevel Study of
Collective Efficacy." *Science* 277(5328): 918–24.

Sampson, Robert J., and William Julius Wilson. 1995. "Toward a
Theory of Race, Crime, and Urban Inequality." Pp. 37–54 in *Crime
and Inequality*, edited by John Hagan and Ruth D. Peterson.
Stanford: Stanford University Press.

Sánchez-Jankowski, Martin. 1991. *Islands in the Street: Gangs and
American Urban Society*. Berkeley: University of California Press.

Saulny, Susan. 2009. "Attorney General, in Chicago, Pledges Youth Violence Effort." *New York Times*, October 7. Retrieved October 8, 2009. http://www.nytimes.com/2009/10/08/us/08 chicago.html?_r=0.

Seper, Jerry. 2012. "Latin Kings Gang Boss Gets 60-Year Prison Sentence." *Washington Times*, January 12. Retrieved January 15, 2012. http://www.washingtontimes.com/news/2012/jan/12/latin-kings-gang-boss-gets-60-year-prison-sentence/.

Sharkey, Patrick. 2010. "The Acute Effect of Local Homicides on Children's Cognitive Performance." *Proceedings of the National Academy of Sciences* 107(26): 11733–38.

Shaw, Clifford Robe, and Henry Donald McKay. 1969. *Juvenile Delinquency and Urban Areas: A Study of Rates of Delinquency in Relation to Differential Characteristics of Local Communities in American Cities*. Chicago: University of Chicago Press.

Sherman, Lawrence W., Denise Gottfredson, Doris MacKenzie, John Eck, Peter Reuter, and Shawn Bushway. 1997. "Preventing Crime: What Works." Pp. 1–19 in *What Doesn't Work, What's Promising: A Report to the United States Congress (NCJ 171676)*. Washington, DC: U.S. Department of Justice, Office of Justice Programs.

Shotts, Kenneth W. 2002. "Gerrymandering, Legislative Composition, and National Policy Outcomes." *American Journal of Political Science* 46: 398–414.

Silver, Eric, and Lisa L. Miller. 2004. "Sources of Informal Social Control in Chicago Neighborhoods." *Criminology* 42(3): 551–84.

Simpson, Richard. 2001. *Rogues, Rebels, and Rubber Stamps: The Politics of the Chicago City Council*. Boulder, CO: Westview.

Skarbek, David. 2014. *The Social Order of the Underworld: How Prison Gangs Govern the American Penal System*. New York: Oxford University Press.

Skogan, Wesley G., and Susan M. Hartnett. 1997. *Community Policing, Chicago Style*. New York: Oxford University Press.

Skogan, Wesley G., Susan M. Hartnett, Natalie Bump, and Jill Dubois. 2008. *Evaluation of Ceasefire-Chicago*. Evanston, IL: Northwestern University Press.

Skolnick, Jerome H. 1966. *Justice without Trial: Law Enforcement in Democratic Society*. New York: Wiley.

Small, Mario Luis. 2008. "Four Reasons to Abandon the Idea of 'the Ghetto.'" *City & Community* 7(4): 389–98.

———. 2009. "How Many Cases Do I Need? On Science and the Logic of Case Selection in Field-Based Research." *Ethnography* 10(1): 5–38.

Small, Mario L., and Monica McDermott. 2006. "The Presence of Organizational Resources in Poor Urban Neighborhoods: An Analysis of Average and Contextual Effects." *Social Forces* 84(3): 1697–724.

Soss, Joe, Richard C. Fording, and Sanford F. Schram. 2011. *Disciplining the Poor: Neoliberal Paternalism and the Persistent Power of Race.* Chicago: University of Chicago Press.

Spergel, Irving A. 1995. *The Youth Gang Problem: A Community Approach.* Oxford: Oxford University Press.

———. 2007. *Reducing Youth Gang Violence: The Little Village Gang Project in Chicago.* Lanham, MD: AltaMira Press.

Spohn, Cassia, and David Holleran. 2000. "The Imprisonment Penalty Paid by Young, Unemployed Black and Hispanic Male Offenders." *Criminology* 38(1): 281–306.

St. Jean, Peter K. B. 2007. *Pockets of Crime: Broken Windows, Collective Efficacy, and the Criminal Point of View.* Chicago: University of Chicago Press.

Stone, Clarence N. 1989. *Regime Politics: Governing Atlanta 1946–1988.* Lawrence: University Press of Kansas.

Strong, James. 1985. "Activists Call Daley Negligent in Probe of Lozano Slaying." *Chicago Tribune*, January 1. Retrieved April 15, 2015. http://articles.chicagotribune.com/1985-01-01/news/ 8501010165_1_richard-m-daley-jesus-garcia-charges.

Suttles, Gerald D. 1968. *The Social Order of the Slum: Ethnicity and Territory in the Inner City.* Chicago: University of Chicago Press.

Sweeney, Annie. 2012. "60 Years for Highest-Ranking Latin King Gang Leader." *Chicago Tribune*, January 11. Retrieved January 11, 2012. http://articles.chicagotribune.com/2012-01-11/news/chi-reputed-king-of-latin-kings-street-gang-to-be-sentenced-today-20120111_1_ latin-kings-augustin-tino-zambrano-gangster-disciples:.

Sweeney, Annie and John Byrne. 2013. "Back of the Yards No Man's Land for Police, Politicians." *Chicago Tribune*, September 21. Retrieved January 15, 2014. http://articles.chicagotribune. com/2013-09-21/news/ct-met-chicago-multiple-shooting-0922-20130922_1_mass-shooting-gang-deering-district-cmdr

Taylor, Carl S. 1990. *Dangerous Society.* East Lansing: Michigan State University Press.

Taylor, Ralph B., and Jeanette Covington. 1993. "Community Structural Change and Fear of Crime." *Social Problems* 40(3): 374–97.

Thomas, Charles. 2010. "Alderman: Weis Shouldn't Bargain with 'Urban Terrorists.'" *ABC.go.com*, August 31. Retrieved September 1, 2010. http://abclocal.go.com/wls/story?section=news/politics& id=7642665:.

Thomas, William Isaac, and Florian Znaniecki. 1918. *The Polish Peasant in Europe and America: Monograph of an Immigrant Group*. Chicago: University of Chicago Press.

Tita, G. E., J. Cohen, and J. Engberg. 2005. "Ecological Study of the Location of Gang Set Space." *Social Problems* 52: 272–299.

Tita, George E., and Andrew Papachristos. 2010. "The Evolution of Gang Policy: Balancing Intervention and Suppression." Pp. 24–50 in *Youth Gangs and Community Intervention: Research, Practice, and Evidence*, edited by Robert J. Chaskin. New York: Columbia University Press.

Tita, George, K. Jack Riley, and Peter Greenwood. 2003. "From Boston to Boyle Heights: The Process and Prospects of a 'Pulling Levers' Strategy in a Los Angeles Barrio." Pp. 102–30 in *Policing Gangs and Youth Violence*, edited by Scott H. Decker. Belmont, CA: Wadsworth.

Tritsch, Shane. 2010. "Why Is Illinois So Corrupt." *Chicago*, December 9. Retrieved December 12, 2010. http://www.chicagomag.com/ Chicago-Magazine/December-2010/Why-Is-Illinois-So-Corrupt-Local-Government-Experts-Explain/.

"2015 Election Results." 2015. *Chicago Tribune*, April 9. Retrieved April 10, 2015. http://elections.chicagotribune.com/results/.

Tyler, Tom R. 2007. *Legitimacy and Criminal Justice: An International Perspective*. New York: Russell Sage Foundation.

U.S. Bureau of the Census. 1970. *American FactFinder*. Retrieved February 21 2015. http://factfinder.census.gov/faces/nav/jsf/pages/ index.xhtml.

———. 1980. *American FactFinder*. Retrieved February 21, 2015. http:// factfinder.census.gov/faces/nav/jsf/pages/index.xhtml.

———. 1990. *American FactFinder*. Retrieved February 21 2015. http:// factfinder.census.gov/faces/nav/jsf/pages/index.xhtml.

———. 2000. *American FactFinder*. Retrieved February 21 2015. http:// factfinder.census.gov/faces/nav/jsf/pages/index.xhtml.

———. 2010. *American FactFinder*. Retrieved February 21, 2015. http:// factfinder.census.gov/faces/nav/jsf/pages/index.xhtml.

U.S. Decennial Census. 2010.

U.S. Department of Justice. 2009a. "'Corona' Augustin Zambrano among 18 Alleged Latin Kings Gang Leaders in Little Village Region Indicted on Federal Charges." Press Release. Retrieved from https://www.fbi.gov/chicago/press-releases/2009/cg100109-1.htm.

———. 2009b. "Criminal Rico: A Guide for Federal Prosecutors." Retrieved July 20, 2015. http://www.justice.gov/sites/default/files/usam/legacy/2014/10/17/rico.pdf.

———. 2009c. *United States of America v. Augustin Zambrano, Vicente Garcia, Valentin Baez, Ruben Caquis, Alphonso Chavez, Juan Dejesus, Danny Dominguez, Luis Garcia, Ernesto Grimaldo, Samuel Gutierrez, Jose Guzman, Nedal Issa, Fernando King, Polin Lopez, Javier Ramirez, Wilfredo Rivera Jr., Fernando Vazquez, Felipe Zamora.* Superseding Indictment, No. 08 CT 746.

Vaughan, Diane. 1986. *Uncoupling: Turning Points in Intimate Relationships.* New York: Oxford University Press.

———. 1996. *The Challenger Launch Decision: Risky Technology, Culture, and Deviance at NASA.* Chicago: University of Chicago Press.

Velez, Maria B. 2009. "Contextualizing the Immigration and Crime Effect: An Analysis of Homicide in Chicago Neighborhoods." *Homicide Studies* 13(3): 325–35.

Vélez, María B., Christopher J. Lyons, and Wayne A. Santoro. 2015. "The Political Context of the Percent Black-Neighborhood Violence Link: A Multilevel Analysis." *Social Problems* 62(1): 93–119.

Venkatesh, Sudhir A. 1997. "The Social Organization of Street Gang Activity in an Urban Ghetto." *American Journal of Sociology* 103(1): 82–111.

———. 2002. *American Project: The Rise and Fall of a Modern Ghetto.* Cambridge, MA: Harvard University Press.

———. 2006. *Off the Books: The Underground Economy of the Urban Poor.* Cambridge, MA: Harvard University Press.

———. 2008. *Gang Leader for a Day: A Rogue Sociologist Takes to the Streets.* New York: Penguin.

Venkatesh, Sudhir A., and Steven D. Levitt. 2000. "'Are We a Family or a Business?' History and Disjuncture in the Urban American Street Gang." *Theory and Society* 29(4): 427–62.

Vevea, Rebecca. 2011. "Culture of Calm Is Threatened by Budget Cuts." *New York Times*, May 8. Retrieved May 9, 2011. http://www.nytimes.com/2011/05/08/us/08cnccalm.html.

Vigil, James D. 1988. *Barrio Gangs: Street Life and Identity in Southern California*. Austin: University of Texas Press.

Vogel, Ronald E., and Sam Torres. 1998. "An Evaluation of Operation Roundup: An Experiment in the Control of Gangs to Reduce Crime, Fear of Crime and Improve Police Community Relations." *Policing: An International Journal of Police Strategies & Management* 21(1): 38–53.

Wacquant, Loïc. 2009. *Prisons of Poverty*. Minneapolis: University of Minnesota Press.

Warner, Barbara D., and Pamela Wilcox Rountree. 1997. "Local Social Ties in a Community and Crime Model: Questioning the Systemic Nature of Informal Social Control." *Social Problems* 44: 520–36.

Weisburd, David L., Elizabeth R. Groff, and Sue-Ming Yang. 2012. *The Criminology of Place: Street Segments and Our Understanding of the Crime Problem*. New York: Oxford University Press.

Weisel, Deborah and Ellen Painter. 1997. *The Police Response to Gangs: Case Studies in Five Cities*. Washington DC: Police Executive Research Forum.

Western, Bruce. 2006. *Punishment and Inequality in America*. New York: Russell Sage Foundation.

"What's Squeezing the Latin Kings—and What That Means to Chicago" 2014. Editorial. *Chicago Tribune*, July 3. Retrieved July 4, 2014. http://www.chicagotribune.com/news/opinion/ct-edit-latin-kings-0706-story.html.

Wilson, William J. 1987. *The Truly Disadvantaged: The Inner City, the Underclass, and Public Policy*. Chicago: University of Chicago Press.

Winett, Liana B. 1998. "Constructing Violence as a Public Health Problem." *Public Health Reports* 113(6): 498.

Winship, Christopher, and Jenny Berrien. 1999. "Boston Cops and Black Churches." *Public Interest* 136(Summer): 52–68.

Winship, Christopher, Jenny Berrien, and Omar McRoberts. 2000. "Religion and the Boston Miracle: The Effect of Black Ministry on Youth Violence." Pp. 266–85 in *Who Will Provide? The Changing Role of Religion in American Social Welfare*, edited by Mary Jo Bane and Brent Coffin. Boulder, CO: Westview Press.

Wirth, Louis. 1938. "Urbanism as a Way of Life." *American Journal of Sociology* 44: 1–24.

INDEX

Figures and notes are indicated by f and n following the page number.